# Functional Management

# Functional Management

M. Abdul Hakkeem

SERIALS PUBLICATIONS
NEW DELHI (INDIA)

First Published - 2011

ISBN: 978-81-8387-412-0



*Published by*

**SERIALS PUBLICATIONS**
4830/24, Prahlad Street, Ansari Road
Darya Ganj, New Delhi-110002 (India)
Phone : 23245225 Fax : 91-11-23272135
E-mail: serials@sify.com

# Contents

# Preface

At present there are about 44 per cent of tile factories in the country are functioning in the State of Kerala. The clay tile industry in Kerala is centered in three districts namely Thrissur, Quilon and Calicut. Thrissur District accounted for the highest agglomeration of 45 per cent of the units in Kerala. This is a labour intensive industry providing not only direct employment but also indirect employment to lot of people. This industry is highly localized in the State due to availability of raw materials, climate condition, abundance of labour etc. But these industries focus a peculiar threat from the general public that it would lead to environmental degradation. In spite of this industry survives successfully.

The performance of a business depends on the effectiveness of various functional areas such as Production, Marketing, Finance and Labour. The Clay Tile Manufacturing Units are no exception. The study covers all the registered small scale tiles manufacturing units located at Thrissur District, Kerala. The availability of raw materials and reasonable labour have acted as a fillip to the growth of the industry in Alagappanagar, Chittissery and Pudukad areas in Thrissur District. What are the techniques and practices adopted in the production process? What are the factors that influence marketing effectiveness? How does the clay tile unit raise funds from different sources? What are the practices followed in the labour management? What are the various problems faced by the units in each functional area? All these functional areas are interdependent in nature. To what extent are they linked with each other? The performance in each functional area affects its overall performance. This lead to many research issues and this study makes an attempt to find out answers to these questions.

Hence, the present research study is undertaken to examine the overall performance of clay tile manufacturing units in Thrissur District, Kerala. They will surely find this study useful and interesting. I hope that this book will be well received by the Scholars, Students and Teachers.

**M. Abdul Hakkeem**

# Acknowledgement

This work is the outcome of my four year Research study on a fascinating topic titled *"A Study of Clay Tiles Manufacturing Units in Thrissur District, Kerala"* under the able supervision and extra-ordinary guidance of Dr. E. Mubarak Ali, Associate Professor, Department of Commerce, Jamal Mohamed College, Trichy. The Guide had critically scrutinized my perspectives and view during the course of my study. The topic was discussed in regard to various aspects at many sittings and ultimately found a fruitful result. The criticisms and precious suggestions offered by my supervisor helped me a great deal in coming out with this successful thesis and in this regard I express my sincere thanks and heartfelt gratitude for his unbound versatility.

I Place record my thanks to the President, Secretary & Correspondent, Treasurer, Assistant Secretary and Members of the Management Committee, Jamal Mohamed College for giving me an opportunity to do this research work. I sincerely place on record my deep sense of gratitude to Dr. M. Sheik Mohamed, Principal & Head, Department of Commerce, Jamal Mohamed College for his constant motivation and valuable suggestions that helped me in constructing my thesis in a good form.

I extend my gratitude to Dr. R. Khader Mohideen, Associate Professor of Commerce, who has given me concrete ideas and support in every movement of this work. In the process of my research study, Dr. A. M. Mohamed Sindhasha, Associate Professor of Commerce had helped me with his ideologies and perspectives to channelise my thesis in a well constructed path.

His expertise and nerve breaking effort is hard to explain. I thus express my sincere sense of gratitude to him. All the members of the staff of Department of Commerce, Jamal Mohamed College, Trichy, assisted me in one way or other during the course of the preparation of the thesis.

It is my pleasure to extend sincere thanks to my colleague Dr. G.S. David Sam Jayakumar for helping me in applying the statistical tools used in the study and Mr. D. Jayachandran, Retired Professor of Jamal Mohamed College, for extending kind cooperation in the construction of this work. I am also grateful to my beloved parents, brother, sisters and my wife who constantly encouraged my to accomplish this task.

The study covers all the registered small scale tiles manufacturing units located at Thrissur District, Kerala and the focus was on the main four functional areas namely Production, Marketing, Finance and Labour. A wide range of primary data was in need to proceed with analysis and leading executives from the tiles manufacturing sectors have extended their helping hand to cater to my demands. But for their dedicated co-operation my thesis would have been only a dream. I propose my appreciation and thanks especially to these eminent persons Mr. Tapas Saha, Mr. Hareeswaran and Mr. Muthu Veerapan, Assistant Directors, SISI, Govt. of India, Ministry of SSI, Thrissur and Mr. Biju P. Abraham, Entrepreneur Guidance Cell, DIC, Thrissur are worth appreciation and I acknowledge my deep sense of gratitude to these gentlemen.

I sincerely record my thanks to Mr. Palanikutty, Sree Lakshmi Clay Products, Chittissery, Mr. Anil Kumar, Chitra Ceramics, Pudukad, Sree Kailas Potteries, Grace Tiles, Smarna Tiles and Siva Sakthi Tiles who helped me in many ways and means.

It is my bounden duty to express my sincere thanks to the editor and other personnel of the Serial Publications, New Delhi who accepted to bring my Research Study into a book form.

**M. Abdul Hakkeem**

# Chapter 1

# Design and Execution of the Study

## INTRODUCTION

Throughout the known history of human race clay has been intimately associated with man's daily life in more ways than one, be it potter's or shelters. Clay has also fascinated man through the ages due to its distinctive features like plasticity which dry or elasticity when wet, its ability to retain any form given when dried and finally burning into a strong body with a beautiful color. Clay-based products are very much a part of modern industry. Development of technologies has established the use of clay more wisely and cleverly for the needs of modern man's habitat. In contemporary architecture, clay roof tiles and floor tiles play a vital role in defining the elegance and character of each building and its interior.

Clay tile has been a prominent component of Kerala architecture for quite sometime and in the 20$^{th}$ century, having a tiled house was a matter of pride. The elders in the state who are reared in such a 'tile dominated' ambience would find it difficult to believe that the clay tile industry was brought here from abroad. The first clay tile factory in the country was established by the Bessel Missionaries of Germany 160 years ago in Mangalore and they had set up the Calicut tile factory at Feroke in 1878. Thrissur, which later became the hub of this industry, had its first tile factory in 1990 at Manaly. The favourable factors like the availability of clay, firewood in abundance and momentum of the early start gave the necessary fillip to the fast growth of the industry in the State. When the tiles industry started using electricity, it was available in the State at a relatively cheap cost.

Due to various favourable factors the clay tile industry grew and spread to different parts of the State and then to other parts of our country, the main concentration being Calicut, Thrissur, and Quilon in Kerala and Mangalore and Kundapur in Karnataka. There are about 800 factories, big and small, in the country engaged in the manufacture of terracotta clay products like Mangalore pattern roofing tiles, flooring tiles and decorative tiles.

The 1970's were the golden period of this industry in Thrissur. There were more than 250 units in Thrissur alone. That was the time when innovation in product range and opening up of new markets took place. The clay tiles manufactured in this region are consistently of superior quality due to better technological process and quality control techniques. Availability of good quality of clay in the locality and high return on the investment can be the probable reasons for the sudden surge of this industry in this district. However, neither a sustainable market nor a willing enterprise was evident. Obviously, in due course this resulted in a degenerative process, which was strongly felt in the 90's. The stereotype of processing and low machination caused serious concern in this region. The product innovation and machination will give a positive impact on productivity and profitability.

An industry which gave direct employment to 20000 people and indirectly fed more than 25000 was not given its due share of attention by planners and economists. Had there been sincere efforts in the field of research and development, probably the present status of this industry would have been different.

## RATIONALE FOR SELECTION OF THE TOPIC

At present there are about 800 tiles factories in India spread over different states namely Kerala, Gujarat, Karnataka, Orissa,

Madhya Pradesh, Maharastra and Andra Pradesh. Around 44 per cent of tiles factories in the country are functioning in the State of Kerala. The clay tiles industry in Kerala is centered in three districts namely Thrissur, Quilon and Calicut. Thrissur district account for the highest concentration of 45 per cent of the units in Kerala. The availability of raw materials and reasonable labour have acted as a fillip to the growth of the industry in Alagappanagar, Chittissery and Pudukad areas in Thrissur district. The researcher's family is doing the tiles business for the last 2 decades. Therefore, the researcher had a natural inclination to choose this topic in this area.

## STATEMENT OF THE PROBLEM

The performance of a unit depends on the effectiveness of various functional areas such as Production, Marketing, Finance and Labour. The clay tiles manufacturing units are no exception. Therefore, a comprehensive understanding of these functional areas is required. What are the techniques and practices adopted in the production process? What are the factors that influence marketing effectiveness? How does the clay tile units raise funds from different sources? To what extent are the funds effectively utilised by these units? What are the practices followed in the labour management? What are the various problems faced by the units in each functional area? All these functional areas are interdependent in nature. To what extent are they linked with each other? The performance in each functional area affects its overall performance. This leads to many research issues and this study makes an attempt to find out answers to these questions. Hence, the present research study is undertaken to examine the overall performance of clay tiles manufacturing units in Thrissur District, Kerala.

## REVIEW OF LITERATURE

A wide variety of research studies have been conducted by a number of individuals. Institutions and agencies have prepared and presented various reports and articles on tile industry. A review of the available literature will be helpful in enlightening the readers on the present status of the industry. An attempt is made to review the literature and it is presented in chronological order.

*KAP India Tiles (2001)* conducted a research on the "Present State of the Tile Industry in Thrissur" and the study concludes that the human force is the key factor behind clay industry, by eliminating or reducing the human element, the clay industry won't survive. At the same time modernization must be accepted where necessary so that the quality and quantity of the products can be improved. By cluster formation these objectives can be achieved. Further, the cluster can be developed and established as a globally competent and preferred source for clay products [1].

*C. G. Narayanan (1995)* examined the efficient use of fuel in clay tiles manufacturing units in different ways: Induced draught purely depends on mechanical efficiency unlike kiln chimney, which mostly depends on atmospheric condition such as humidity, rain, cloud etc; Control of fuel such as depth and clear suction possibility and the damper control; Yearly maintenance of kiln chambers and the application of heat conserving materials such as pozzolana, rice husk etc., in the crevices of inside chamber to avoid loss of heat[2].

*V. Easwaran (1995)* reported on the process of tiles, use of ammonium chloride, varying between 0.1 to 1.0 per cent according to the physico-chemical properties of the soil, as in admixture with the soil. It was found out that the drying firing losses were reduced to 3 to 4 per cent compared with the factory losses of 25 to 30 per cent [3].

*R. S. Prasad (1994)* studied the cluster group of industries on clay tiles. This study is mainly concentrated on identifying the problems faced by the existing tiles manufacturing units including technology, financial problems facing modernization, availability of suitable clays, firewood and their cost, marketing etc.[4].

*Anantha Subramaniam (1993)* stated in his study that, modernization is needed without delay. This is possible only by providing required financial assistance to the industry. The Government and the financing institutions should be persuaded to chalk out a programme for providing finance for implementing a modernization programme [5].

*K.G.K. Warrier (1992)* critically examined raw material processing and technology. The important parameters on the raw material quality, processing conditions and quality of products have been listed and explained. Some of the recent developments in the clay industry such as the concept of vitrified clay tiles and firing practices have been examined[6].

*M. K. Nair (1991)* studied the modernization of clay industry and this study mainly concentrates on enabling any small scale unit to introduce modernization measures, facilitate identification of appropriate process of producing clay articles, conforming to standard specifications and list possible improvements that could be brought about in the existing process of manufacture for modernization, with minimal dislocation and investments[7].

*K. P. Mani (1990)* studied the economics of tile industry in Kerala, According to him the industry can diversify towards the production of burnt bricks and low cost building products; the technology prevailing in the industry is out-dated, tile factories which face financial and marketing problems are to be declared sick and unnecessary competition among the factories leads to the destruction of the industry[8].

*National Productivity Council (1987)* made an attempt to measure the productivity of tile industry in Kerala. Though the number of tile factories in Kerala increases the capital and productivity have declined particularly since 1985, due to high cost of labour and raw materials[9].

*P. F. Thomas (1986)* mentioned the urgency of modernizing the tile factories in Kerala to recapture the earlier eminence in tile production[10].

*Karnataka State Financial Corporation (1986)* conducted a State Level Seminar on modernization of roofing and flooring tile industry at Mangalore. It evaluated the problems and prospects of the industry in Karnataka[11].

*The Government of Gujarat (1984)* reported on the tile industry concentrated in Morvi in Gujarat. It was observed that the problems prevailing in the state were quite similar to those in Kerala[12].

*M.R. Sreedharan Nair and M.K. Bala Krishnan Nair (1980)* studied the stressed need for using pugmill and revolving press to reduce labour cost and to better the quality of tiles. Mechanisation is required for material handling also. It is noted that fuel is the biggest problem of the industry. It is also suggested that furnaces have to be scientifically designed[13].

*B.R. Ananthan (1975)* examined the origin, history, features and problems of tile industry in south Kerala District. Most of the factories were not dependent on banks for long term or short-term financial assistance. During the Second World War, the tile industry made very high profits. He found that most of the tile units were not able to take advantage of the facilities of small scale Industries since they were not registered as SSI's due to the ignorance of the entrepreneurs[14].

*John Thomas Chirayath (1969)* conducted a study of the tile industry in Kerala. In addition to the origin and history of the industry, a number of statistical data and other structural ratios were also included in the study[15].

*L.C. Jain and V. K. Jain (1966)* assessed the major problems in increasing production, stabilizing prices and improving quality. Increase in drying cracks and warps, rough appearance warped surface, crooked alignment, cracks, air bubbles, blocked holes are some of the defects of Indian tiles. Breakage during transit is 8.9% but in the monsoon it may be 10 to 15 per cent[16].

*V. K. Ghatge (1966)* studied the building bricks and tiles manufacturing in India from the very ancient period. It exists as a village industry and is run on a seasonal basis. Agricultural labourers are mainly employed in the industry, simple and locally available equipment are used for its manufacture[17].

*Devaraja Iyer (1966)* has traced the origin and development of the tile industry in Thrissur district. He was the engineer in charge of the construction of Manali river-bridge who discovered the suitability of soil around the Manali river for manufacturing tiles. It was the dawn of the tiles industry in the district[18].

*D. Sorabji (1966)* stated that the deterioration in the quality of tiles adversely affected the foreign exchange earnings capacity. Overcharging and liberalized factory rules, restriction and paucity of power, clay and heavy taxation are the bottlenecks of the industry. It is suggested that only a concerted effort by Government, manufacturers and labourers can overcome the problems of the tile industry. Neither the Government nor the manufacturers have realized the gravity of the situation[19].

*U.P. Mahaswary (1966)* has identified the problems of small-scale tile factory in Madras, Andhra Pradesh and Kerala. These are; unsatisfactory preparation of clay mix, lack of driers fitted with humidity and temperature controllers, excessive breakage during drying stage, high fuel consumption, high percentage rejects of tiles from kilns and poor quality of finished products and very low percentage of first quality tiles[20].

*National Council of Economic Research (1962)* stated in the report "Techno Economic Survey of Kerala", have discussed the factors responsible for the development of tile industry in Kerala [21].

*Department of Economics and Commerce, Govt. of Madras (1957)* reported that tiled roofing is comparatively cheap and ideal to Indian climate conditions in comparison with reinforced cement concrete roofing and flooring[22].

*"History and Development of Tile Industry in Mangalore" was the work of B.G. Karat (1955).* He examined the factors responsible for the concentration and development of tile industry in Mangalore. He pointed out that the availability of high quality clay, cheap labour and good demand for the product were the chief factors responsible for the concentration of the industry in Mangalore[23].

*H. Hoffman (1913)* in his book "The Basel Mission Industries" has discussed the socio-economic conditions then existing and the background of undertaking the industry. The object of starting the first tile factory in Mangalore was to provide livelihood to the Christian converts[24].

*Edward Dobson wrote his book in 1889,* which had been claimed as the first book in English on the subject. He has discussed the importance of tiles and bricks in the ancient period, with regard to their use in temples and other places of worship. The use of high quality bricks and tiles in monuments and public buildings was a prestigious practice[25].

A review of earlier studies cited enabled the researcher to identify the fact that no comprehensive study has so far been made to study the organizational and functional areas of the clay tile units and their contribution to the overall growth of Thrissur, a backward but fast developing district in Kerala.

## DEFINITIONS OF THE CONCEPTS USED

*Small scale unit:* Unit which has invested less than Rs. 1 crore.

*Small Scale Clay tiles manufacturing unit:* A unit engaged in manufacturing the roofing tiles, flooring tiles and other decorative clay tiles.

*Small Scale Clay tiles manufacturing Industry:* Group of units engaged in manufacturing the roofing tiles, flooring tiles and other decorative clay tiles.

*Production performance:* A comprehensive working of production components such as production process, employment of materials and problems related to production activities.

*Marketing performance:* Adopting marketing practices and encountering problems related to marketing activities.

*Finance performance:* Arranging, utilizing the funds, managing the working capital and problems related to financial activities.

*Labour performance:* Recruiting, selecting, paying, promoting and motivating the employees and then providing with other benefits and problems related to labour.

*Overall performance:* The combination of the performance of functional areas such as production, marketing, finance and labour.

## OBJECTIVES OF THE STUDY

The following are the objectives of the study:

1. To study the profile of the Clay Tiles Industry, Study area and the functions of clay tiles manufacturing units in Thrissur District (Kerala).

2. To analyse the Production and Marketing performance of the units and the problems associated with them.
3. To analyse the Financial and Labour performance of the units and the problems related to them.
4. To examine the overall performance of clay tiles manufacturing units in Thrissur District.

## SCOPE OF THE STUDY

The study covers all the registered small-scale clay tiles manufacturing units located at Thrissur district in Kerala State. The four functional areas namely Production, Marketing, Finance and Labour can be analysed from different angles such as "finding the correlation between the various factors involved in the functional areas and organizational variable", "contribution of the factors towards the performance of the respective functional areas" and "contribution of the functional areas to the overall performance of these units". Though other small-scale industries are scattered all over the district, clay tiles manufacturing units are located mainly in three areas namely Chittissery, Alagappanagar and Pudukad. So, the researcher has chosen the above-mentioned three areas for this research study. The focus was on the roofing tiles, flooring tiles and other decorative tiles manufactured by the units.

## PERIOD OF STUDY

The study period is divided into different parts based on the date used in this research work. The primary data from all the units were collected between 2005 and 2006. The secondary data were collected between the year 1998 and 2006.

## HYPOTHESES

The study has the following hypotheses:

1. There is no significant relationship between the various factors of the functional areas and the organizational variables of the clay tiles manufacturing units.
2. There are no significant factors emerging in the various functional areas that contributed to the performance of the respective functions.

3. The problems in the functional areas did not reduce the performance of the respective functions.
4. There are no significant functions emerging and contributing to the overall performance of the units.
5. There is no significant difference in the level of performance among the clay tiles manufacturing units in Thrissur district.

## METHODOLOGY

In Thrissur district, there are three major clusters of clay tiles manufacturing units—Chittissery, Alagappanagar and Pudukad. 84 units are registered under small-scale units category as per the records of District Industrial Centre—39 in Chittissery, 23 in Alagappanagar and 22 in Pudukad. Census method was adopted for selecting the units in this study.

### Pilot Study

A pilot study was conducted by the researcher. The researcher prepared a draft interview schedule which comprised 96 conceptual questions from the functional areas: Production (32), Marketing (17), Finance (28), and Labour (19). 30 units were drawn at random for the pilot study. After collecting the data, the 96 questions were reduced to 68 based on the judgmental validity procedure. Similarly, the researcher also had a discussion with the experts and owners of the units and identified a total of 37 problems in the functional areas.

### Primary Data

A structured interview schedule was prepared to collect the primary data from the units. The schedule consisted of two parts. Part–I is organisational background, which consisted of 8 questions. Part–II includes a total of 68 conceptual questions based on the functional areas namely Production (24), Marketing (10), Finance (22) and Labour (12). Similarly it also includes the problems identified in each functional area.

### Secondary Data

The secondary data were gathered from the records of Small Industries Service Institute, District Industries Centre and Magazines, Books, Published documents, websites and discussions with experts.

### Data Analysis

The collected data were analysed with the help of statistical package namely SPSS (Statistical Package for Social Science) and Alyuda Neural Forecaster. The analysis was done at three stages. In stage–1 after classification and tabulation of data, statistical techniques were used to find the relationship between the variables of functional areas and the organizational variables. In stage–2 Neural Networks technique was used to scrutinize the effect of functional variables on the performance of various functional areas. Multiple regression analysis was used to find out the effect of each functional area on the overall performance of the factories. Similarly, in stage–3 control chart was used to classify the performance of the units into high and low and finally discriminant analysis was employed to identify the best predictors which will discriminate the level of units into high and low.

## LIMITATIONS OF THE STUDY

The study is mainly focused on registered small-scale clay tiles manufacturing units in Thrissur District and results of the study are applicable only to small-scale units located in Thrissur District. Generalisation of results is not possible for the units functioning in the other parts of Kerala or elsewhere in the country. The questions raised by the researcher were purely categorical in nature, so he did not prove the reliability and validity of the items by employing statistical tools. Therefore the reliability and validity of the data depends on the information supplied by them. The owners or managers of certain units were not at all co-operative during the data collection, in spite of the assurance given to them that the data would be kept confidential and would be used only for the study purpose.

## CHAPTER SCHEME

Following are the various chapters organized in this research study:

*Chapter I:* Design and execution of the study.

*Chapter II:* Profile of the clay tiles manufacturing units–An overview

*Chapter III:* Analysis of Production and Marketing functions.

*Chapter IV:* Analysis of Finance and Labour functions.

*Chapter V:* Analysis of the overall performance of clay tiles manufacturing units.

*Chapter VI:* Summary of findings, suggestions and conclusion.

### *Notes References*

1. KAP India Tiles, "Present State of the Tile Industry in Thrissur", Survey report, Thrissur, 2001.
2. Narayanan, C.G., Vice President, All Kerala Tile Manufacturers' Association, "Fuels for Tile Industry", Survey report of Chithra Ceramics, Pudukad, Thrissur, 1995.
3. Easwaran, V., "Improved Bricks and Tiles Through CBRI Research", Survey report of Central Building Research Institute, Trivandrum, 1995.
4. Prasad, R.S., "Cluster Group of Industries on clay tiles, Study report of Small Industries Service Institute (SISI), Thrissur, (1994).
5. Dr. Anantha Subramaniam, President, All Kerala Tile Manufacturers' Association, Survey report on "Financing for Modernisation of Tile Industry", Thrissur, 1993.
6. Warrier, K.G.K., "Clay Based Ceramic Products – An Overview", Report of Regional Research Laboratory, Trivandrum, 1992.
7. Nair, M.K., "Modernization Guide for clay products industry", Study report of Small Industries Service Institute (SISI), Thrissur, 1991.
8. Mani, K.P., "Tile Industry in Kerala – Economics, Problems & Prospects", doctoral thesis, Cochin University of Science & Technology, 1990.
9. National Product Council, "Productivity of tile Industry in Kerala", NPC, Thrissur, 1987.

10. Thomas, P. F., "Need for Development of Technology in tile Industry", Status report of State Product Council, Thrissur, 1986.

11. Karnataka State Financial Corporation, "Modernisation of Roofing & Flooring tile Industry, A State Level Seminar Report, Mangalore, 1986.

12. Government of Gujarat, Department of Economics, "Roofing & Flooring Tile Industry in Morvi", Status report of Government of Gujarat, 1984.

13. Sreedharan Nair, M.R. & Bala Krishnan Nair, M. K., "Tiles Industry in Kerala–Mangalore type roofing tiles", Status Report of Small Industries Service Institute (SISI) Thrissur, 1980.

14. Ananthan, B. R., "Tile Industry in South Kerala District–A Case Study", *Indian Journal of Commerce*, 1975.

15. John Thomas Chirayath, "A Study on the Tile Industry in Kerala", Doctoral Thesis, Calicut University, 1969.

16. Jain, L.C. and Jain, V. K., "Bricks and Tile Research in India", Report of All India Seminar on Ceramic Industries, Small Industries Service Institute (SISI) Thrissur, 1966.

17. Ghatge, V. K., "A Note on Building Bricks and Roofing Tile Industries", Report of All India Seminar on Ceramic Industries, Small Industries Service Institute (SISI) Thrissur, 1966.

18. Devaraja Iyer, "Origin, Growth and Present Position of Tile Industry", Report of All India Seminar on Ceramic Industries, Small Industries Service Institute (SISI) Thrissur, 1966.

19. Sorabji, D., "Brick and Tile Industry", Report of All India Seminar on Ceramic Industries, Small Industries Service Institute (SISI) Thrissur, 1962.

20. Maheswary, U.P., "Development Research vs Small Scale Roofing Tile Industry", Report of All India Seminar on Ceramic Industries, Small Industries Service Institute (SISI) Thrissur, 1962.

21. The National Council of Economic Research, "Techno Economic Survey of Kerala", Survey Report, New Delhi, 1962.

22. Department of Economics and Commerce, Govt. of Madras, "Manufacturing of Building Materials", Unpublished Research Project, Madras, 1957.

23. Kart, B. G., "History and Development of the Tile Industry in Mangalore", Doctoral Thesis, University of Bombay 1955.

24. Hoffman, H., "The Basel Mission Industries", New Publications, Mangalore, 1913.

25. Edward Dobson, "A Rudimentary Treatise on the Manufacturing of Bricks and Tiles", London, 1889.

CHAPTER 2

# Profile of Clay Tiles Manufacturing Units–An Overview

This chapter consists of four sections.

- A profile of clay tiles industry.
- A profile of clay tiles manufacturing industry in Kerala.
- A profile of Thrissur District.
- Functional areas of clay tiles manufacturing units—Production, Marketing, Finance and Labour.

## PROFILE OF CLAY TILES INDUSTRY

Clay tiles are one of the most distinctive and decorative historic roofing and flooring materials because of their great variety of shapes, colours, profiles, patterns, and textures. Traditionally, clay tiles were formed by hand, and later by machine extrusion of natural clay, textured or glazed with color, and fired in high-temperature kilns. The unique visual qualities of a clay tiles often make it a prominent feature in defining the overall character of a historic building. The significance and inherently fragile nature of tiles dictate that special care and precaution be taken to preserve and repair them.

*Clay tiles* have been used for thousands of years all over the world. In fact, the original roof tiles are still in use on many ancient buildings in Italy and other parts of Europe. The original tiles used by most European cultures were barrel-type tiles or "cap & pan" tiles as we refer to them today. Barrel clay tiles made their way to the New World with the Spanish explorers and were used for roofing and flooring their Mission churches. From St. Augustine, Florida to Southern Mexico, the Spaniards built their missions continuing north along the California coast.

It may be either handcrafted or machine-made; in general, roofs installed before the end of the 19th century consist of hand formed tiles, with machine-made tiles becoming more dominant as technology improved during the 20th century. Clay tile itself, whether made by hand or by machine, can vary in quality from tile to tile. Terracotta red is the colour most commonly associated with historic clay roofing and flooring tiles. The reddish colour comes from clay with a large percentage of iron oxide, and there are many variations of this natural colour to be found in tiles, ranging from deep reddish browns to softer and paler oranges and pinks. Lighter buff and beige colors, as well as black, also appear on traditional tile roofed buildings. Buff-colored tiles were made from nearly pure fire clay, and pouring manganese dissolved in water over the tile before firing resulted in smoke brown or black glazed tiles. Towards the end of the 19th century the popularity of coloured glazes for roofing tiles increased, and their use and the range of colours continues to expand today.

**Historical Background**

The origin of clay tiles can be traced independently to two different parts of the world: China, during the Neolithic Age, beginning around 10,000 B.C; and the Middle East, a short time later. From these regions, the use of clay tiles spread throughout Asia and Europe. Not only the ancient Egyptians and Babylonians, but also the Greeks and Romans roofed their buildings with clay tiles, and adaptations of their practice continue in Europe to the present. European settlers brought this roofing tradition to America where it was established in many places by the 17$^{th}$ century.

Archeologists have recovered specimens of clay tiles from 1585 settlement of Roanoke Island in North Carolina. Clay tiles were also used in the early English settlements in Jamestown, Virginia, and nearby St.Mary's in Maryland. Clay tiles were also used in the Spanish settlement of St. Augustine in Florida, and by both the French and Spanish in New Orleans.

Dutch settlers on the east coast first imported clay tiles from Holland. By 1650, they had established their own full-scale production of clay tiles in the upper Hudson River Valley, shipping tiles south to New Amsterdam. Several tile-manufacturing operations were in business around the time of the American Revolution, offering both coloured and glazed tile and unglazed natural terracotta tile in the New York City area, and in neighboring New Jersey. A 1774 New York newspaper advertised the availability of locally produced, clay tiles for sale that were guaranteed to "stand any weather". On the west coast clay tile was first manufactured in wooden moulds in 1780 at Mission San Antonio de Padua in California by Indian neophytes under the direction of Spanish missionaries.

By far the most significant factor in popularizing clay tiles during the Colonial period in America was the concern with fire like the devastating fires of London (1666) and Boston. These fire codes, which remained in effect for almost two centuries, encouraged the use of tile for roofs and floors, because of its fireproof qualities. Clay roofing, flooring and other decorative tiles were also preferred because of its durability, ease of maintenance, and lack of thermal conductivity.

Although more efficient production methods had lowered the cost of the clay tile, its use began to decline in much of the northeastern United States during the second quarter of the 19th century. Wood shingles were becoming popular and new fire-resistant materials slate and metals such as copper, iron, tin-plate, zinc, and galvanized iron were available. The metal roofing materials were available at a lower cost. Even the appearance of clay tile was no longer fashionable, and by the 1830s clay roofing tiles had slipped temporarily out of popularity in many parts of the world.

## Revival Styles and Renewed Interest in Clay Tiles

By the mid-19th century, the introduction of the Italianate villa style of architecture in the United States prompted a new interest in clay tiles. This had the effect of revitalizing the clay tile manufacturing industry, and by the 1870s, new factories were in business, including large operations in Akron, Ohio, Baltimore and Maryland. The Centennial Exhibition in Philadelphia promoted clay tiles in 1876. Tile-making machines were first patented in the 1870s, and although much roofing and flooring tile continued to be made by hand, by the 1880s more and more factories were beginning to use machines.

Clay tiles fell out of fashion again for a short time at the end of the 19th century, but once again gained acceptance in the 20th century, due primarily to the popularity of the Romantic Revival of architectural styles. With the availability of machines capable of extruding clay in a variety of forms in large quantities, clay tiles became more readily available across the nation. More regional manufacturing plants were established in areas with large natural deposits of clay, including Alfred, New York; New Lexington, Ohio; Lincoin, California; and Atlanta, Georgia; as well as Indiana, Illinois and Kansas. The popularity of clay tiles continued in the 20th century.

## The Colourful World of Clay

In and around Kent and Sussex, Wealden clay gives tiles a warm, deep, reddish hue that has become a feature of the local built landscape. Variations in colour are obtained by controlling the kiln atmosphere whereby the iron content occurring naturally in clay undergoes a chemical change during firing, producing a wide spectrum of colours. This unusual colouring is the result of 'smut', a black glaze used on tiles in the area. In and around London, the city atmosphere with its pollution and smoke has resulted in roofs becoming covered in grime, which means that roofs which started out being the characteristic red and orange of clay roof tiles now look black and red. The main source of clay in the Midlands is Etruria Marl in the Staffordshire area where production methods have influenced the characteristic Blue and Brindled tiles. Blue tiles are produced by close control of the kiln atmosphere upon iron-rich Etruria Marl clay.

## The Preferred Roofing Material

A look upwards at the ceiling today reveals many different styles and types of roofing. Clay roof tiles have been around since the 13th century and have proved their durability. Their colour is permanent and, unlike other materials, does not fade with time. Indeed, the elements work with the clay to produce a weathered and mellow appearance, improving their looks with age. What is more, clay tiles are fire resistant, able to withstand harsh chemicals and are not susceptible to biological degradation, they do not harbour excessive mould growth and are not affected by extremes of heat or cold. These properties coupled with the fact that clay tiles are a natural and sustainable product make clay tiles an ideal roofing option for new building and refurbishment work. One of the greatest challenges to architects, planners and designers must be to consider not only how the building will look in the immediate future, but also how it will look in 10, 20, 40, 50, or 100 years' time. This is the greatest legacy that they can bequeath to future generations-an architecture that is as beautiful, if not more so, in decades to come as it was when first constructed.

The roof is undoubtedly the most exposed face of any structure. It has to withstand rain, wind, ice, and ultra-violet light and, increasingly, the effects of damaging acids caused by atmospheric pollution. Not only will a clay roof tile hold an authentic time worn appeal but also its maintenance cost will mean that its whole life cost is relatively low. The life span of a clay tile is influenced by the type of clay, the way it is manufactured, the dampness of the atmosphere, the position of the building and the pitch of the roof. All these factors will influence the speed of the weathering process.

## Early Tiles

During the 17th and 18th centuries the most common type of clay tiles used in America were flat and rectangular. They measured approximately 10" x 6" x ½" (25cm x 15cm x 1.25cm), and had two nail or peg holes at one end through which they were anchored to the roofing and flooring laths. Sometimes a strip of mortar was placed between the overlapping rows of tile to prevent the tiles from lifting in high winds. In addition to flat tiles, interlocking S-shaped pantiles were also used in the 18th century. These were formed by moulding clay over tapered sections of logs, and were generally quite large. Alternately termed pan, crooked, or Flemish tiles, and measuring approximately 14 ½ " x 9 ½ " (37cm x 24cm), these interlocking tiles were hung on roofing lath by means of a ridge or lug located on the upper part of the underside of each tile. Both plain (flat) tile and pantile (S-shaped or curved) roofs and floors were capped at the ridge with semicircular ridge tiles.

The accurate dating of the early roofing tiles is difficult and often impossible. Fragments of tile found at archeological sites may indicate the existence of clay tile roofs and floors, but the same type of tile was also sometimes used for other purposes such as outlasted many of the earliest, less permanent structures, it was often reused on later buildings.

## Clay Tile Substitutes

In addition to sheet metal "tile" roofs introduced in the middle of the 19th century, concrete roofing tile was developed as another substitute for clay tile in the later part of the 19th century. It became quite popular by the beginning of the 20th century. Concrete tile is composed of a dense mixture of Portland cement blended with aggregates, including sand, and pigment, and extruded from high-pressure machines. Although it tends to lack the colour permanence and the subtle colour variations inherent in natural clay tiles, concrete tile continues to be a popular roofing material today because it reproduces the general look of clay tile, if not always the exact profile or proportions of historic clay tile, at a somewhat lower cost and weight.

**Roof Tiles Used in Modern Houses**

Floor Tile Used in Interiors

Floor Tile Used in Exteriors

## A PROFILE OF CLAY TILES MANUFACTURING INDUSTRY IN KERALA

### The State of Kerala

Kerala, one of the smallest states in the Republic of India, was formed in 1956. It has an area of 15005 square miles (38,863 square kilometers), about one per cent of the total area of India. The state stretches for about 360 miles (580 kilometers) along the Malabar Coast on the southwestern side of the Indian peninsula; its width varies from 20 to 75 miles. It is bordered by Karnataka state in the north, Tamilnadu State in the east. The capital is Trivandrum. Kerala has evolved a unique culture. It is a highly politicized region, but it has a long tradition of religious amity. The temperature normally varies between 80$^0$F to 90$^0$F in the plains but drops to about 70$^0$F in the high lands. Kerala gets both southwest and northwest monsoons with seasonal rainfall in many parts of the State that exceeds 118" (3000mm).

Kerala's population as per the census of 2001 is 318 million comprising 15,468,664 males and 16,369,955 females. 2001 Census figure shows that Kerala has achieved the highest literacy rate of 90.92% as against All India rate of 65.38%. Kerala has 10.3 million workers accounting for 2.6% of the country's total workforce.

### Profile of Clay Tiles Manufacturing Industry in Kerala

More than a century old, the tiles industry can legitimately be called a traditional industry of Kerala State. Due mainly to the natural advantages, the industry gradually spread to different parts of the State. In the matter of both total value of production and diversity of products manufactured, Kerala is foremost among the tile making States. It is used for roofing, flooring and decorative purposes. More than three fourths of the houses constructed in the rural areas and more than one fourth of the houses in the urban areas use tiles and slates as the roofing and flooring materials.

It was in the year 1878 that the Bessel Missionaries of Germany in Mangalore established the first clay tile factory in the country and they had set up the Calicut Tile Factory at Feroke. These tiles have won really worldwide reputation. They have been exhibited in many exhibitions in different centers like Madras, Bombay, Allahabad and Banaras and more than a dozen gold and silver medals were awarded at these exhibitions. At present there are about 800 tile factories in India spread over different states—Kerala, Gujarat, Karnataka, Orissa, Madhya Pradesh, Maharastra and Andra Pradesh. Around 44 per cent of tile factories in the country are in the state of Kerala.

The clay tile industry in Kerala is centered in three districts namely Thrissur, Quilon and Calicut. There are 350 tile factories in Kerala providing direct employment to more than 20000 persons and indirect employment to 25000 persons. Thrissur district accounts for the highest concentration of 45% of the units are located in the areas of Alagappanagar, Chittissery and Pudukad. In Quilon district 26% units are located in the areas of Ithikkara, Asramam, Mynagappally, Kallada etc., and around 19 % of the tiles units are situated in Calicut district. The installed capacity of the tile industry in Kerala is 100 crores tiles per annum. The present production is only 55 crores tiles accounting for 55% of the installed capacity.

## Mining and Minerals

The mineral resources in the State and its contribution to the State's economy are insignificant. Major minerals in the State are beach sands comprising Illuminate, Monazite, Zircon, China clay, Tile clay, Lime shell, Lime stone, Bauxite, Silica sand, Graphite and Quartz which are being explored and exploited by the State Department of Mining and Geology, Kerala Mineral Exploration and Development Project and Kerala State Mineral Development Corporation.

## Land Utilisation Pattern

Important crops of the State are paddy, coconut, cashew nut, coffee, areca nut, rubber, tea, cocoa, banana, pineapple and spices like ginger, cardamom, pepper etc. The present land utilization at 86% including forests is high compared with other regions of the country.

## Level of Technology

The tile factories in Kerala vary greatly in the degree of mechanization and the level of technology employed. As a matter of fact, the tile industry in Kerala presents a vivid picture of the obsolete and the modern. In general, the tile factories can be broadly classified into three groups as small, medium and big. The small factories employ rudimentary and antiquated methods where almost all the operations are done by manual labour. In most of the big factories the operations are highly mechanized. They employ modern techniques and are run by electricity. These big factories thus have higher efficiency of production and hence stand out from the rest. In between these two extreme groups come the medium factories, which use only the minimum machinery required and rely on manual labour to a great extent. Because of the preponderance of small and medium factories, the tile industry is generally considered a labour intensive one.

## Concentration in the Tiles Industry

Even though there are tile factories in all the nine districts of the State, the highest concentration of factories is found in Thrissur (45%) followed by Quilon (26%) and Calicut (19%). The proliferation of the tile factories in these centers and their spread to other parts of the State were due mainly to the natural advantages in the matter of essential raw materials, cheap transport facilities and the rise of a local entrepreneurial class to patronize the industry. The primary factors influencing the location of a tile factory is the easy availability of suitable types of clay and firewood in the near vicinity. Both clay and firewood are heavy and voluminous material and the cost of their transport is a major factor in the cost of production. A special feature in the location of most of the older factories in the State is that they are located in places which have the advantage of cheap canal or river transport. These factories were thus able to keep down their cost of production by making use of cheap water transport. Many factories located in Quilon, Feroke and Alwaye have even now the advantage of cheap water transport. In Ollur and Pudukkad area of Thrissur district factories do not have the facilities for water transport. But these factories enjoy a complementary advantage in that both clay and firewood are available in close proximity.

Most of the tiles manufacturing centres are located near railway heads having a good network of railway connections. Probably this is the single major factor that has greatly helped the dispersal of the finished products of the tile factories in Kerala to far-flung corners of the country. Similarly, the proximity of a Harbour near Feroke (Calicut) was responsible for the development of a flourishing export trade in tiles. Since tile industry is a labour intensive one, the availability of labour can normally be considered to influence the location of tile factories.

## MATERIALS USED IN THE PRODUCTION PROCESS

### Clay

What is clay? Different answers may be given. The chemist would call it a hydrous silicate of alumina; the little boy, a nice sticky mud-and they would both be right. But only in part, clay is not a single substance but a mixture of several substances; while aluminum silicate is the chief ingredient, impurities are also present. These impurities affect the working properties; hence there are two essential properties when: moist it is plastic, and when heated it becomes hard.

Feldspar is the parent of clay. Feldspar is important to the potter because it is used in most glazer and almost all clay bodies. It is the chief ingredient of granite and many other rocks. There are several different kinds of feldspar, but all of them contain alumina and silica plus something else. During the weathering process, these substances are dissolved out of the feldspar, while alumina and silica remain to form clay.

## TYPES OF CLAY

### Residual clay

Pure clay is composed of alumina, silica and chemically combined water; but absolutely pure clay is almost non-existent.

The clay most nearly pure is that which has remained in the same spot where it was formed. This is called residual clay.

### Sedimentary Clay

Most clay has not remained where it was formed, but has moved great distances, carried by streams, winds and glaciers. Such clay is called sedimentary clay. As a result of its transportation it has been ground finer in grain and contains many impurities; hence it is more plastic and less refractory than residual clay. Its colour in the natural state may be almost anything—blue, green, yellow, red, brown, gray, or even black. When fired it is usually some shade of red or buff.

### Plastic Kaolin

Plastic kaolin is almost a contradiction, for actually no kaolin is really plastic. The term refers to certain clays which have been transported without becoming contaminated, and so burn white. Because of their finer grain size, they are a little more workable than regular kaolins and are therefore valuable as body ingredients.

### Ball Clay

Ball clay is sedimentary clay, which, in most cases, has been carried in a stream and deposited on the bottom of some body of water. It is extremely fine in grain and usually has carbonaceous material mixed with it. As a result, it is highly plastic. It is often dark in colour, but if heated, turns white.

### Terracotta Clay

Terracotta may be made from any fine red-burning clay, but the best varieties require material which has been many times deposited by natural causes in order that it may be sufficiently fine in texture, it must also produce a pleasant colour when fired. The term 'Terracotta' usually applies to objects of a certain shade of red, but originally it was used for all kinds of baked earth. At present, any vases and similar objects made of unglazed clay are classed as 'Terracotta' by dealers, quite irrespective of their colour.

## Fire Clay

Fire clay is found throughout the coal measures. It burns to a white or cream colour, though some of the less pure ones are reddish when fired. The composition and qualities of fire clay vary very greatly, and many varieties are known. The best type of fire clay contains almost as much alumina as silica. The highest grades of fire clay are difficult to work with, on account of their low plasticity, but highly refractory clays, which are at the same time plastic are very valuable, though rather scarce. Fire clays are used commercially in the manufacture of refractory brick.

## Stoneware Clay

Like fire clay, stoneware clay will stand high temperatures, but it is smoother and more plastic and usually fire to a light buff colour. In a reducing fire they become gray or brown. Monmouth and Jordan are stoneware clays.

## Common Clay

Common clay is the material used to make tiles and bricks. It is abundant throughout our county, usually fires dark red or brown, and hardens at low temperatures. Common clays vary widely in their characteristics, but they have much to offer the potter who will take the trouble to learn their secrets.

The clay tiles are usually of low grade. Red burning type of clays should easily burn hard at comparatively low temperatures. These clays have fusion point around 950$^0$C to 1000$^0$C. The vast resources of alluvial clays in the paddy lands and valleys are used by this industry. The clays available for the manufacture of tiles are mostly found in the districts of Thrissur, Alappuzha, Kannanur, Ernakulam, Kottayam, Kozhikode, Palakkad, Kollam and Thruvananthapuram. There are two main types of tile clays in the State – terracotta clay and china clay. The china clays are confined mainly to Kannanur district, whereas, the terracotta clays are found in all other districts mentioned above. Tile and brick clays are included in the group of minor minerals. The industry consumes about 10 lakhs tones of clay in a year.

### Firewood

It is the most commonly used fuel in these industries in Kerala for burning tiles. More than 40% of the cost of production of tile is the cost of firewood in small size units having intermittent kilns while this is about 25% in medium and large size units having long continuous kilns. To reduce fuel consumption is to reduce the cost of production. The firewood price is increasing rapidly due to many reasons such as reduction in the forest area and utilization of land for cultivation, increasing demand for wood for other industries, increasing demand for wood as fuel in the domestic sector and increase in the cost of all fuels etc. These trends are beyond the control of tile manufacturers. Firewood is a renewable source of energy. Producing more firewood by cultivating fast growing trees and maintaining forest has to be attempted.

### Kerosene and Other Oil Mix

Kerosene is most commonly one used as lubricating oil. Nowadays kerosene is not available in plenty. The producers get kerosene on the basis of quota. Kerosene and other oils can be used for burning terracotta clay tiles but the sulphur in some oil tends to spoil clay tiles. Oil is particularly useful in countries where coal is difficult to obtain. As oil has 1 ½ to 2 ½ times the heating power of coal and needs much less attention in handling; so, the difference between the cost of oil and the cost of coal is not as serious as it appears at first sight. With oil firing, the chimney-heat losses are low, no smoke is produced, and the control of the temperature of the kiln is easier. There are the advantages but there is a greater risk of explosion and of fire and the insurance rates are higher than with coal.

### Other Clay-related Products

Most of the modern tile factories in Kerala are making a variety of products besides ordinary roofing tiles and bricks. The range of products includes ornamental ceiling and flooring tiles, ridge and valley tiles, terrace tiles, elephant tongue tiles, ridge ventilators, ventilators - single tile and double tile, skylights – single tile and double tile, finials and crested ridges, terracotta vases in attractive designs, and filters, flower pots and drainage pipes. These are made with the same tile clay by making suitable changes in the dies used or by slightly altering the manufacturing process.

## A PROFILE OF THRISSUR DISTRICT

Thrissur District came into existence on the 1st of April 1958. The name Thrissur is derived from the Malayalam word 'Thrissivaperur' which means the sacred land of Lord Shiva. A temple of Lord Shiva known as 'Vadakkannathan' at the heart of the town is the major attraction of the town. In addition, the famous temple of Lord Srikrishna at Guruvayur is situated in the District at a distance of 30 Kms from the town. Thrissur is known as the Cultural Capital of Kerala. A number of cultural institutions have their headquarters in this District. It is bounded by Malappuram and Palakkad Districts in the North, Ernakulam and Idukki Districts in the South, Arabian Sea in the West and Palakkad and Coimbatore Distrcit of Tamilnadu in the East. The District has an area of 3032 Sq Kms, which constitutes 7.8 per cent of the total area of the State.

### Administrative Set-up

For administrative set-up, the District has 225 villages in five Taluks. The Taluks are Chavakkad, Kodungallur, Mukundapuram, Thalappilly and Thrissur. For the purpose of Development activities, there are 1 corporation (Thrissur), 5 Municipalities, 17 Blocks, 209 Villages and 92 Panchayaths with 1220 Panchayat Wards after reconstitution effected during 2001. The area of the corporation is 101.42 Sq.Kms.

### Rainfall, Soil and River

Thrissur has a pleasing climate throughout the year. The District receives heavy rainfall during the South-West Monsoon, from June to November. The normal annul rainfall is estimated to 3263 mm. January to May is generally dry and the mild winter is limited to November-December. The soil in the District is generally well-drained and mixed. Sandy soil, graveled clay soil and clayey soil characterize the district.

The Bharathapuzha, one of the longest rivers in the State with length of 204 Km and Chalakudy River pass through the District. The river water is used both for irrigation and drinking. The soil in the river basins is extremely fertile, suitable for cultivation.

### Population and Literacy

The District population, as per 2001 Census is 29,75,440. Which is 9.34 per cent of the total population of the State. Out of the total population of the District, 14,22,047 are males and 15,53,393 are females. The Census Report 2001 estimates 24,56,081 literates in the District, out of that 12,00,247 are male and 12,55,834 are females. The literacy rate of the District, excluding children below 7 years is 92.56% in 2001 against 90.18% in 1991.

**Table 1**
**Demographic Features of Thrissur District**

| *Description* | *District* | *State* |
|---|---|---|
| Area (sq.km) | 3032 | 38863 |
| Population (in lakhs) | 29.75 | 318.39 |
| Density (per sq.km.) | 981 | 819 |
| Sex ratio (M/F) | 1000/1092 | 1000/1058 |
| Literacy rate ( % ) | 92/56 | 90/92 |
| Percentage growth rate in the decade (1991-2001) | 8.70 | 9.42 |
| Rural (%) | 71.8 | - |

*Source:* Census of India 2001.

### Material Resources

Agriculture is the main economic activity of the people at the District. The irrigation system in the District is basically meant for paddy cultivation. For the successful cultivation of paddy, the State Department of Irrigation concentrates on developing surface water resources and the lion's share of investments is in major and medium irrigation projects. For the benefit of agriculturists four major irrigation projects are located in the District.

Thrissur District has good potential for fisheries development as it is endowed with marine and inland water fishing facilities. The District has 91,415 fishermen population of which 71,183 are in marine sector and 20,232 are in inland sector. The District is not rich in mineral resources except for clay and sand. Preliminary investigation has been conducted to assess the availability of tile/brick clay in various parts of the District.

### Physical Infrastructure for Industrial Development

The total geographical area of Thrissur District is 2,99,390 hectare. Barren and uncultivable land is 296 hectare and cultivable wasteland is 2,807 hectare. The land under fallow other than current fallow is 3,209 hectare and current fallow is 7, 450 hectare. To provide modern factory accommodation to the small-scale industries in the District, two major industrial estates, ten mini industrial estates and two development plots have been established. Electricity has reached almost all parts of the District. The District receives heavy rainfall during monsoon season and hence has abundant surface water resource. Water availability is quite satisfactory.

### Social Infrastructure

The important industrial lending institutions in the District are Banks, Kerala Financial Corporation (KFC), Small Industries Development Bank of India (SIDBI) and National Small Industries Corporation Limited (NSIC). Twenty-nine commercial Banks have their branches in this District. Canara Bank is the lead bank of the District, South Malabar Gramin Bank (SMGB), a regional rural bank, opened its 15 branches in Thrissur District in 1999 to 2001. Besides the commercial banks there are Thrissur District Co-operative Bank, Irinjalakuda Co-operative Agricultural Land Development Bank, Cochin Co-operative Agricultural Land Development Bank, South Malabar Gramin Bank, Kerala Financial Corporation and 159 Primary Service Co-operative Banks. SISI provides some short-term training courses in various disciplines like Industrial Management, Financial Management, Marketing Management, Quality and Inventory Control, Accounting procedures and Labour law, Export Packaging etc. Entrepreneurial Development and Skill Oriented Training Programmes are also organized in association with Technical Institution and NGOs.

### Resource-Based Industries

The District is agriculturally developed with a good network of irrigation schemes. The principal agricultural products in the District include paddy, coconut, rubber, tea, areca nut, cashew nut, tamarind, jackfruit, banana, tapioca, papaya, mango, pulses, ginger and turmeric. The surplus agricultural produce is transported to other States in its raw form for value added process. Lots of medicinal plants are growing in the forest. Treated rubber-wood is a good substitute for manufacturing furniture and building materials. The clay tiles industry is the most important industry in the District employing the largest number of labourers. At present there are 160 tile factories in the District. 84 units are registered, as small-scale units as per the record of District Industrial Centre and rest of the units are unregistered units. There are three major centres for clay tiles manufacturing units located in Allagappanagar, Chittichery, and Pudukad.

### District Industries Centre (DIC)

The District Industries Centre in Thrissur was established in 1978. It is located at Ayyanthole, and is about 3 Kms from Thrissur Railway station. The key role of DIC's is promoting small-scale industries. The establishment of the District Industries Centre carries was a revolutionary strategy aiming at rapid industrialization. The DIC is a nucleus representing all agencies connected with industries and would act as the nerve centre for future industrial development of the district.

## FUNCTIONAL AREAS OF CLAY TILES MANUFACTURING UNITS

### Organisational Background

The tiles industry in Kerala is a traditional one and due to various reasons like availability of suitable clay, labour, firewood and climatic conditions, they have a certain regional

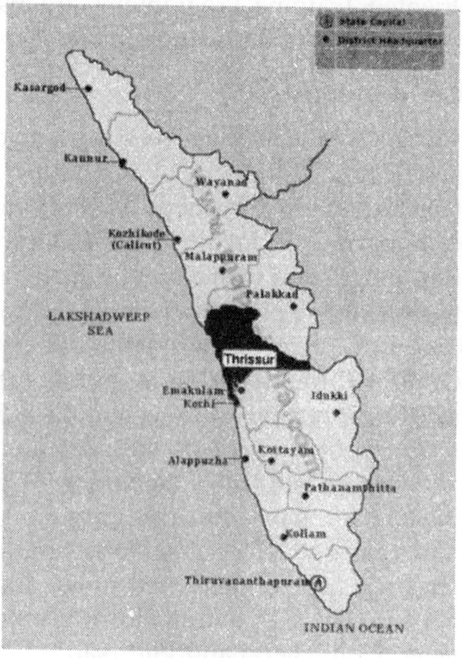


State of Kerala

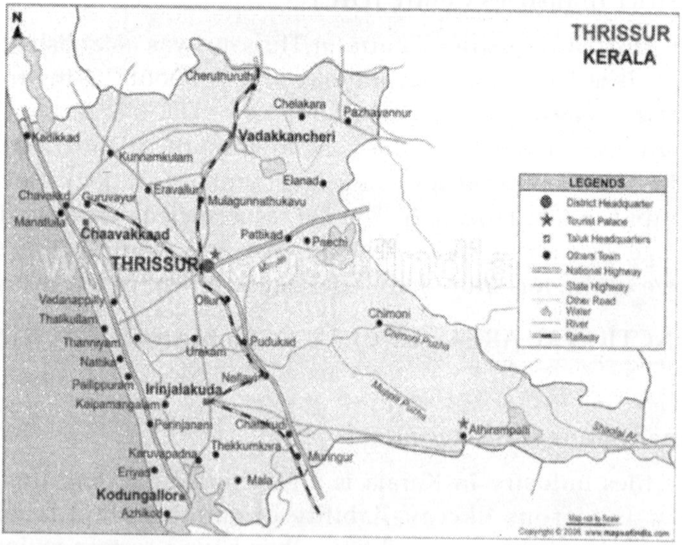


Thrissur District

effect of concentration. The factories located in certain areas have common characteristics of manufacturing, processing and distribution of clay tiles.

There are three prominent localities of Thrissur District where the Clay tiles manufacturing units are found – Alagappanagar, Chittissery and Pudukad. Pudukad is near Thrissur railway station and the other two are about 6 km from the railway station. In the' course of research, the researcher identified that the units were randomly established between 1970 and 2000. These units manufactured different varieties of clay tiles for roofing, flooring and decorative tiles. These units are classified into sole trading concerns, partnership concerns, private limited companies and co-operative societies. Most of the small units are of sole proprietorship but some are partnership. The medium factories are mostly of partnership and a few big units are limited companies. The installed production capacities of the units are below 8000, 8000 to 16000 and 16000 to 24000 clay products per day.

## Functional Areas

After discussions with experts and entrepreneurs, the researcher identified four functional areas – Production, Marketing, Finance and Labour. All the functional areas are equally important. The functional areas and the variables associated with them are briefly described below.

## Production

Production is the most important function of any manufacturing unit. In the course of research, the researcher identified some of the important factors related to the production function.

### Clay Procurement and Storages

Clay is the only raw material used in the manufacture of tiles. The clay is obtained from the paddy fields about three to four feet below the ground. The clay is dug out manually and transported by means of trucks or boats to the factory sites. Clay used in the manufacture of tiles are two types – terracotta clay and china clay. The terracotta clay is normally blue or black in colour and has high cohesiveness. The china clay is yellow in colour and is less cohesive and has higher sand content. Clay from different fields differs widely in their plasticity and other properties.

Great importance needs to be given to the choice of clay. Clay is transported by trucks, lorries and boats. Clay is generally procured through contractors or from farmers. In the latter case practically no difficulties exist. But if contractors supply clay, procurement is not so smooth. The clay is procured before the rainy season starts and is left for weathering. It is recommended that raw material stock of clay need not be kept for more than ten to fifteen days at a time. The only time higher stocks need be held is during the rainy season when procurement becomes difficult on account of rains. The rains generally last for three or four months; stock can be gradually built up a month before the rains start. If the unit is using only a single type of clay it could be stored in heaps. If the unit processes more than one type and if production is more than 15000 tiles per day separate storage of clay is recommended. Unit having a capacity of less than 15000 tiles per day but using more that one type of clay will have to stock clay in alternate layers.

**Pugging and De-airing**

The first stage of manufacture is to determine the nature of clay i.e. its properties like plasticity and sand content. Plasticity is required to an extent but too much plasticity leads to disproportionate shrinkage. This will further lead to cracks and breakages while drying and burning. To control the plasticity it will have to be mixed proportionately with China clay.

The sand content of the clay is an important factor and has to be held at the optimum level, which is around 20 per cent. While the de-airing pugmill requires 20 to 22 per cent sand, the ordinary pugmill works fairly well when it is around 15 to 18 per cent. Sand testing can control the percentage of sand content. At present most of the units do not bother about the sand testing.

The clay is sent through a pair of rollers, with a gap of 1/8", which acts as the coarse grinder. From the coarse grinder the clay goes through a double shaft mixer. Here the clay is thoroughly mixed so that a homogeneous mass is obtained. In some units, the clay passes through double shaft mixer first and later through the coarse grinder. This is a wrong practice, as the clay will be in comparatively hard lumps to begin with, and if processed through the double shaft mixed directly, the blades of the mixer will get worn out too soon. Moreover thorough mixing will be difficult as some clay lumps will be present. The coarse grinder should precede double shaft mixer, so that clay is broken up and some grinding has been already done when it is fed to the mixer.

From the mixer the clay is conveyed to a high-speed roller. The high-speed rollers should have a gap of 1/16" to achieve fine grinding which contributes to quality. The clay is then pugged in a pugmill. Before pugging, the clay should be de-aired by a vacuum pump, which is attached to the pugmill. A de-airing pugmill breaks the clay mass into small particles and the air is sucked out by the vacuum pump. The vacuum pressure is generally maintained at a level of 600mm of Hg. However a de-airing pugmill is not suitable for all types of clay. Clay of high plasticity does not require de-airing. For clays with average plasticity and other inferior types of clay, de-airing is an absolute necessity. The quality of the block is good and it can go straight to the press. The curing of the blocks can thus be eliminated if de-airing is employed.

It was noticed that some units adopt the practice of storing de-aired blocks. This is not correct as the de-aired blocks will again absorb air and the de-airing process is made ineffective. For clays that are highly plastic the de-airing is unnecessary and pugging can be done directly. The pugged blocks will however have to be stored for two or three days for curing. At the pugmill, the cutting of the blocks is mostly done manually. In this case the block size is not consistent and slight variations occur. If the blocks are larger, this will lead to more clay being recycled from the press. After pressing the tiles, excess clay is trimmed off. If the blocks are smaller than required, the tiles pressed become underweight and less strong due to insufficient clay.

In order to avoid this the pugged blocks must be cut by an automatic cutter installed at the mouth of the pugmill so that the size of blocks are controlled and a counter could be used in order to indicate the number of blocks cut per day. Presently the worker puts a number on each block to indicate how many blocks have been made per day.

### Pressing

The sliced blocks if de-aired can go directly to the press. The de-aired slabs are separated from the blocks, oiled and placed on the die. The oil used is rice bran or light diesel oil or some times kerosene. If no de-airing has been done the blocks must be cured. The blocks are placed on a trolley and transported to the shed close by for curing. The blocks remain here for two days for curing. After curing, the blocks are taken to the press. The individual slabs are separated, placed on the table, beaten and oiled. After oiling it is placed on the die.

Both power and manually operated presses are employed for pressing. The power press generally has 5 dies and a speed of fifteen strokes per minute. This will give a capacity of 12000 tiles per 8 hours. The hand press, generally gives about 4000 to 5000 tiles per 8 hours. The pressed tiles are then trimmed so that the extra clay is removed. The trimming can be done either manually, or by an automatic trimmer. When done manually, the pressed tile is taken out into a pallet and the pallet placed on a revolving stand and then trimmed. If trimming is automatic the tiles are directly taken on to the pallet.

The percentage of tiles that do not get pressed properly is rather large about 5 to 10 per cent in some of the companies. Proper pressing is not achieved because the slabs are not cut to correct lengths or because the slabs are not placed where atmospheric conditions are uniform (i.e. avoiding window opening etc.) Natural airflow is to be maintained. The second stage involves exposing the tiles to slightly hot conditions and at the final stage to more hot conditions. To achieve this, storage space has to be properly laid out and in each of the stages, proper conditions have to be maintained. The period of each stage of drying has to be found out experimentally for each type of clay.

### Method of Producing Hot Air

The air from the cooling chamber of the kiln can be drawn by a blower and this hot air is taken through an underground duct (if possible) or by a pipe to the storage space and distributed by means of controllable valve over those tiles which are at the third stage of drying. For slight hot air (about 95°C) required in the second stage the hot air obtained from the cooling chambers can be diluted by means of cold air obtained from a fan or blower and this slight hot air can be distributed over those tiles at the second stage of drying. In some cases, second stage of drying may be avoided. In that case the initial natural drying and hot air drying will be sufficient.

In order to have good draught it is advisable to use an exhaust blower or fan for exhausting the air that has absorbed the moisture, the fan location and capacity have to be decided on the capacities of individual factories. It is better to have an enclosed chamber to have uniform conditions. Another method of drying is using hot air again. Now the hot air is obtained from flue gases of the chambers. In intermittent chambers with ten or fifteen chambers, the exhaust temperature of the flue gases leaving the chimney is about 900 to 1000°C. This waste heat is considerable. This can be used to heat air in a duct system and this hot air can be used for drying.

These two systems can be adopted for units producing tiles about 10000 to 15000 tiles per day. Below this production level, it may not be economical to have these systems. The most efficient system of drying is humidity drier system. This is an enclosed chamber in which hot air is circulated and the condition of air is maintained in such a way that humidity is about 60 to 80%. This is the normal humidity required for good drying. Hence, hot water circulation may also have to be done inside the chamber to maintain the humidity control. This humidity control obviously leads to constant rate of drying and leads to better quality. The cost of humidity drier is exorbitantly high and it is normally recommended for those units having production of above 25000 tiles per day. However, total cost has to be considered before the installation of any such humidity drier.

**Burning**

Tiles are burnt in different types of kiln, which incidentally depends on production capacity of the units. The most modern type is the Hoffmann Kiln. Firewood is the common fuel used in most of these Kilns. Fuel cost is a major component of the total cost of production. There are three types of burning of tiles – (i) Downdraught Kilns (ii) Semi-continuous or Intermittent Kilns and (iii) Continuous Chamber or Hoffmann Kiln.

*Downdraught Kilns*

Many small size factories are using one or two single chamber downdraught kilns of either round or rectangular shape having capacity ranging from 3500 to 5000 tiles. Rectangular-shaped kilns are more advantageous in stacking tiles. Most of the tiles manufacturers in Kerala use firewood as fuel and very few use other fuels like cashew shell, paddy husk, coconut shell, saw dust occasionally whenever available. This type of kiln gives good results with careful burning which suits batch production. Since the air and tiles are not pre-heated and the waste gases leave at high temperature during burning and cooling through the chimney, the thermal efficiency of the kiln is very low. The firewood consumption varies from 0.8 to 1.2 tonnes per 1000 tiles. The maximum temperature observed in this kiln is 700°C to 800°C.

***Semi-continuous or Intermittent Kilns***

Most of the medium size factories have the semi-continuous or Intermittent Kilns with 4 to 16 chambers with a capacity of 3000 to 3500 tiles per chamber. In this type of kiln, the waste heat while heating and cooling can be transferred from one to the other and the work is continued without stopping. The consumption of firewood varies from 0.5 to 0.8 tones per 1000 tiles. It the number of chambers are more, consumption of firewood is reduced. The maximum temperature observed in this kiln is 750°C to 850° C.

### *Continuous Chamber or Hoffmann Kiln*

Originally, Hoffman kiln was circular in shape with chimney at the center. Now, it has been modified with two rectangular tunnels connected at the end by cross tunnels. The number of channels varies from 18 to 36 with a capacity of 3000 to 5800 per chamber. The chambers are properly interconnected with the control of dampers for efficient utilization of hot gases while operating the kiln so that the consumption of fuel is reduced to a large extent. One round of firing usually takes five to seven days. The consumption of wood comes to 0.33 to 0.5 tonnes per 1000 tiles with maximum temperature of 850° C to 950° C and the consumption of firewood can be reduced further depending on the number of chambers. Hoffman kiln can be designed for production of 10000 to 30000 tiles per day. Most of the units are observing the temperature by drawing samples by practical experience. Almost all the tiles manufacturing are using firewood because of its availability and the coal is not used due to high transport cost and losses during transit.

### Testing

The burnt tiles are released from the kiln and transported to a shed close by. While the tiles are being unloaded the temperature within the chamber is around 100°C. To facilitate easy working it is suggested that a coir mat be used on the floor of the kiln. A fan can be used so that conditions are made more conductive for the workers to work in the chamber.

The unloaded tiles are garbled i.e. the tiles are inspected for cracks, breakages and colours. The presence of cracks and breakage are determined by striking the tile; if a good quality tile is struck then the ring or sound produced is metallic and clear. If any damages or cracks are present, the ring sounds hollow. The colours are examined visually. An over burnt tile has a darker color and an unburnt one has a lighter shade.

← Press for hand-made clay tiles

Power-Driven press →

← Hand-Driven cutting table

Automatic cutting table →

← De-Airing Machine

Clays on chain conveyer →

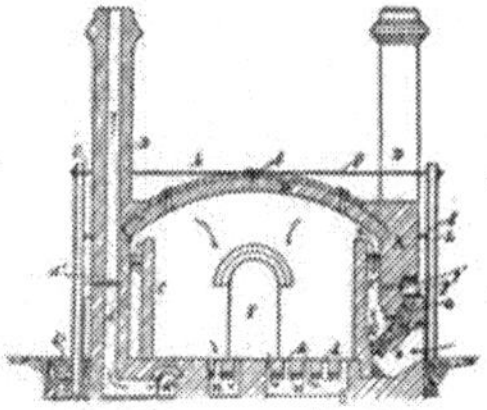

Plan of Down-Draught Kiln

Plan of Semi-Continuous Kiln

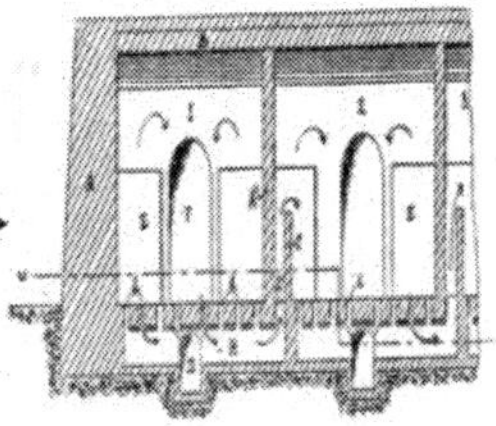

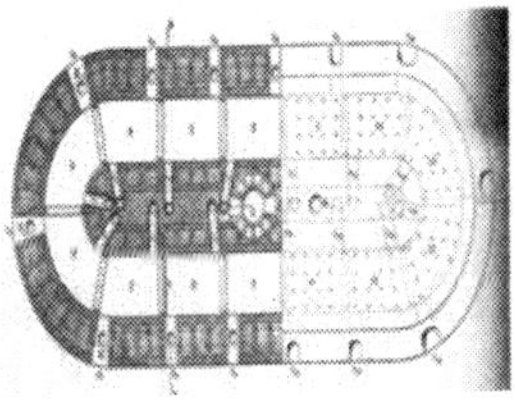

Plan of Modern Hoffman Kiln

**Machineries in Clay Tiles Manufacturing Units**

These are the only tests normally done in the old method. However it is recommended that other tests like sand content analysis, water absorption test and shrinkage test be done from time to time. The weight of the tile should be standardized and maintained for future verification. The breaking strength test can also be done so as to ensure the quality of the tiles.

## MARKETING

In ancient times man discovered that scarce resources can be conserved with division of labour. Specialization of labour requires trade, when people produce more of some products and services than they use, they seek to exchange them for needed goods and services, which others have. Thus trade and marketing activities arise to facilitate the exchange of goods and services and they also influence what will be produced and exchanged. This is the essence of marketing system i.e. to allocate scarce resources efficiently in such a way as to satisfy the needs of man to the greatest extent possible.

All the economic activities are based on marketing, because the use of men, money materials and machinery are rewarded through marketing. The production practices are influenced by the marketing activity. "Marketing includes the searching activities of prospective sellers and buyers as they attempt to find out the products and services which they want and those which others want and also includes the facilitating activities such as financing, storing and transporting.

In the following pages the marketing of tiles in Thrissur District is examined. Though the marketing practices followed by the units were unstructured, the researcher identified six different aspects of marketing. They are demand, supply, pricing, sales, competition and promotion.

**Demand for Tiles**

Demand is the major determinant of the success of any clay tiles manufacturing units. Here demand refers to the work orders given to the units. The work orders taken by the units are purely based on the nature and location of their customers. The customers of the units were of different types namely regular customers, agents and Government contractors. The regular customers of the units were located within the state of Kerala as well as from other States. Though the regular customers are primary for the units, agents and Government contractors also purchase the clay tiles. Most of the work orders came through the Government contractors and this would lead to the survival and success of the units.

**Supply of Tiles**

Supply is another important determinant of the performance of marketing. Absence of supply of tiles to their customers results in the reduction in the performance of the units. Though the units get work orders within the state of Kerala, they also supply tiles to other parts of South India—Tamilnadu, Pondicherry, Andhra Pradesh and Karnataka. Customers from Tamilnadu, were do bulk purchase and sell retail in their own

State. So the State of Tamilnadu plays a vital role in the increase of the marketing of the units.

### Pricing

Pricing is another dominating factor, which enhances marketing. The methods of pricing followed by the units differ according to the demand and competition. The units adopt three different methods of pricing—cost-based, demand-based and competition-based.

### Competition and Sale of Tiles

Competition is another extraneous factor, which determines the strength, survival and the success of the clay units. The major competitors units are located within and outside Thrissur District, because all the units were located as a cluster area. The units sell the clay tiles on cash and on credit. Customers were allowed a credit period of less than one week. They sold tiles directly to their customers as well as through the agents.

### Promotion

In order to increase the sales volume of the clay tiles, the units adopted different types of promotional techniques. The units appointed special agents for increasing the sales volume. Giving discounts, giving compensation for the breakages and arranging the transport facilities for their regular customers were some of the promotional techniques adopted by them. Due to normal breakages in the clay tiles, they allowed 120 clay tiles per load as the compensation at free of cost. Moreover, they also adopted certain strategies to maintain the sale of clay tiles. The units thought that supply of clay tiles to their customers in a prompt manner might enhance the sales. Similarly, by giving good quality clay tiles, by extension of credit period and replacing the broken tiles they can promote sales.

## FINANCE

Finance plays a vital role in determining the performance of the units. Though there are various determinants, the units concentrate on the four different factors-Capital, Loans, Investment made by the units and Returns expected.

### Capital

Finance is the life-blood of any business. In order to meet the short-term as well as long-term requirements of the units, the amount of capital invested by the units is the most important one. The capital invested can be divided into fixed capital and working capital. Fixed capital is the amount invested by the units at the time of starting the business. This fixed capital may be raised through the owned fund invested by the unit owners and also by raising the borrowed funds. Similarly, the working capital determines and meets the short-term requirements of the units. This may be raised through the various sources like collection from the debtors, cash sales, short term loans, funds from the friends and relatives and advance amount from the customers for the work order given by them.

### Loans

Though the units raised the capital through their owned funds, loans also play a vital role in meeting the short-term and long-term requirements. The units raised the loans from various sources such as Kerala Finance Corporation, through their friends and relatives and loans from the small financial institutions. The units raised a long- term loan upto rupees twenty lakhs from the financial institutions for the purchase of machinery. The institutions charged a maximum interest of 15 per cent on the loans got by the units. Moreover the unit availed themselves of subsidies from the State Government but the Government of Kerala imposed a lot of rules, regulations and restrictions regarding the subsidies in the year 1995.

### Investment

Investment here refers to the amount of investment made by the units in fixed assets. Though the units raised the funds through various sources to meet the short-term requirements, they are in a need of investing their funds to meet the long-term requirements such as Investment in land and buildings, Procurement and establishment of plant and machinery, purchasing electrical fittings, pallets and frames, chimney and furniture and fittings. These fixed assets also determine the performance of the units.

### Returns

As the aim of any business is profit, profit alone determines its success. The returns earned by the units were classified into two categories such as expected returns and the actual returns. Expected returns refer to the rate of return expected by the owners of the units after capital invested, loans raised and investment made in fixed assets but before the actual business was started. Contrarily the actual returns are the returns achieved by the units at present. Usually the units expect a return of 25 to 50 per cent and the present scenario of returns is below 15 per cent.

## LABOUR

The clay tiles manufacturing units were purely the labour-intensive units. Like finance, labour also determines the working and the success of the units. The average number of labour employed in small-units is 40 to 60 and units producing below 8000 tiles have an average labour of 60 to 75 per day and those producing 8000 to 16000 tiles per day employ 75 to 100. The number of supervisory and managerial staff are three to four in small size, five to eight in medium size and seven to ten in big size units. The labour function is categorized as three factors (i) Recruitment and Selection, (ii) Working shifts and leaves and (iii) Remuneration and Compensation

### Recruitment and Selection

Recruitment and selection is the most important factor among the three determinants of the labour function. The units recruited their workers by conducting personal interview, through the contractors, recruiting from the factory gate and on the recommendations by the present labourers. There are various criteria for selecting the workers. Usually, the units selected the workers based on the apprenticeship qualification, technical qualification and previous experience. The selected workers were employed and classified as skilled labours, semi-skilled labours, unskilled labours, and employee in supervisory & administrative level.

**Shifts and Leaves**

The productivity of the workers determines the performance of labour function. Usually at the production level the units are in need of labour such as skilled, semi-skilled and unskilled. For these types of labour, the units categorized the work into three shifts a day. Every shift consists of eight hours of work in a day for each type of workers. In the normal seasons the units adopted a single shift working day and in the peak seasons they had two or three shifts in a day. As for as the leaves are concerned, the owners of the units did not allow weekend leave with wages for the workers. Other than this, the owners unemploy the workers on various occasions. This may be due to the shortage of raw materials, inadequate demand for their product, stoppage of production and shortage of working capital.

**Remuneration and Compensation**

Remuneration and compensation are other important factors in determining the survival and performance of the labourers. The owners of the units adopted two different methods of payment of remuneration-time rate and piece rate. Usually most of the units followed the time rate system of remuneration. In addition, the owners allowed over-time remuneration to their workers. The over time remuneration given to the workers is purely based on three different criteria namely a normal rate system, 1.5 times of normal rate and 2 times of normal rate. As far as the compensation is concerned, if there is any accident for the workers inside the factory, some units meet the medical expenses wholly, some units partly. Money compensation also made by some units. In addition to this the workers, the units make the contribution of small amount to the employees' provident fund and employees' group insurance schemes. The workers also got their membership in the workers trade unions namely Centre for Indian Trade Union (CITU) and Indian National Trade union Congress (INTUC).

# Chapter 3

# Analysis of Production and Marketing Functions

This chapter is an analysis of the functional areas of Production and Marketing of Clay tiles manufacturing units. The analysis was done at three different stages for production and marketing.

At the first stage, simple frequency tables and cross tabulations were used to present the organisational background and the various factors of production and marketing. Moreover the technique of contingency co-efficient was also used to identify the association between organisational background and the various factors of production and marketing.

At the second stage, multiple regression analysis was used to scrutinize the contribution of various factors of production and marketing to its performance.

At the third stage, various problems in production and marketing were cross-classified and stepwise multiple regression analysis was used to identify the impact of the problems on the performance of production and marketing.

Table 1 shows the location of the units. From the total of 84 units, 46.4 per cent (39) of the units were located in

Chittissery followed by 27.4 per cent (23) in Alagappanagar and 26.2 per cent (22) in Pudukad.

**Table 1**
**Location of the Units**

| *Place* | *No. of Units* | *Per cent* |
|---|---|---|
| Alagappanagar | 23 | 27.4 |
| Chittissery | 39 | 46.4 |
| Pudukad | 22 | 26.2 |
| Total | 84 | 100.0 |

*Source:* Primary Data.

Hence, a majority of 46.4 per cent of the units were located in Chittissery area.

**Table 2**
**Year of Establishment of the Units**

| *Year* | *No. of Units* | *Per cent* |
|---|---|---|
| Before 1981 | 5 | 6.0 |
| 1981–1985 | 7 | 8.3 |
| 1985–1990 | 30 | 35.7 |
| After 1990 | 42 | 50.0 |
| Total | 84 | 100.0 |

*Source:* Primary Data.

Table 2 provides the year of establishment of each unit. Exactly 50 per cent (42) of the units were established after 1990, 35.7 per cent (30) started functioning between 1985 and 1990.

Hence, the maximum of 50 per cent of the units were established after 1990.

**Table 3**
**Jurisdiction of the Units**

| *Area* | *No. of Units* | *Per cent* |
|---|---|---|
| Panchayat | 74 | 88.1 |
| Municipality | 9 | 10.7 |
| Corporation | 1 | 1.2 |
| Total | 84 | 100.0 |

*Source:* Primary Data

Table 3 gives the jurisdiction of the clay tiles manufacturing units in Thrissur District. Out of 84 units, 88.1 per cent (74) were within the jurisdiction of panchayat followed by 10.7 per cent (9) in municipality area and 1.2 per cent (1) within the corporation.

Hence, the maximum of 88.1 per cent (74) of the units were located within the jurisdiction of the panchayat.

**Table 4**
**Tiles Manufactured by the Units**

| *Types* | *Number of Units* | *Per cent* |
|---|---|---|
| Roofing tiles | 4 | 4.8 |
| Flooring tiles | 42 | 50.0 |
| Other clay tiles | 9 | 10.7 |
| Roofing and Flooring tiles | 8 | 9.5 |
| Flooring and Decorative tiles | 20 | 23.8 |
| Decorative and other clay tiles | 1 | 1.2 |
| Total | 84 | 100.0 |

*Source:* Primary Data.

Table 4 provides the particulars of the various types of tiles manufactured by the units. From the total of 84 units, exactly 50 per cent (42) were manufacturing flooring tiles; 23.8 per cent (20) flooring and decorative tiles and 10.7 per cent (9) decorative and other tiles.

Hence, the maximum of 50 per cent of the units manufactured flooring tiles only.

**Table 5**
**Type of Ownership of the Units**

| *Types* | *No. of Units* | *Per cent* |
|---|---|---|
| Sole Proprietorship | 48 | 57.1 |
| Partnership | 29 | 34.5 |
| Co-operative society | 4 | 4.8 |
| Private company | 3 | 3.6 |
| Total | 84 | 100.0 |

*Source:* Primary Data.

Table 5 shows the nature of ownership of the units. 57.1 per cent (48) of the units have sole proprietors, 34.5 per cent

(29) are partnership concern and 4.8 per cent (4) are co-operative societies.

Hence, the maximum of 57.1 per cent of the units were owned by sole proprietors.

**Table 6**
**Educational Qualification of the Owner**

| *Qualifications* | *No. of Units* | *Per cent* |
|---|---|---|
| Below S.S.L.C | 9 | 10.7 |
| Pre-degree | 34 | 40.5 |
| Technical | 9 | 10.7 |
| Graduate | 29 | 34.5 |
| Post-graduate | 3 | 3.6 |
| Total | 84 | 100.0 |

*Source:* Primary Data.

Table 6 lists the educational qualifications of the owners of units. 40.5 per cent (34) of the unit owners had education upto pre-degree; 34.5 per cent (29) had a graduate degree and 10.7 per cent (9) were technicians.

Hence, 40.5 per cent of the unit owners had pre-degree.

**Table 7**
**Installed Production Capacity Per Day**

| *Capacity (in tiles)* | *No. of Units* | *Per cent* |
|---|---|---|
| Below 8000 | 34 | 40.5 |
| 8000–16000 | 33 | 39.3 |
| 16000–24000 | 17 | 20.2 |
| Total | 84 | 100.0 |

*Source:* Primary Data.

Table 7 gives the installed production capacity of the clay tiles manufacturing units. The maximum of 40.5 per cent (34) of the units had a production capacity of below 8000 tiles per day, 39.3 per cent (33) from 8000 to 16000 tiles and 20.2 per cent (17) from 16000 to 24000 tiles per day.

Hence, 40.5 per cent of the units had 8000 or less tiles as the production capacity per day.

**Table 8**
**Factors Influenced to Establish the Units in Thrissur District**

| | Rank | | | | | | |
|---|---|---|---|---|---|---|---|
| *Factors* | *1* | *2* | *3* | *4* | *5* | *6* | *7* |
| Availability of raw material | 77 (91.7) | 06 (7.1) | 01 (1.2) | - | - | - | - |
| Availability of labour | - | - | - | 03 (3.6) | 12 (14.3) | 40 (47.6) | 29 (34.5) |
| Traditional | - | 04 (4.8) | 01 (1.2) | 04 (4.8) | 11 (13.1) | 17 (20.2) | 47 (56) |
| Good demand | 07 (8.3) | 36 (42.9) | 29 (34.5) | 10 (11.9) | 02 (2.4) | - | - |
| Good Transport facilities | - | 11 (13.1) | 29 ) (34.5 | 27 (32.1) | 14 (16.7) | 02 (2.4) | 01 (1.2) |
| Availability of capital or loan | - | 25 (29.8) | 16 (19) | 10 (11.9) | 17 (20.2) | 13 (15.5) | 03 (3.6) |
| Previous experience in the field | - | 02 (2.4) | 08 (9.5) | 30 (35.7) | 28 (33.3) | 12 (14.3) | 04 (4.8) |

( ) in Percentage.

Table 8 ranks the various factors, which influenced the owners to establish the clay tiles manufacturing units. 91.7 per cent (77) of the units rank the factor "Availability of raw materials" first, 42.9 per cent (36) rank "Good demand" the second and 29.8 per cent (25) "Availability of capital or loan". This reveals, the factors such as availability of raw material, good demand and availability of capital or loan were the most dominating factors that influenced them to establish the units in Thrissur District.

**Table 9**
**Actual Production Per Day**

| *Tiles (in Numbers)* | *No. of Units* | *Per cent* |
|---|---|---|
| Below 6000 | 60 | 71.4 |
| 6000– 12000 | 12 | 14.3 |
| 12000–18000 | 12 | 14.3 |
| Total | 84 | 100.0 |

*Source:* Primary Data.

Table 9 shows the actual production by the units. The maximum of 71.4 per cent of the units manufactured below

6000 tiles per day, 14.3 per cent (12) units manufactured from 6000 to 12000 tiles and another 14.3 per cent (12) units from 12000 to 18000 tiles.

Hence, a majority of 71.4 per cent of the units manufactured below 6000 tiles per day.

**Table 10**
**Place of Procurement of Clay**

| *Area* | *No. of Units* | *Per cent* |
|---|---|---|
| Within Panchayat | 32 | 38.1 |
| Outside the Panchayat but within the District | 52 | 61.9 |
| Outside the District | - | - |
| Total | 84 | 100.0 |

*Source:* Primary Data.

Table 10 shows the place of procurement of clay by the units. 61.9 per cent (52) of the units procured the clay from outside the Panchayat but within the same district and the remaining units procured from within the Panchayat.

Hence, the maximum of 61.9 per cent of the units were procuring the clay from outside the Panchayat but within the district.

**Table 11**
**Distance from the Factory to Procure Clay**

| *Distance (in Kms.).* | *No. of Units* | *Per cent* |
|---|---|---|
| Less than 5 | - | - |
| 5–10 | 29 | 34.5 |
| 10–15 | 33 | 39.3 |
| Above 15 | 22 | 26.2 |
| Total | 84 | 100.0 |

*Source:* Primary Data.

Table 11 reveals the distance from the factory to source of clay. 39.3 per cent (33) of the units procure the clay within 10 to 15 kilometres from the factory followed by 34.5 per cent (29) from 5 to 10 kilometres and 26.2 per cent (22) in 15 kilometers and above.

Hence, 39.3 per cent of the units procure the clay within 10 to 15 kilometres from the factory.

**Table 12**
**Methods Adopted for Procuring Clay**

| *Methods* | *No. of Units* | *Per cent* |
|---|---|---|
| Own land/farm | 4 | 4.8 |
| Leasehold land/farm | 19 | 22.6 |
| Through contractors | 60 | 71.4 |
| Other agencies | 1 | 1.2 |
| Total | 84 | 100.0 |

*Source:* Primary Data.

Table 12 shows the various methods adopted for collecting the clay. 71.4 per cent (60) of the units are collecting the clay through contractors followed by 22.6 per cent (19) from leasehold land while 4.8 per cent (4) dig the clay from their own land.

Hence, the maximum of 71.4 per cent of the units are collecting the clay through contractors.

**Table 13**
**Clay Used for Production**

| *Type* | *No. of Units* | *Per cent* |
|---|---|---|
| Terracotta clay | 67 | 79.8 |
| China clay | - | - |
| Both | 17 | 20.2 |
| Total | 84 | 100.0 |

*Source:* Primary Data.

Table 13 lists the types of clay used. 79.8 per cent (67) of the units used terracotta clay for production and remaining 20.2 per cent (17) of units utilized both terracotta and china clay for their production.

Hence, the maximum of 79.8 per cent of the units are using terracotta clay for production of tiles.

**Table 14**
**Methods Adopted for Storing Clay**

| *Methods* | *No. of Units* | *Per cent* |
|---|---|---|
| Heap | 67 | 79.8 |
| Box feeder | 1 | 1.2 |
| Both | 16 | 19.0 |
| Total | 84 | 100.0 |

*Source:* Primary Data.

Table 14 explains the methods adopted by the units to store the clay. 79.8 per cent (67) of units followed the heap method and 19 per cent (16) of them adopted heap as well as box feeder method.

Hence, the maximum 79.8 per cent of the units adopt the heap method to store the clay.

**Table 15**
**Methods of Cutting Clay Blocks**

| *Methods* | *No. of Units* | *Per cent* |
|---|---|---|
| Manual cutting | 28 | 33.3 |
| Automatic cutting | 22 | 26.2 |
| Both | 34 | 40.5 |
| Total | 84 | 100.0 |

*Source:* Primary Data.

Table 15 lists the methods of cutting the clay blocks. 40.5 per cent (34) of the units adopted both the manual and automatic machine cutting; 33.3 per cent (28) only manual cutting and 26.2 per cent (22) only automatic cutting machine.

Hence, 40.5 per cent of the units were using both manual and automatic methods for cutting the clay blocks.

**Table 16**
**Sources of Water**

| *Sources* | *No. of Units* | *Per cent* |
|---|---|---|
| Well | 27 | 32.2 |
| Bore-Well | 41 | 48.8 |
| Outside source | 16 | 19.0 |
| Total | 84 | 100.0 |

*Source:* Primary Data.

Table 16 shows the sources of water for manufacturing the clay tiles. 48.8 per cent (41) of the units procured the water from their own bore-well followed by 32.2 per cent (27) of the units from their well and 19 per cent (16) purchasing the water through outside sources.

Hence, 48.8 per cent of the units were procuring the water from their own bore-wells.

**Table 17**
**Methods Used for Pressing the Tiles**

| *Methods* | *No. of Units* | *Per cent* |
|---|---|---|
| Manual pressing | 20 | 23.8 |
| Power operated pressing | 23 | 27.4 |
| Both | 41 | 48.8 |
| Total | 84 | 100.0 |

*Source:* Primary Data.

Table 17 gives the methods of pressing the clay. 48.8 per cent (41) of the units adopted the manual and also used power operated revolving machines for pressing the clay, 27.4 per cent (23) only power operated revolving machines and 23.8 per cent (20) used only the manual pressing.

Hence, 48.8 per cent of the units used both manual and machine pressing.

**Table 18**
**De-airing Machine Used in Production**

| *Response* | *No. of Units* | *Per cent* |
|---|---|---|
| Yes | 43 | 51.2 |
| No | 41 | 48.8 |
| Total | 84 | 100.0 |

*Source:* Primary Data.

Table 18 shows the units' responses to the use of de-airing machine in their factory. More than 50 per cent (43) of the units have accepted the de-aired vacuum pump and the remaining 48.8 per cent (41) have not.

Hence, a majority of 51.2 per cent of the units used the de-airing machine in their production process.

**Table 19**
**Methods of Trimming Tiles**

| *Methods* | *No. of Units* | *Per cent* |
|---|---|---|
| Manual trimming | 18 | 21.4 |
| Automatic trimming | 25 | 29.8 |
| Both | 41 | 48.8 |
| Total | 84 | 100.0 |

*Source:* Primary Data.

Table 19 explains the methods of trimming the clay tiles. 48.8 per cent (41) of the units adopted the manual and machine trimming; 29.8 per cent (25) used automatic machines and 21.4 per cent (18) only the manual trimming.

Hence, 48.8 per cent of the units had both manual and machine trimming.

**Table 20**
**Oil Used in Production**

| *Types* | *No. of Units* | *Per cent* |
|---|---|---|
| Rice bran oil | 12 | 14.3 |
| Light diesel oil | 42 | 50.0 |
| Kerosene | 30 | 35.7 |
| Total | 84 | 100.0 |

*Source:* Primary Data.

Table 20 lists the types of oil used in the production process. Exactly 50 per cent (42) of the units used light diesel oil; 35.7 per cent (30) used kerosene and 14.3 per cent (12) rice bran oil.

Hence, a half of (50 per cent) the total units were using light diesel oil in their production process.

**Table 21**
**Oil Used Per Load**

| *Litres* | *No. of Units* | *Per cent* |
|---|---|---|
| Less than 10 | 1 | 1.2 |
| 10 - 20 | 62 | 73.8 |
| 20 - 30 | 1 | 1.2 |
| 30 - 40 | 9 | 10.7 |
| More than 40 | 11 | 13.1 |
| Total | 84 | 100.0 |

*Source:* Primary Data.

Table 21 explains the quantity of oil used per load of 6000 tiles. It is inferred that 73.8 per cent (62) of the units used 10 to 20 litres of oil for manufacturing a load of 6000 tiles followed by 13.1 per cent (11) 40 litres and above and 10.7 per cent (9) 30 to 40 litres of oil for manufacturing a load of tiles.

Hence, the maximum of 73.8 per cent of the units used 10 to 20 litres of oil to manufacture a load of 6000 clay tiles.

**Table 22**
**Methods Adopted for Transporting the Clay to Machines**

| *Methods* | *No. of Units* | *Per cent* |
|---|---|---|
| Coir belt | 29 | 34.5 |
| Rubber belt | 12 | 14.3 |
| Chain conveyor | 20 | 23.8 |
| Elevator | 3 | 3.6 |
| Manual | 20 | 23.8 |
| Total | 84 | 100.0 |

*Source:* Primary Data.

Table 22 presents the methods adopted for transporting the clay to various places in the factory for production process. 34.5 per cent (29) of the units used coir belt for transporting clay; 23.8 per cent (20) adopted chain conveyor and through manual labour, 14.3 per cent (12) with rubber belt and 3.6 per cent (3) used elevators.

Hence, 34.5 per cent of the units were using coir belt for transporting the clay.

**Table 23**
**Methods Used to Dry Tiles**

| *Methods* | *No. of Units* | *Per cent* |
|---|---|---|
| Natural | 66 | 78.6 |
| Smoke drying system | 2 | 2.4 |
| Steam heating system | 3 | 3.6 |
| Natural and smoke drying system | 13 | 15.4 |
| Total | 84 | 100.0 |

*Source:* Primary Data.

Table 23 shows the various methods used for drying the clay tiles. More than 75 per cent (66) of the units adopted natural sunlight to dry the clay tiles followed by 15.4 per cent (13) natural as well as smoke drying system.

Hence, a maximum of 78.6 per cent of the units were exposing the tiles to natural sunlight to dry them.

Table 24 shows the place of procuring the firewood. More than 60 per cent (51) of the units purchased the firewood from outside the panchayat but within the same district; 32.1 per cent (27) of the units from within the panchayat and remaining 7.1 per cent (6) made their purchase from outside the district.

Hence, a majority of 60.7 per cent of the units were purchasing the firewood from outside the panchayat but within the district.

Table 24

Place of Procurement of Firewood

| *Area* | *No. of Units* | *Per cent* |
|---|---|---|
| Within panchayat | 27 | 32.1 |
| Outside the panchayat within district | 51 | 60.8 |
| Outside the District | 6 | 71 |
| Total | 84 | 100.0 |

*Source:* Primary Data.

Table 25

Season of Purchasing Firewood

| *Season* | *No. of Units* | *Per Cent* |
|---|---|---|
| Summer | 32 | 38.1 |
| All seasons | 52 | 61.9 |
| Total | 84 | 100.0 |

*Source:* Primary Data.

Table 25 gives particulars of the season of purchasing firewood. 61.9 per cent (52) of the units purchased the firewood in all the seasons and 38.1 per cent (32) of the units bought firewood in summer season.

Hence, the maximum of 61.9 per cent of the units were purchasing the firewood in all seasons.

Table 26

Distance from the Factory to Procure Firewood

| *Kilometers* | *No. of Units* | *Per cent* |
|---|---|---|
| Less than 5 | - | - |
| 5–10 | 25 | 29.8 |
| 10–15 | 23 | 27.4 |
| More than 15 | 36 | 42.8 |
| Total | 84 | 100.0 |

*Source:* Primary Data.

Table 26 reveals the distance of the source of firewood from the factory. 42.8 per cent (36) of the units procured the firewood from a distance of 15 kilometres from the factory; 29.8 per cent

(25) from 5 to 10 kilometres and 27.4 per cent (23) from 10 to 15 kilometers.

Hence, 42.8 per cent of the units were procuring the firewood traveling a distance of 15 kilometres or above from the factory.

**Table 27**
**Firewood Used Per Load**

| *Tonnes* | *No. of Units* | *Per cent* |
|---|---|---|
| Less than 3 | 20 | 23.8 |
| 3–6 | 50 | 59.5 |
| 6–9 | 12 | 14.3 |
| More than 9 | 2 | 2.4 |
| Total | 84 | 100.0 |

*Source:* Primary Data.

Table 27 shows the quantity of firewood used to manufacture a load of 6000 clay tiles. It is inferred that 59.5 per cent (50) of the units used 3 to 6 tonnes of firewood for manufacturing a load of 6000 tiles followed by 23.8 per cent (20) below 3 tonnes, 14.3 per cent (12) 6 to 9 tonnes and 2.4 per cent (2) of the units used 9 tonnes and above.

Hence, the maximum of 59.5 per cent of the units used 3 to 6 tonnes of firewood to manufacture a load of 6000 clay tiles.

**Table 28**
**Fuel Used in Production**

| *Types* | *No. of Units* | *Per cent* |
|---|---|---|
| Sawdust | 51 | 60.7 |
| Cashew shell | 33 | 39.3 |
| Paddy husk | - | - |
| Total | 84 | 100.0 |

*Source:* Primary Data.

Table 28 describes the fuels used in the production process. More than 60 per cent (51) of the units used sawdust as fuel and remaining 39.3 per cent (33) used Cashew shell.

Hence, a majority of 60.7 per cent of the units were using sawdust as fuel in their production process.

Table 29
**Methods Followed for Burning the Tiles**

| *Methods* | *No. of Units* | *Per cent* |
|---|---|---|
| Downdraught kiln | 34 | 40.5 |
| Semi- continuous down draught chamber type kiln | 33 | 39.3 |
| Hoffman continuous Horizontal draught type kiln | 17 | 20.2 |
| Total | 84 | 100.0 |

*Source:* Primary Data.

Table 29 lists the methods followed for burning the tiles. 40.5 per cent (34) of the units used the downdraught kiln for burning the tiles; 39.3 per cent (33) semi-continuous downdraught chamber type kiln and 20.2 per cent (17) Hoffman continuous horizontal draught type kiln.

Hence, 40.5 per cent of the units were adopting downdraught kiln for burning the tiles.

Table 30
**Methods Adopted for Measuring the Burning Temperature**

| *Methods* | *No. of Units* | *Per cent* |
|---|---|---|
| Judgment by practical experience | 79 | 94.0 |
| Thermocouple | 5 | 6.0 |
| Other indicator | - | - |
| Total | 84 | 100.0 |

*Source:* Primary Data.

Table 30 shows the methods adopted for measuring burning temperature of finished tiles. 94 per cent (79) of the units judged the temperature by practical experience and the remaining 6 per cent (5) of the units used the thermocouple instrument.

Hence, the maximum of 94 per cent of the units were using the practical experience to measure the burning temperature of finished tiles.

Table 3.31 provides the tests adopted to check the finished tiles. 56 per cent (47) of the units adopted judgement by experienced supervisors to check finished tiles; 22.6 per cent (19) water absorption and 21.4 per cent (18) breaking strength test to check the quality of finished tiles.

Hence, a majority of 56 per cent of the units used their experienced supervisors to check the quality of finished tiles.

**Table 31**
**Test Adopted to Check Finished Tiles**

| *Test* | *No. of Units* | *Per cent* |
|---|---|---|
| Water absorption | 19 | 22.6 |
| Breaking strength | 18 | 21.4 |
| Shrinkage test | - | - |
| Judgement by experienced supervisors | 47 | 56.0 |
| Total | 84 | 100.0 |

*Source:* Primary Data.

**Table 32**
**Average Number of Breakage of Tiles Per Load**

| *Numbers* | *No. of Units* | *Per cent* |
|---|---|---|
| Less than 50 | 26 | 31.0 |
| 50–100 | 23 | 27.4 |
| 100–150 | 27 | 32.1 |
| More than 150 | 8 | 9.5 |
| Total | 84 | 100.0 |

*Source:* Primary Data.

Table 32 shows the average number of breakage of tiles per load. 32.1 per cent (27) of the units agreed that the average breakage was 100 to 150 tiles per load, followed by 31 per cent (26) below 50 tiles and 27.4 per cent (23) from 50 to 100 tiles but 9.5 per cent (8) of the units had the breakage of 150 tiles and above per load.

Hence, 32.1 per cent of the units agreed that the average breakage was 100 to 150 tiles per load.

**Table 33**
**Performance of Production Function**

| *Level* | *No. of Units* | *Per cent* |
|---|---|---|
| Bad | 8 | 9.5 |
| Moderate | 16 | 19.0 |
| Good | 54 | 64.4 |
| Excellent | 6 | 7.1 |
| Total | 84 | 100.0 |

*Source:* Primary Data.

Table 33 shows the levels of production of the units. 64.4 per cent (54) of the units stated that their performance of production was good; 19 per cent (16) moderate and 9.5 per cent (8) bad.

Hence, a majority of 64.4 per cent of the units stated that their performance was good.

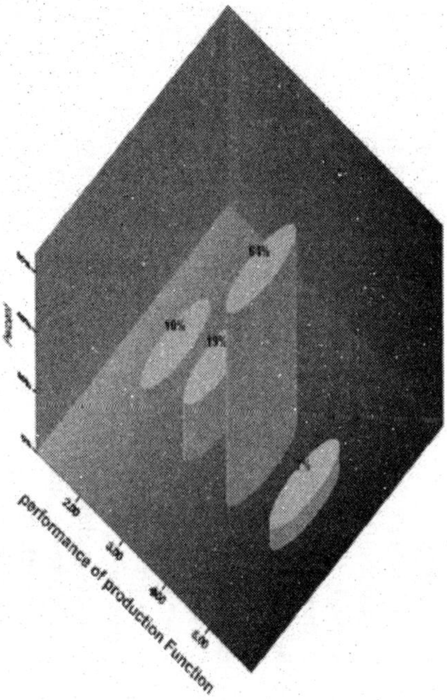


**Diagram 1**

Table 34 gives particulars of production based on the location of the units. The following code may be used

A = units situated in Alagappanagar

B = units situated in Chittissery

C = units situated in Pudukad

When three figures are given, they refer to A, B and C respectively.

- Most of the units produced 6000 tiles (or fever) a day – 65.2 per cent of A, 74.4 per cent of B and 72.7 per cent of C.

**Table 34**
**Factors of Production Based on the Location of the Units**

| Factors | | Location | | |
|---|---|---|---|---|
| | | *Alagappanagar* (*n*=23) | *Chittissery* (*n*=39) | *Pudukad* (*n*=22) |
| Actual production per day(in Numbers) | Below 6000 | 15 (65.2) | 29 (74.4) | 16 (72.7) |
| | 6000-12000 | 4 (17.4) | 6 (15.4) | 2 (9.1) |
| | 12000-18000 | 4 (17.4) | 4 (10.3) | 4 (18.2) |
| Place of procurement of clay | Within the Panchayat | 5 (21.7) | 16 (41.0) | 11 (50.0) |
| | Outside the Panchayat but within the District | 18 (78.3) | 23 (59.0) | 11 (50.0) |
| Distance from the factory to procure clay (in Kms.) | 5-10 | 7 (30.4) | 14 (35.9) | 8 (36.4) |
| | 10-15 | 10 (43.5) | 15 (38.5) | 8 (36.4) |
| | Above 15 | 6 (26.1) | 10 (25.6) | 6 (27.3) |
| Methods adopted for procuring clay | Own land / farm | 1 (4.3) | 2 (5.1) | 1 (4.5) |
| | Lease hold land / farm | 3 (13.0) | 11 (28.2) | 5 (22.7) |
| | Through contractors | 19 (82.6) | 25 (64.1) | 16 (72.7) |
| | Other agencies | - | 1 (2.6) | - |
| Clay used for production | Terracotta clay | 18 (78.3) | 31 (79.5) | 18 (81.8) |
| | Terracotta & China clay | 5 (21.7) | 8 (20.5) | 4 (18.2) |
| Methods adopted for storing clay | Heap method | 16 (69.6) | 35 (89.7) | 16 (72.7) |
| | Box feeder | - | - | 1(4.5) |
| | Both | 7 (30.4) | 4 (10.3) | 5 (22.7) |
| Methods of cutting clay blocks | Manual cutting | 7 (30.4) | 14 (35.9) | 7 (31.8) |
| | Automatic cutting | 8 (34.8) | 9 (23.1) | 5 (22.7) |
| | Both | 8 (34.8) | 16 (41.0) | 10 (45.5) |

*Contd...*

| Factors | | Location | | |
|---|---|---|---|---|
| | | *Alagappanagar (n=23)* | *Chittissery (n=39)* | *Pudukad (n=22)* |
| Sources of water | Well | 7 (30.4) | 11 (28.2) | 9 (40.9) |
| | Bore-Well | 11 (47.8) | 20 (51.3) | 10 (45.5) |
| | Outside source | 5 (21.7) | 8 (20.5) | 3 (13.6) |
| Methods used for pressing the tiles | Manual pressing | 5 (21.7) | 8 (20.5) | 7 (31.8) |
| | Power operated pressing | 8 (34.8) | 11 (28.2) | 4 (18.2) |
| | Both | 10 (43.5) | 20 (51.3) | 11 (50.0) |
| De-airing machine used in production | Yes | 13 (56.5) | 17 (43.6) | 13 (59.1) |
| | No | 10 (43.5) | 22 (56.4) | 9 (40.9) |
| Methods of trimming tiles | Manual trimming | 5 (21.7) | 8 (20.5) | 5 (22.7) |
| | Automatic trimming | 8 (34.8) | 12 (30.8) | 5 (22.7) |
| | Both | 10 (43.5) | 19 (48.7) | 12 (54.5) |
| Oil used in production | Rice Bran oil | 3 (13.0) | 6 (15.4) | 3 (13.6) |
| | Light diesel oil | 9 (39.1) | 22 (56.4) | 11 (50.0) |
| | Kerosene | 11 (47.8) | 11 (28.2) | 8 (36.4) |
| Oil used per load(in Litres) | Below 10 | - | 1 (2.6) | - |
| | 10-20 | 16 (69.6) | 28 (71.8) | 18 (81.8) |
| | 20-30 | - | 1 (2.6) | - |
| | 30-40 | 3 (13.0) | 4 (10.3) | 2 (9.1) |
| | 40 and Above | 4 (17.4) | 5 (12.8) | 2 (9.1) |
| Methods for transporting the clay to machines [d] | Coir belt | 9 (39.1) | 16 (41.0) | 4(18.2) |
| | Rubber belt | 1 (4.3) | 4 (10.3) | 7 (31.8) |
| | Chain conveyor | 5 (21.7) | 9 (23.1) | 6 (27.3) |
| | Elevators | 3 (13.0) | - | - |
| | Manual | 5 (21.7) | 10 (25.6) | 5 (22.7) |

*Contd...*

| Factors | | Location | | |
|---|---|---|---|---|
| | | *Alagappanagar (n=23)* | *Chittissery (n=39)* | *Pudukad (n=22)* |
| Methods used to dry tiles | Natural | 14 (60.9) | 34 (87.2) | 18 (81.8) |
| | Smoke drying system | 1 (4.3) | - | 1 (4.5) |
| | Steam Heating system | 1 (4.3) | 2 (5.1) | - |
| | Natural and Smoke drying system | 7 (30.4) | 3 (7.7) | 3 (13.6) |
| Place of procurement of firewood | Within Panchayat | 8 (34.8) | 11 (28.2) | 8 (36.4) |
| | Outside the District | - | 6 (15.4) | - |
| | Outside the Panchayat but within district | 15 (65.2) | 22 (56.4) | 14 (63.6) |
| Season of purchasing firewood | Summer | 9 (39.1) | 13 (33.3) | 10 (45.5) |
| | All seasons | 14 (60.9) | 26 (66.7) | 12 (54.5) |
| Distance from the factory to procure firewood(in Kms.) | 5-10 | 8 (34.8) | 9 (23.1) | 8(36.4) |
| | 10-15 | 8 (34.8) | 10 (25.6) | 5 (22.7) |
| | Above 15 | 7 (30.4) | 20 (51.3) | 9 (40.9) |
| Firewood used per load(in Tonnes) [d] | Below 3 | 2 (8.7) | 13 (33.3) | 5 (22.7) |
| | 3-6 | 16 (69.6) | 20 (51.3) | 14 (63.6) |
| | 6-9 | 5 (21.7) | 6 (15.4) | 1 (4.5) |
| | 9 and Above | - | - | 2 (9.1) |
| Fuel used in production | Sawdust | 10 (43.5) | 28 (71.8) | 13 (59.1) |
| | Cashew shell | 13 (56.5) | 11 (28.2) | 9 (40.9) |
| Methods followed for burning the tiles | Down draught Kiln | 9 (39.1) | 14 (35.9) | 11 (50.0) |
| | Semi-continuous down draught chamber type Kiln | 7 (30.4) | 19 (48.7) | 7(31.8) |

*Contd...*

| Factors | | Location | | |
|---|---|---|---|---|
| | | *Alagappanagar (n=23)* | *Chittissery (n=39)* | *Pudukad (n=22)* |
| | Hoffman continuous Horizontal draught type Kiln | 7 (30.4) | 6 (15.4) | 4(18.2) |
| Methods adopted for measuring the burning temperature | Judged by practical experience | 22 (95.7) | 37 (94.9) | 20(90.9) |
| | Thermocouple | 1(4.3) | 2 (5.1) | 2 (9.1) |
| Test adopted to check finished tiles | Water absorption test | 5(21.7) | 7 (17.9) | 7 (31.8) |
| | Breaking strength test | 4(17.4) | 8 (20.5) | 6 (27.3) |
| | Judgement by experienced supervisors | 14(60.9) | 24 (61.5) | 9 (40.9) |
| Breakage of tiles per load(in Numbers) | Below 50 | 7(30.4) | 12 (30.8) | 7 (31.8) |
| | 50-100 | 7(30.4) | 8 (20.5) | 8 (36.4) |
| | 100-150 | 8(34.8) | 12 (30.8) | 7 (31.8) |
| | Above 150 | 1(4.3) | 7 (17.9) | - |
| Performance of production function | Bad | 3(13.0) | 3 (7.7) | 2 (9.1) |
| | Moderate | 6(26.1) | 3 (7.7) | 7 (31.8) |
| | Good | 13(56.5) | 29 (74.4) | 12 (54.5) |
| | Excellent | 1(4.3) | 4 (10.3) | 1 (4.5) |

( ) in Percentage Contingency Coefficient ≥ 0.5 P-Value <0.01[a]
Contingency Coefficient ≥ 0.5 P-Value <0.05[b]
Contingency Coefficient ≤ 0.5 P-Value <0.01
Contingency Coefficient ≤ 0.5 P-Value <0.05[c]

- 78.3 per cent of A, 59 per cent of B and 50 per cent of C procure clay from sources outside their own Panchayat area but within the district.
- Most of the units (43.5 per cent of A, 38.5 per cent of B and 36.4 per cent of C) procure clay from sources situated within 15 kilometres from the unit. Only 22 units go more than 15 kilometres.
- Through 23 units take clay either from own land or lease-held land; a majority 82.6 per cent of A, 64.1 per cent of B and 72.7 per cent of C procure clay through contractors.
- Terracotta is the type of clay mostly used though a few units used both terracotta and china clay.
- Clay kept in heaps is the traditional method of storing it (69.6 per cent of A, 89.7 per cent of B and 72.7 per cent of C) though a few units use the box feeder method, which is the modern method.
- Most of the units adopt both manual cutting and machine cutting depending on the capacity of the units.
- Bore-wells are the major suppliers of water to the units, majority of 47.8 per cent of A, 51.3 per cent of B and 45.5 per cent of C.
- Both manual pressing and power-operated pressing play an equal part in the production process.
- 56.5 per cent of A, 43.6 per cent of B and 59.1 per cent of C used de-airing machine and the other units did not use.
- Manual trimming of tiles and automatic trimming are used in 43.6 per cent of A, 48.7 per cent of B and 54.5 per cent of C.
- Light diesel oil is used by 56.4 per cent of B and 50 per cent of C, whereas kerosene is used by 47.8 per cent of A
- Most units (69.6 per cent of A, 71.8 per cent of B and 81.8 per cent of C) keep the oil used at 10 to 20 litres per load and all other units exceed this quantity.

- Coir belt is the most used conveyance of clay, a majority 39.1 per cent of A, 41 per cent of B and 18.2 per cent of C, though 31.8 per cent of C use rubber belt.
- Natural method of allowing the tiles to dry in sunlight is the most favoured one, a maximum of 60.9 per cent of A, 87.2 per cent of B and 81.8 per cent of C were adopting this method.
- 51 units out of 84 procure firewood from outside their own Panchayat area, but within the district.
- Though some units procure firewood only during summer, the activity goes on all the year round, a majority 60.9 per cent of A, 66.7 per cent of B and 54.5 per cent of C.
- The distance between the units and the source of firewood varies: it is 5 to 10 kilometres for 25 units, 10 to 15 kilometres for 23 units and above 15 kilometres for 36 units.
- Most units of all three localities (69.6 per cent of A, 51.3 per cent of B and 63.6 per cent of C) keep the consumption of firewood as low as possible between 3 and 6 tonnes per load.
- Sawdust is used by a larger number of units (51) than cashew shell (33).
- For burning the tiles Hoffman is least used. Downdraught kiln and semi-continuous downdraught kiln are used by an almost equal number of units.
- All the units except 5 units measure the burning temperature with the help of practical experience, rather than with the use of thermocouple.
- Similarly, to check the finished tiles, Judgement by experienced supervisors is the prevalent method, a maximum 60.9 per cent of A, 61.5 per cent of B and 40.9 per cent of C were following this techniques.
- Regarding breakage of tiles per load, one unit of A and 7 units of B record the maximum of 150 tiles or above. Of the other units there are 3 slabs with almost

an equal number in each–below 50, 50 to 100 and 100 to 150 tiles.

- Leaving out 30 units, 54 have recorded good performance of production.

Moreover, the results of the contingency co-efficient suggest that the factors of production such as Methods for transporting the clay to machines and firewood used per load were associated with the location of the units. Hence, it can be concluded that the location of the units played a vital role in determining the Methods for transporting the clay to machines and firewood used per load.

Table 35 shows particulars of production on the basis of the year of establishment. The code is adopted:

A = units established before 1981

B = units established 1981 to 1985

C = units established 1985 to 1990

D = units established 1990 and after

Where four figures are mentioned successively, they refer to A, B, C and D respectively.

- Irrespective of the year of establishment, 60 units produce about 6000 tiles a day.
- Most units procure clay from outside the Panchayat limit, but within the district.
- The distance between the unit and the source of clay is below 10 kilometres for 29 unit, 10 to 15 for 33 units and more than 15 kilometres for 22 units.
- Though 60 per cent of A procure clay from lease-held land, most units of all categories (60 units) get clay through contractors.
- Terracotta is most widely used than china clay.
- Only one unit of C uses box feeder to store clay. All the other units use either heap method or both heap and box feeder.
- Both manual cutting and machine cutting alternate in almost equal measures.

**Table 35**
**Factors of Production Based on the Year of Establishment**

| *Factors* | | *Year* | | | |
|---|---|---|---|---|---|
| | | *Before 1981 (n=5)* | *1981-1985 (n=7)* | *1985-1990 (n=30)* | *1990 and After (n=42)* |
| Actual production per day(in Numbers) | Below 6000 | 3 (60.0) | 3 (42.9) | 21 (70.0) | 33 (78.6) |
| | 6000-12000 | - | 3 (42.9) | 3 (10.0) | 6 (14.3) |
| | 12000-18000 | 2 (40.0) | 1 (14.3) | 6 (20.0) | 3 (7.1) |
| Place of procurement of clay | Within the Panchayat | 2 (40.0) | 3 (42.9) | 11 (36.7) | 16 (38.1) |
| | Outside the Panchayat but within the District | 3 (60.0) | 4 (57.1) | 19 (63.3) | 26 (61.9) |
| Distance from the factory to procure clay (in Kms.) | 5-10 | 2 (40.0) | 2 (28.6) | 12 (40.0) | 13 (31.0) |
| | 10-15 | 1 (20.0) | 3 (42.9) | 11 (36.7) | 18 (42.9) |
| | Above 15 | 2 (40.0) | 2 (28.6) | 7 (23.3) | 11 (26.2) |
| Methods adopted for procuring clay | Own land/farm | - | 1 (14.3) | 1 (3.3) | 2 (4.8) |
| | Lease hold land/farm | 3 (60.0) | 1 (14.3) | 6 (20.0) | 9 (21.4) |
| | Through contractors | 2 (40.0) | 5 (71.4) | 23 (76.7) | 30 (71.4) |
| | Other agencies | - | - | - | 1 (2.4) |
| Clay used for production | Terracotta clay | 3 (60.0) | 6 (85.7) | 23 (76.7) | 35 (83.3) |
| | Terracotta & China clay | 2 (40.0) | 1 (14.3) | 7 (23.3) | 7 (16.7) |
| Methods adopted for storing clay | Heap method | 4 (80.0) | 5 (71.4) | 23 (76.7) | 35 (83.3) |
| | Box feeder | - | - | 1 (3.3) | - |
| | Both | 1 (20.0) | 2 (28.6) | 6 (20.0) | 7 (16.7) |

*Contd...*

| Factors | | Year | | | |
|---|---|---|---|---|---|
| | | Before 1981 (*n*=5) | 1981-1985 (*n*=7) | 1985-1990 (*n*=30) | 1990 and After (*n*=42) |
| Methods of cutting clay blocks | Manual cutting | - | 1 (14.3) | 9 (30.0) | 18 (42.9) |
| | Automatic cutting | 3 (60.0) | 3 (42.9) | 8 (26.7) | 8 (19.0) |
| | Both | 2 (40.0) | 3 (42.9) | 13 (43.3) | 16 (38.1) |
| Sources of water | Well | - | 3 (42.9) | 13 (43.3) | 11 (26.2) |
| | Bore-Well | 2 (40.0) | 4 (57.1) | 14 (46.7) | 21 (50.0) |
| | Outside source | 3 (60.0) | - | 3 (10.0) | 10 (23.8) |
| Methods used for pressing the tiles | Manual pressing | - | - | 8 (26.7) | 12 (28.6) |
| | Power operated pressing | 2 (40.0) | 3 (42.9) | 8 (26.7) | 10 (23.8) |
| | Both | 3 (60.0) | 4 (57.1) | 14 (46.7) | 20 (47.6) |
| De-airing machine used in production | Yes | 4 (80.0) | 4 (57.1) | 15 (50.0) | 20 (47.6) |
| | No | 1 (20.0) | 3 (42.9) | 15 (50.0) | 22 (52.4) |
| Methods of trimming tiles | Manual trimming | - | 1 (14.3) | 5 (16.7) | 12 (28.6) |
| | Automatic trimming | 2 (40.0) | 3 (42.9) | 9 (30.0) | 11 (26.2) |
| | Both | 3 (60.0) | 3 (42.9) | 16 (53.3) | 19 (45.2) |
| Oil used in production | Rice Bran oil | - | 1 (14.3) | 3 (10.0) | 8 (19.0) |
| | Light diesel oil | 3 (60.0) | 1 (14.3) | 18 (60.0) | 20 (47.6) |
| | Kerosene | 2 (40.0) | 5 (71.4) | 9 (30.0) | 14 (33.3) |
| Oil used per load(in Litres)[a] | Below 10 | 1 (20.0) | - | - | - |
| | 10-20 | 2 (40.0) | - | 25 (83.3) | 35 (83.3) |
| | 20-30 | - | - | 1 (3.3) | - |
| | 30-40 | - | 3 (42.9) | 1 (3.3) | 5 (11.9) |
| | 40 and Above | 2 (40.0) | 4 (57.1) | 3 (10.0) | 2 (4.8) |

*Contd...*

| Factors | | Year | | | |
|---|---|---|---|---|---|
| | | *Before 1981 (n=5)* | *1981-1985 (n=7)* | *1985-1990 (n=30)* | *1990 and After (n=42)* |
| Methods for transporting the clay to machines | Coir belt | - | 3 (42.9) | 7 (23.3) | 19 (45.2) |
| | Rubber belt | 1 (20.0) | - | 7 (23.3) | 4 (9.5) |
| | Chain conveyor | 3 (60.0) | 2 (28.6) | 6 (20.0) | 9 (21.4) |
| | Elevators | - | 1 (14.3) | 2 (6.7) | - |
| | Manual | 1 (20.0) | 1 (14.3) | 8 (26.7) | 10 (23.8) |
| Methods used to dry tiles | Natural | 4 (80.0) | 4 (57.1) | 23 (76.7) | 35 (83.3) |
| | Smoke drying system | - | - | 2 (6.7) | - |
| | Steam Heating system | - | 1 (14.3) | - | 2 (4.8) |
| | Natural and Smoke drying system | 1 (20.0) | 2 (28.6) | 5 (16.7) | 5 (11.9) |
| Place of procurement of firewood | Within Panchayat | 1 (20.0) | 2 (28.6) | 11 (36.7) | 13 (31.0) |
| | Outside the District | - | 2 (28.6) | - | 4 (9.5) |
| | Outside the Panchayat but within district | 4 (80.0) | 3 (42.9) | 19 (63.3) | 25 (59.5) |
| Season of purchasing firewood | Summer | 1 (20.0) | 1 (14.3) | 11 (36.7) | 19 (45.2) |
| | All seasons | 4 (80.0) | 6 (85.7) | 19 (63.3) | 23 (54.8) |
| Distance from the factory to procure firewood (in Kms.) | 5-10 | 1 (20.0) | 2 (28.6) | 9 (30.0) | 13 (31.0) |
| | 10-15 | 1 (20.0) | 2 (28.6) | 12 (40.0) | 8 (19.0) |
| | Above 15 | 3 (60.0) | 3 (42.9) | 9 (30.0) | 21 (50.0) |
| Firewood used per load(in Tonnes)[c] | Below 3 | 2 (40.0) | 1 (14.3) | 8 (26.7) | 9 (21.4) |
| | 3-6 | 1 (20.0) | 1 (14.3) | 20 (66.7) | 28 (66.7) |
| | 6-9 | 2 (40.0) | 4 (57.1) | 2 (6.7) | 4 (9.5) |
| | 9 and Above | - | 1 (14.3) | - | 1 (2.4) |

*Contd...*

| Factors | | Year | | | |
|---|---|---|---|---|---|
| | | *Before 1981 (n=5)* | *1981-1985 (n=7)* | *1985-1990 (n=30)* | *1990 and After (n=42)* |
| Fuel used in production | Sawdust | 4 (80.0) | 4 (57.1) | 17 (56.7) | 26 (61.9) |
| | Cashew shell | 1 (20.0) | 3 (42.9) | 13 (43.3) | 16 (38.1) |
| Methods followed for burning the tiles | Down draught Kiln | - | 2 (28.6) | 11 (36.7) | 21 (50.0) |
| | Semi-continuous down draught chamber type Kiln | 3 (60.0) | 3 (42.9) | 12 (40.0) | 15 (35.7) |
| | Hoffman continuous Horizontal draught type Kiln | 2 (40.0) | 2 (28.6) | 7 (23.3) | 6 (14.3) |
| Methods adopted for measuring the burning temperature | Judged by practical experience | 5 (100.0) | 7 (100.0) | 28 (93.3) | 39 (92.9) |
| | Thermocouple | - | - | 2 (6.7) | 3(7.1) |
| Test adopted to check finished tiles [d] | Water absorption test | - | 4 (57.1) | 6 (20.0) | 9 (21.4) |
| | Breaking strength test | 2 (40.0) | 3 (42.9) | 9 (30.0) | 4 (9.5) |
| | Judgement by experienced supervisors | 3 (60.0) | - | 15 (50.0) | 29 (69.0) |
| Breakage of tiles per load (in Numbers) | Below 50 | 2 (40.0) | 3 (42.9) | 10 (33.3) | 11 (26.2) |
| | 50-100 | 1 (20.0) | 2 (28.6) | 8 (26.7) | 12 (28.6) |
| | 100-150 | 2 (40.0) | 2 (28.6) | 9 (30.0) | 14 (33.3) |
| | Above 150 | - | - | 3 (10.0) | 5 (11.9) |
| Performance of production function | Bad | 1 (20.0) | - | 2 (6.7) | 5 (11.9) |
| | Moderate | - | 1 (14.3) | 6 (20.0) | 9 (21.4) |
| | Good | 3 (60.0) | 4 (57.1) | 21 (70.0) | 26 (61.9) |
| | Excellent | 1 (20.0) | 2 (28.6) | 1 (3.3) | 2 (4.8) |

( ) in Percentage Contingency Coefficient $\geq 0.5$ P-Value $<0.01$[a] Contingency Coefficient $\geq 0.5$ P-Value $<0.05$[b]
Contingency Coefficient $\leq 0.5$ P-Value $<0.01$[c] Contingency Coefficient $\leq 0.5$ P-Value $<0.05$[d]

- Bore-well are the main suppliers of water for 41 units and the other units draw water from well or from outside sources.
- Both manual pressing and power-operated pressing were adopted by 60 per cent of A, 57.1 per cent of B and nearly 47 per cent of C and D.
- The use of de-airing machine has declined over the year from 80 per cent of A to 47.6 per cent of D.
- Manual trimming and automatic trimming of tiles are both adopted by most of the units (60 per cent of A, 42.9 per cent of B, 53.3 per cent of C and 45.2 per cent of D).
- The use of light diesel oil dominates – 60 per cent of each A and C, and 47.6 per cent of D, but 71.4 per cent of B use Kerosene.
- 40 per cent of A and 83.3 per cent of C and D keep the use of oil at 10 to 20 litres per load whereas 40 per cent of A and 57.1 per cent of B exceed 40 litres.
- For transporting the clay to the machines, chain conveyor is used by 60 per cent of A; but coir belt is the most favoured method for 42.9 per cent of B, 23.3 per cent of C and 45.2 per cent of D.
- Exposure to the natural sunlight is the most favoured method of drying the tiles, a maximum 80 per cent of A, 57.1 per cent of B, 76.7 per cent of C and 83.3 per cent of D.
- Most of the units procure firewood from outside the Panchayat area, a majority of 80 per cent of A, 42.9 per cent of B, 63.3 per cent of C and 59.5 per cent of D.
- Though 32 units procure firewood only during summer, the activity is carried on in all the seasons by 52 units.
- The average of firewood used is 3 to 6 tonnes per load (20 per cent of A, 14.3 per cent of B, 66.7 per cent each of C and D), but 40 per cent of A and 57.1 per cent of B consume more than 6 tonnes.

- Sawdust is more used as fuel than cashew shell, a maximum of 80 per cent of A, 57.1 per cent of B, 56.7 per cent of C and 61.9 per cent of D.
- Semi-continuous downdraught kiln is most used for burning the tiles, a majority 60 per cent of A, 42.9 per cent of B, 40 per cent of C and 35.7 per cent of D.
- Except 2 units of C, and 3 of D, all the other units measure burning temperature by practical experience, instead of with the use of thermocouple.
- Similarly, to check the finished tiles, judgement by experienced supervisors prevail, except in the case of B, which use water absorption test and breaking strength test.
- Breakage is kept at the minimum (below 50 tiles per load) by 40 per cent of A, 42.9 per cent of B, 33.3 per cent of C and 26.2 per cent of D, totally 26 units. An almost equal number incurs breakage of 50 to 100 and 100 to 150.
- One unit of A, 2 of C and 5 of D have recorded bad performance and on the other hand, average performance has been good - 60 per cent of A, 57 per cent of B, 70 per cent of C and 62 per cent of D.

Moreover, the results of the contingency co-efficient suggest that the factors of production namely firewood & oil used per load and test adopted to check the finished tiles were associated with the year of establishment of the units and these were statistically significant at five per cent and one per cent level.

Table 36 gives particulars of production on the basic of the jurisdiction of the units. The following code may be used.

A = units in Panchayat limits

B = Municipality limits

C = Corporation

When three numbers occur successively, they refer to A, B and C respectively.

**Table 36**
**Factors of Production Based on the Jurisdiction of the Units**

| *Factors* | | *Jurisdiction* | | |
|---|---|---|---|---|
| | | *Panchayat* (*n*=74) | *Municipality* (*n*=9) | *Corporation* (*n*=1) |
| Actual production per day (in Numbers) | Below 6000 | 53 (71.6) | 6 (66.7) | 1 (100.0) |
| | 6000-12000 | 11 (14.9) | 1 (11.1) | - |
| | 12000-18000 | 10 (13.5) | 2 (22.2) | - |
| Place of procurement of clay | Within the Panchayat | 31 (41.9) | 1 (11.1) | - |
| | Outside the Panchayat but within the District | 43 (58.1) | 8 (88.9) | 1 (100.0) |
| Distance from the factory to procure clay (in Kms.)[d] | 5-10 | 28 (37.8) | 1 (11.1) | - |
| | 10-15 | 31 (41.9) | 2 (22.2) | - |
| | Above 15 | 15 (20.3) | 6 (66.7) | 1 (100.0) |
| Methods adopted for procuring clay | Own land/farm | 4 (5.4) | - | - |
| | Lease hold land/farm | 17 (23.0) | 2 (22.2) | - |
| | Through contractors | 52 (70.3) | 7 (77.8) | 1 (100.0) |
| | Other agencies | 1 (1.4) | - | - |
| Clay used for Production | Terracotta clay | 59 (79.7) | 7 (77.8) | 1 (100.0) |
| | Terracotta & China clay | 15 (20.3) | 2 (22.2) | - |
| Methods adopted for storing clay | Heap method | 60 (81.1) | 6 (66.7) | 1 (100.0) |
| | Box feeder | 1 (1.4) | - | - |
| | Both | 13 (17.6) | 3 (33.3) | - |
| Methods of cutting clay blocks | Manual cutting | 25 (33.8) | 2 (22.2) | 1 (100.0) |
| | Automatic cutting | 19 (25.7) | 3 (33.3) | - |
| | Both | 30 (40.5) | 4 (44.4) | - |

*Contd...*

| Factors | | Jurisdiction | | |
|---|---|---|---|---|
| | | *Panchayat (n=74)* | *Municipality (n=9)* | *Corporation (n=1)* |
| Sources of water | Well | 21 (28.4) | 5 (55.6) | 1 (100.0) |
| | Bore-Well | 39 (52.7) | 2 (22.2) | - |
| | Outside source | 14 (18.9) | 2 (22.2) | - |
| Methods used for pressing the tiles | Manual pressing | 17 (23.0) | 2 (22.2) | 1 (100.0) |
| | Power operated pressing | 20 (27.0) | 3 (33.3) | - |
| | Both | 37 (50.0) | 4 (44.4) | - |
| De-airing machine used in production | Yes | 38 (51.4) | 5 (55.6) | - |
| | No | 36 (48.6) | 4 (44.4) | 1 (100.0) |
| Methods of trimming tiles | Manual trimming | 16 (21.6) | 1 (11.1) | 1 (100.0) |
| | Automatic trimming | 22 (29.7) | 3 (33.3) | - |
| | Both | 36 (48.6) | 5 (55.6) | - |
| Oil used in production | Rice Bran oil | 10 (13.5) | 2 (22.2) | - |
| | Light diesel oil | 37 (50.0) | 4 (44.4) | 1 (100.0) |
| | Kerosene | 27 (36.5) | 3 (33.3) | - |
| Oil used per load(in Litres) | Below 10 | 1 (1.4) | - | - |
| | 10-20 | 52 (70.3) | 9 (100.0) | 1 (100.0) |
| | 20-30 | 1 (1.4) | - | - |
| | 30-40 | 9 (12.2) | - | - |
| | 40 and Above | 11 (14.9) | - | - |
| Methods for transporting the clay to machines | Coir belt | 27 (36.5) | 2 (22.2) | - |
| | Rubber belt | 9 (12.2) | 3 (33.3) | - |
| | Chain conveyor | 18 (24.3) | 2 (22.2) | - |
| | Elevators | 3 (4.1) | - | - |
| | Manual | 17 (23.0) | 2 (22.2) | 1 (100.0) |

*Contd...*

| Factors | | Jurisdiction | | |
|---|---|---|---|---|
| | | *Panchayat (n=74)* | *Municipality (n=9)* | *Corporation (n=1)* |
| Methods used to dry tiles | Natural | 58 (78.4) | 7 (77.8) | 1 (100.0) |
| | Smoke drying system | 2 (2.7) | - | - |
| | Steam Heating system | 3 (4.1) | - | - |
| | Natural and Smoke drying system | 11 (14.9) | 2 (22.2) | - |
| Place of procurement of firewood | Within Panchayat | 26 (35.1) | 1 (11.1) | - |
| | Outside the District | 6 (8.1) | - | - |
| | Outside the Panchayat but within district | 42 (56.8) | 8 (88.9) | 1 (100.0) |
| Season of purchasing firewood | Summer | 28 (37.8) | 4 (44.4) | - |
| | All seasons | 46 (62.2) | 5 (55.6) | 1 (100.0) |
| Distance from the factory to procure firewood (in Kms.) | 5-10 | 24 (32.4) | 1 (11.1) | - |
| | 10-15 | 19 (25.7) | 4 (44.4) | - |
| | Above 15 | 31 (41.9) | 4 (44.4) | 1 (100.0) |
| Firewood used per load(in Tonnes) | Below 3 | 17 (23.0) | 3 (33.3) | - |
| | 3-6 | 43 (58.1) | 6 (66.7) | 1 (100.0) |
| | 6-9 | 12 (16.2) | - | - |
| | 9 and Above | 2 (2.7) | - | - |
| Fuel used in production | Sawdust | 48 (64.9) | 3 (33.3) | - |
| | Cashew shell | 26 (35.1) | 6 (66.7) | 1 (100.0) |
| Methods followed for burning the tiles | Down draught Kiln | 31 (41.9) | 2 (22.2) | 1 (100.0) |
| | Semi-continuous down draught chamber type Kiln | 29 (39.2) | 4 (44.4) | - |
| | Hoffman continuous Horizontal draught type Kiln | 14 (18.9) | 3 (33.3) | - |

*Contd...*

| Factors | | Jurisdiction | | |
|---|---|---|---|---|
| | | Panchayat (n=74) | Municipality (n=9) | Corporation (n=1) |
| Methods adopted for measuring the burning temperature | Judged by practical experience | 71 (95.9) | 7 (77.8) | 1 (100.0) |
| | Thermocouple | 3 (4.1) | 2 (22.2) | - |
| Test adopted to check finished tiles | Water absorption test | 17 (23.0) | 2 (22.2) | - |
| | Breaking strength test | 16 (21.6) | 1 (11.1) | 1 (100.0) |
| | Judgement by experienced supervisors | 41 (55.4) | 6 (66.7) | - |
| Breakage of tiles per load (in Numbers) | Below 50 | 22 (29.7) | 4 (44.4) | - |
| | 50-100 | 21 (28.4) | 1 (11.1) | 1 (100.0) |
| | 100-150 | 23 (31.1) | 4 (44.4) | - |
| | Above 150 | 8 (10.8) | - | - |
| Performance of production function | Bad | 8 (10.8) | - | - |
| | Moderate | 14 (18.9) | 2 (22.2) | - |
| | Good | 46 (62.2) | 7 (77.8) | 1 (100.0) |
| | Excellent | 6 (8.1) | - | - |

( ) in Percentage

Contingency Coefficient ≥ 0.5 P-Value <0.01[a]
Contingency Coefficient ≥ 0.5 P-Value <0.05[b]
Contingency Coefficient ≤ 0.5 P-Value <0.01[c]
Contingency Coefficient ≤ 0.5 P-Value <0.05[d]

- Only 24 units of A and B produce more than 6000 tiles per day and the remaining units of A, B and C produce less than 6000 tiles per day.
- 58.1 per cent of A, 88.9 per cent of B and the only unit of C procure clay from outside the Panchayat area.
- The distance between the unit and the source of clay is 10 to 15 km for 41.9 per cent of A and about 15 km for 66.7 per cent of B and the one unit of C.
- 70.3 per cent of A, 77.8 per cent of B and the one unit of C procure clay through contractors.
- Terracotta dominates (79.7 per cent of A, 77.8 per cent of B and 100 per cent of C), though 17 units are both terracotta and china clay.
- Though one unit of A uses box feeder for storing the clay, the keeping of the clay in heaps is the most practiced method.
- Except for the unit of C, which uses only manual cutting, all the units use both manual and machine cutting, according to the needs and circumstances.
- The only unit of C draws all its water from the wells. 28.4 per cent of A and 55.6 per cent of B also use the same source. 39 units of A and 2 units of B draw water from bore-wells.
- Both manual pressing and power-operated pressing are adopted by 50 per cent of A and 44.4 per cent of B. The only unit of C adopts manual pressing alone.
- The use and the absence of de-airing machine balance each other-43 units use it and 41 do not use it.
- Both manual pressing and machine pressing are practiced by 48.6 per cent of A and 55.6 per cent of B. The only unit in C practices manual pressing alone.
- The use of light diesel oil dominates with 50 per cent of A, 44.4 per cent of B and 100 per cent of C use the same.

- The norm of oil used is 10 to 20 litres for a load with a maximum 70.3 per cent of A, 44.4 per cent of B and 100 per cent of C.
- Coir belt, rubber belt and chain conveyor are the three most used methods of transporting the clay to the machines.
- As for drying the tiles, exposure to sunlight is the natural and easy way with a majority of 78.4 per cent of A, 77.8 per cent of B and 100 per cent of C using the method.
- In most cases the source of firewood lies outside the Panchayat area, but within the district with a maximum of 56.8 per cent of A, 88.9 per cent of B and one unit of C utilise this source.
- 28 units of A and 4 of B limit their purchase of firewood to summer, but all the other units do it the year round.
- 48 units get firewood from sources within a distance of 15 km and 36 units farther.
- 20 units manage to keep the consumption of firewood at a low level – below 3 tonnes per load and the norm is 3 to 6 tonnes, a maximum of 58.1 per cent of A, 66.7 per cent of B and one unit of C.
- 64.9 per cent of A use sawdust, but 66.7 per cent of B and one unit of C use cashew shell as fuel.
- 41.9 per cent of A and 100 per cent of C for burning the tiles uses downdraught kiln, whereas 44.4 per cent of B use semi-continuous downdraught kiln. 14 units of A and 3 units of B also use Hoffman kiln.
- Except that 3 units of A and 2 of B use thermocouple, all the other units measure burning temperature by practical experience.
- Similarly, to check finished tiles, judgement by experienced supervisors is popular with 55.4 per cent of A and 66.7 per cent of B.
- Though 8 units of A suffer a breakage of 150 or more tiles per load, the norm is 100 to 150 (31.1 per cent of A and 44.4 per cent of B).

- 6 units of A have done excellent production performance and good performance is found in 62.2 per cent of A, 77.8 per cent of B and 100 per cent of C.

Moreover, the results of the contingency co-efficient suggest that the factor of production namely distance from the factory to procuring the clay was associated with the year of establishment of the units and this was statistically significant at five per cent level.

Table 37 gives particulars of production based on the type of tiles manufactured by the units. The following code is used.

A = Roofing tiles

B = Flooring tiles

C = Other tiles

D = Roofing and flooring

E = Flooring and decorative

F = Decorative and other tiles

- 6 units of B, 2 of C and 4 of E produce more than 12000 tiles per day. But, most of the units' produce only less than 6000 tiles per day.
- The source of clay for most units is outside the Panchayat but within the district.
- The source of clay is within 15 km for a majority of units i.e. 75 per cent of A, 45.2 per cent of B, 44.4 per cent of C, 37.5 per cent of D and 20 per cent of E.
- Most of the units get clay through contractors.
- 11 units of B, 2 of C, 1 of D and 3 of E use both terracotta and china clay. But the rest of the units use only terracotta.
- Most of the units store the clay in heaps.
- Both manual cutting and automatic cutting are practised by 75 per cent of A, 40.5 per cent of B, 22.2 per cent of C, 25 per cent of D and 50 per cent of D. The unit of F does only manual cuttings.
- Bore-wells supply water to most units.

**Table 37**
**Factors of Production Based on Type of Clay Tiles Manufactured by the Units**

| *Factors* | | *Type of Clay Tiles* | | | | | |
|---|---|---|---|---|---|---|---|
| | | *Roofing (n=4)* | *Flooring (n=42)* | *Other tiles (n=9)* | *Roofing & Flooring (n=8)* | *Flooring & Decorative (n=20)* | *Decorative & other tiles (n=1)* |
| Actual production per day(in Numbers) | Below 6000 | 3 (75.0) | 27 (64.3) | 5 (55.6) | 8 (100.0) | 16 (80.0) | 1 (100.0) |
| | 6000-12000 | 1 (25.0) | 9 (21.4) | 2 (22.2) | - | - | - |
| | 12000-18000 | - | 6 (14.3) | 2 (22.2) | - | 4 (20.0) | - |
| Place of procurement of clay | Within the Panchayat | 1 (25.0) | 16 (38.1) | 4 (44.4) | 5 (62.5) | 6 (30.0) | - |
| | Outside the Panchayat but within the District | 3 (75.0) | 26 (61.9) | 5 (55.6) | 3 (37.5) | 14 (70.0) | 1 (100.0) |
| Distance from the factory to procure clay(in Kms.) | 5-10 | - | 14 (33.3) | 2 (22.2) | 3 (37.5) | 10 (50.0) | - |
| | 10-15 | 3 (75.0) | 19 (45.2) | 4 (44.4) | 3 (37.5) | 4 (20.0) | - |
| | Above 15 | 1 (25.0) | 9 (21.4) | 3 (33.3) | 2 (25.0) | 6 (30.0) | 1 (100.0) |
| Methods adopted for procuring clay [d] | Own land / farm | - | 1 (2.4) | - | 3 (37.5) | - | - |
| | Lease hold land / farm | 1 (25.0) | 10 (23.8) | 2 (22.2) | 2 (25.0) | 4 (20.0) | - |
| | Through contractors | 3 (75.0) | 31 (73.8) | 7 (77.8) | 3 (37.5) | 15 (75.0) | 1 (100.0) |
| | Other agencies | - | - | - | - | 1 (5.0) | - |
| Clay used for production | Terracotta clay | 4 (100.0) | 31 (73.8) | 7 (77.8) | 7 (87.5) | 17 (85.0) | 1 (100.0) |
| | Terracotta & China clay | - | 11 (26.2) | 2 (22.2) | 1 (12.5) | 3 (15.0) | - |
| Methods adopted for storing clay | Heap method | 4 (100.0) | 31 (73.8) | 6 (66.7) | 8 (100.0) | 17 (85.0) | 1 (100.0) |
| | Box feeder | - | - | - | - | 1 (5.0) | - |
| | Both | - | 11 (26.2) | 3 (33.3) | - | 2 (10.0) | - |
| Methods of cutting clay blocks | Manual cutting | 1 (25.0) | 13 (31.0) | 2 (22.2) | 5 (62.5) | 6 (30.0) | 1 (100.0) |
| | Automatic cutting | - | 12 (28.6) | 5 (55.6) | 1 (12.5) | 4 (20.0) | - |
| | Both | 3 (75.0) | 17 (40.5) | 2 (22.2) | 2 (25.0) | 10 (50.0) | - |

*Contd...*

| Factors | | Type of Clay Tiles | | | | | |
|---|---|---|---|---|---|---|---|
| | | *Roofing (n=4)* | *Flooring (n=42)* | *Other tiles (n=9)* | *Roofing & Flooring (n=8)* | *Flooring & Decorative (n=20)* | *Decorative & other tiles (n=1)* |
| Sources of water | Well | 1 (25.0) | 16 (38.1) | 2 (22.2) | 1 (12.5) | 6 (30.0) | 1 (100.0) |
| | Bore-Well | 1 (25.0) | 21 (50.0) | 5 (55.6) | 5 (62.5) | 9 (45.0) | - |
| | Outside source | 2 (50.0) | 5 (11.9) | 2 (22.2) | 2 (25.0) | 5 (25.0) | - |
| Methods used for pressing the tiles | Manual pressing | 1 (25.0) | 10 (23.8) | 1 (11.1) | 3 (37.5) | 4 (20.0) | 1 (00.0) |
| | Power operated pressing | - | 15 (35.7) | 4 (44.4) | - | 4 (20.0) | - |
| | Both | 3 (75.0) | 17 (40.5) | 4 (44.4) | 5 (62.5) | 12 (60.0) | - |
| De-airing machine used in production | Yes | 3 (75.0) | 22 (52.4) | 5 (55.6) | 2 (25.0) | 11 (55.0) | - |
| | No | 1 (25.0) | 20 (47.6) | 4 (44.4) | 6 (75.0) | 9 (45.0) | 1 (100.0) |
| Methods of trimming tiles | Manual trimming | - | 7 (16.7) | 1 (11.1) | 4 (50.0) | 5 (25.0) | 1 (100.0) |
| | Automatic trimming | 1 (25.0) | 16 (38.1) | 3 (33.3) | 1 (12.5) | 4 (20.0) | - |
| | Both | 3 (75.0) | 19 (45.2) | 5 (55.6) | 3 (37.5) | 11 (55.0) | - |
| Oil used in production | Rice Bran oil | 1 (25.0) | 7 (16.7) | - | 1 (12.5) | 3 (15.0) | - |
| | Light diesel oil | 2 (50.0) | 24 (57.1) | 3 (33.3) | 2 (25.0) | 10 (50.0) | 1 (100.0) |
| | Kerosene | 1 (25.0) | 11 (26.2) | 6 (66.7) | 5 (62.5) | 7 (35.0) | - |
| Oil used per load(in Litres)[a] | Below 10 | - | 1 (2.4) | - | - | - | - |
| | 10-20 | 1 (25.0) | 40 (95.2) | - | - | 20 (100.0) | 1 (100.0) |
| | 20-30 | - | 1 (2.4) | - | - | - | - |
| | 30-40 | 2 (50.0) | - | 2 (22.2) | 5 (62.5) | - | - |
| | 40 and Above | 1 (25.0) | - | 7 (77.8) | 3 (37.5) | - | - |
| Methods for transporting the clay to machines | Coir belt | 2 (50.0) | 13 (31.0) | 1 (11.1) | 5 (62.5) | 8 (40.0) | - |
| | Rubber belt | 1 (25.0) | 7 (16.7) | 1 (11.1) | - | 3 (15.0) | - |
| | Chain conveyor | - | 12 (28.6) | 4 (44.4) | - | 4 (20.0) | - |
| | Elevators | - | 1 (2.4) | 1 (11.1) | - | 1 (5.0) | - |
| | Manual | 1 (25.0) | 9 (21.4) | 2 (22.2) | 3 (37.5) | 4 (20.0) | 1 (100.0) |

*Contd...*

| Factors | | Type of Clay Tiles | | | | | |
|---|---|---|---|---|---|---|---|
| | | *Roofing (n=4)* | *Flooring (n=42)* | *Other tiles (n=9)* | *Roofing & Flooring (n=8)* | *Flooring & Decorative (n=20)* | *Decorative & other tiles (n=1)* |
| Methods used to dry tiles | Natural | 4 (100.0) | 33 (78.6) | 5 (55.6) | 7 (87.5) | 16 (80.0) | 1 (100.0) |
| | Smoke drying system | - | 1 (2.4) | - | - | 1 (5.0) | - |
| | Steam Heating system | - | 1 (2.4) | 1 (11.1) | 1 (12.5) | - | - |
| | Natural and Smoke drying system | - | 7 (16.7) | 3 (33.3) | - | 3 (15.0) | - |
| Place of procurement of firewood | Within Panchayat | - | 17 (40.5) | 2 (22.2) | 3 (37.5) | 5 (25.0) | - |
| | Outside the District | 1 (25.0) | 3 (7.1) | 1 (11.1) | 1 (12.5) | - | - |
| | Outside the Panchayat but within district | 3 (75.0) | 22 (52.4) | 6 (66.7) | 4 (50.0) | 15 (75.0) | 1 (100.0) |
| Season of purchasing firewood [c] | Summer | 2 (50.0) | 11 (26.2) | 1 (11.1) | 3 (37.5) | 14 (70.0) | 1 (100.0) |
| | All seasons | 2 (50.0) | 31 (73.8) | 8 (88.9) | 5 (62.5) | 6 (30.0) | - |
| Distance from the factory to procure firewood (in Kms.) | 5-10 | - | 16 (38.1) | 1 (11.1) | 2 (25.0) | 6 (30.0) | - |
| | 10-15 | 1 (25.0) | 11 (26.2) | 4 (44.4) | 2 (25.0) | 5 (25.0) | - |
| | Above 15 | 3 (75.0) | 15 (35.7) | 4 (44.4) | 4 (50.0) | 9 (45.0) | 1 (100.0) |
| Firewood used per load (in Tonnes) [a] | Below 3 | 1 (25.0) | 16 (38.1) | - | - | 3 (15.0) | - |
| | 3-6 | 2 (50.0) | 26 (61.9) | 1 (11.1) | 3 (37.5) | 17 (85.0) | 1 (100.0) |
| | 6-9 | 1 (25.0) | - | 6 (66.7) | 5 (62.5) | - | - |
| | 9 and Above | - | - | 2 (22.2) | - | - | - |
| Fuel used in production | Sawdust | 3 (75.0) | 30 (71.4) | 5 (55.6) | 5 (62.5) | 8 (40.0) | - |
| | Cashew shell | 1 (25.0) | 12 (28.6) | 4 (44.4) | 3 (37.5) | 12 (60.0) | 1 (100.0) |
| Methods followed for burning the tiles | Down draught Kiln | 1 (25.0) | 15 (35.7) | 3 (33.3) | 6 (75.0) | 8 (40.0) | 1 (100.0) |
| | Semi-continuous down draught chamber type Kiln | 3 (75.0) | 17 (40.5) | 3 (33.3) | 2 (25.0) | 8 (40.0) | - |
| | Hoffman continuous Horizontal draught type Kiln | - | 10 (23.8) | 3 (33.3) | - | 4 (20.0) | - |

*Contd...*

| Factors | | Type of Clay Tiles | | | | | |
|---|---|---|---|---|---|---|---|
| | | *Roofing (n=4)* | *Flooring (n=42)* | *Other tiles (n=9)* | *Roofing & Flooring (n=8)* | *Flooring & Decorative (n=20)* | *Decorative & other tiles (n=1)* |
| Methods adopted for measuring the burning temperature | Judged by practical experience | 4 (100.0) | 38(90.5) | 9(100.0) | 8 (100.0) | 19 (95.0) | 1 (100.0) |
| | Thermocouple | - | 4 (9.5) | - | - | 1 (5.0) | - |
| Test adopted to check finished tiles | Water absorption test | 1 (25.0) | 12 (28.6) | 2 (22.2) | 1 (12.5) | 3 (15.0) | - |
| | Breaking strength test | 1 (25.0) | 8 (19.0) | 4 (44.4) | 2 (25.0) | 3 (15.0) | - |
| | Judgement by experienced supervisors | 2 (50.0) | 22 (52.4) | 3 (33.3) | 5 (62.5) | 14 (70.0) | 1 (100.0) |
| Breakage of tiles per load(in Numbers) | Below 50 | 1 (25.0) | 16 (38.1) | 2 (22.2) | 1 (12.5) | 6 (30.0) | - |
| | 50-100 | 1 (25.0) | 11 (26.2) | 5 (55.6) | 1 (12.5) | 5 (25.0) | - |
| | 100-150 | 1 (25.0) | 13 (31.0) | 2 (22.2) | 4 (50.0) | 6 (30.0) | 1 (100.0) |
| | Above 150 | 1 (25.0) | 2 (4.8) | - | 2 (25.0) | 3 (15.0) | - |
| Performance of production function [d] | Bad | 2 (50.0) | 1 (2.4) | 1 (11.1) | 2 (25.0) | 2 (10.0) | - |
| | Moderate | - | 8 (19.0) | - | 1 (12.5) | 6 (30.0) | 1 (100.0) |
| | Good | 2 (50.0) | 31 (73.8) | 6 (66.7) | 4 (50.0) | 11 (55.0) | - |
| | Excellent | - | 2 (4.8) | 2 (22.2) | 1 (12.5) | 1 (5.0) | - |

( )in Percentage Contingency Coefficient $\geq$ 0.5 P-Value <0.01[a]
Contingency Coefficient $\geq$ 0.5 P-Value <0.05[b]
Contingency Coefficient $\leq$ 0.5 P-Value <0.01[c]
Contingency Coefficient $\leq$ 0.5 P-Value <0.05[d]

- Manual pressing and machine pressing both methods are adopted by 75 per cent of A, 40.5 per cent of B, 44.4 per cent of C, 62.5 per cent of D and 60 per cent of D. F believes in manual pressing.
- Most units use de-aired vacuum pumps, but F does not.
- Both manual trimming and automatic trimming of tiles are done in most units, but F does only manual trimming.
- Light diesel oil (42 units) and Kerosene (30) are more used than rice bran oil (only 12).
- One unit of B keeps oil consumption lowest – below 10 litres per load; otherwise the norm is 10 to 20 litres (62 units).
- Though chain conveyor is used by 44 per cent of C, the coir belt is the most common conveyance to transport the clay to the machines (50 per cent of A, 31 per cent of B, 11.1 per cent of C, 62.5 per cent of D and 40 per cent of E. F does not use any thing).
- The natural method of exposing the tiles to sunlight is popular with most of the units.
- The source of firewood for most units lies outside the Panchayat area.
- 32 units procure firewood only during summer, whereas the other units carry on the activities of procuring firewood the year round.
- For 36 units the source of firewood is 15 km away and for the rest, it is nearer.
- 50 units maintain the consumption of firewood at 3 to 6 tonnes per load, but 2 units of C exceed 9 tonnes.
- Sawdust is more used as fuel than cashew shell (51 units).
- 17 units use Hoffman Kiln for burning the tiles, whereas the use of downdraught kiln and the semi-continuous downdraught kiln is almost equal.

- Burning temperature is measured by practical experience, rather than by the use of thermocouple (only4 units of B and 1 of E).
- Similarly, judgement is passed by experienced supervisors to check finished tiles, a majority 50 per cent of A, 52.4 per cent of B, 33.3 per cent of C, 62.5 per cent of D, 70 per cent of E and 100 per cent of F.
- 26 units manage to keep breakage low (below 50 per load), 8 units exceed 150; otherwise the norm is between 50 and 150.
- Two units each of B and C, and one unit each of D and E have performed excellently, and the overall picture of performance is Good.

Moreover, the results of the contingency co-efficient suggest that the factors of production such as methods adopted for procuring the clay, oil used per load, season of purchasing firewood, firewood used per load and performance of production function were associated with the types of clay tiles manufactured by the units and these were statistically significant at five per cent and one per cent level.

Table 38 shows particulars of production on the basis of ownership. The following code is used:

A = Sole proprietorship

B = Partnership

C = Co-operative society

D = Private Company

When 4 figures appear successively, they refer to A, B, C and D respectively.

- Most of the units produce less than 6000 tiles per day whereas only 6 of A, 5 of B and 1 of D manage to produce more than 12000 tiles.
- The source of clay is outside the Panchayat for most of the units.
- 12 units of A, 8 of B, 2 of C have their source of clay beyond 15 km, whereas the rest of the units get it within 15 km.

**Table 38**
**Factors of Production Based on the Ownership of the Units**

| Factors | | Ownership | | | |
|---|---|---|---|---|---|
| | | *Sole Proprietor (n=48)* | *Partnership (n=29)* | *Co-op. Society (n=4)* | *Private company (n=3)* |
| Actual production per day (in Numbers) | Below 6000 | 36 (75.0) | 19 (65.5) | 4 (100.0) | 1 (33.3) |
| | 6000-12000 | 6 (12.5) | 5 (17.2) | - | 1 (33.3) |
| | 12000-18000 | 6 (12.5) | 5 (17.2) | - | 1 (33.3) |
| Place of procurement of clay | Within the Panchayat | 14 (29.2) | 16 (55.2) | - | 2 (66.7) |
| | Outside the Panchayat but within the District | 34 (70.8) | 13 (44.8) | 4 (100.0) | 1 (33.3) |
| Distance from the factory to procure clay (in Kms.) | 5-10 | 15 (31.3) | 12 (41.4) | - | 2 (66.7) |
| | 10-15 | 21 (43.8) | 9 (31.0) | 2 (50.0) | 1 (33.3) |
| | Above 15 | 12 (25.0) | 8 (27.6) | 2 (50.0) | - |
| Methods adopted for procuring clay [d] | Own land / farm | 3 (6.3) | 1 (3.4) | - | - |
| | Lease hold land / farm | 10 (20.8) | 8 (27.6) | 1 (25.0) | - |
| | Through contractors | 34 (70.8) | 20 (69.0) | 3 (75.0) | 3 (100.0) |
| | Other agencies | 1 (2.1) | - | - | - |
| Clay used for production | Terracotta clay | 36 (75.0) | 25 (86.2) | 4 (100.0) | 2 (66.7) |
| | Terracotta & China clay | 12 (25.0) | 4 (13.8) | - | 1 (33.3) |
| Methods adopted for storing clay | Heap method | 37 (77.1) | 25 (86.2) | 4 (100.0) | 1 (33.3) |
| | Box feeder | 1 (2.1) | - | - | - |
| | Both | 10 (20.8) | 4 (13.8) | - | 2 (66.7) |
| Methods of cutting clay blocks | Manual cutting | 18 (37.5) | 9 (31.0) | 1 (25.0) | - |
| | Automatic cutting | 12 (25.0) | 8 (27.6) | - | 2 (66.7) |
| | Both | 18 (37.5) | 12 (41.4) | 3 (75.0) | 1 (33.3) |

*Contd...*

| Factors | | *Ownership* Sole Proprietor (n=48) | Partnership (n=29) | Co-op. Society (n=4) | Private company (n=3) |
|---|---|---|---|---|---|
| Sources of water | Well | 16 (33.3) | 7 (24.1) | 3 (75.0) | 1 (33.3) |
| | Bore-Well | 23 (47.9) | 16 (55.2) | - | 2 (66.7) |
| | Outside source | 9 (18.8) | 6 (20.7) | 1 (25.0) | - |
| Methods used for pressing the tiles [d] | Manual pressing | 17 (35.4) | 2 (6.9) | 1 (25.0) | - |
| | Power operated pressing | 13 (27.1) | 8 (27.6) | - | 2 (66.7) |
| | Both | 18 (37.5) | 19 (65.5) | 3 (75.0) | 1 (33.3) |
| De-airing machine used in production | Yes | 22 (45.8) | 17 (58.6) | 1 (25.0) | 3 (100.0) |
| | No | 26 (54.2) | 12 (41.4) | 3 (75.0) | - |
| Methods of trimming tiles | Manual trimming | 14 (29.2) | 3 (10.3) | 1 (25.0) | - |
| | Automatic trimming | 14 (29.2) | 9 (31.0) | - | 2 (66.7) |
| | Both | 20 (41.7) | 17 (58.6) | 3 (75.0) | 1 (33.3) |
| Oil used in production | Rice Bran oil | 6 (12.5) | 4 (13.8) | - | 2 (66.7) |
| | Light diesel oil | 27 (56.3) | 13 (44.8) | 2 (50.0) | - |
| | Kerosene | 15 (31.3) | 12 (41.4) | 2 (50.0) | 1 (33.3) |
| Oil used per load(in Litres) | Below 10 | - | 1 (3.4) | - | - |
| | 10-20 | 36 (75.0) | 19 (65.5) | 4 (100.0) | 3 (100.0) |
| | 20-30 | 1 (2.1) | - | - | - |
| | 30-40 | 6 (12.5) | 3 (10.3) | - | - |
| | 40 and Above | 5 (10.4) | 6 (20.7) | - | - |
| Methods for transporting the clay to machines [d] | Coir belt | 14 (29.2) | 15 (51.7) | - | - |
| | Rubber belt | 8 (16.7) | 3 (10.3) | 1 (25.0) | - |
| | Chain conveyor | 9 (18.8) | 8 (27.6) | - | 3 (100.0) |
| | Elevators | 2 (4.2) | 1 (3.4) | - | - |
| | Manual | 15 (31.3) | 2 (6.9) | 3 (75.0) | - |

*Contd...*

| Factors | | Ownership | | | |
|---|---|---|---|---|---|
| | | *Sole Proprietor (n=48)* | *Partnership (n=29)* | *Co-op. Society (n=4)* | *Private company (n=3)* |
| Methods used to dry tiles | Natural | 38(79.2) | 23(79.3) | 4(100.0) | 1(33.3) |
| | Smoke drying system | 2(4.2) | - | - | - |
| | Steam Heating system | 2(4.2) | 1(3.4) | - | - |
| | Natural and Smoke drying system | 6(12.5) | 5(17.2) | - | 2(66.7) |
| Place of procurement of firewood | Within Panchayat | 15(31.3) | 9(31.0) | 1(25.0) | 2(66.7) |
| | Outside the District | 2(4.2) | 4(13.8) | - | - |
| | Outside the Panchayat but within district | 31(64.6) | 16(55.2) | 3(75.0) | 1(33.3) |
| Season of purchasing firewood | Summer | 23(47.9) | 7(24.1) | 2(50.0) | - |
| | All seasons | 25(52.1) | 22(75.9) | 2(50.0) | 3(100.0) |
| Distance from the factory to procure firewood (in Kms.) | 5-10 | 16(33.3) | 6(20.7) | 1(25.0) | 2(66.7) |
| | 10-15 | 15(31.3) | 7(24.1) | 1(25.0) | - |
| | Above 15 | 17(35.4) | 16(55.2) | 2(50.0) | 1(33.3) |
| Firewood used per load (in Tonnes) | Below 3 | 10(20.8) | 7(24.1) | 2(50.0) | 1(33.3) |
| | 3-6 | 31(64.6) | 15(51.7) | 2(50.0) | 2(66.7) |
| | 6-9 | 7(14.6) | 5(17.2) | - | - |
| | 9 and Above | - | 2(6.9) | - | - |
| Fuel used in production | Sawdust | 29(60.4) | 19(65.5) | 1(25.0) | 2(66.7) |
| | Cashew shell | 19(39.6) | 10(34.5) | 3(75.0) | 1(33.3) |

Contd...

| Factors | | *Ownership* | | | |
|---|---|---|---|---|---|
| | | *Sole Proprietor (n=48)* | *Partnership (n=29)* | *Co-op. Society (n=4)* | *Private company (n=3)* |
| Methods followed for burning the tiles | Down draught Kiln | 23(47.9) | 9(31.0) | 2(50.0) | - |
| | Semi-continuous down draught chamber type Kiln | 16(33.3) | 14(48.3) | 2(50.0) | 1(33.3) |
| | Hoffman continuous Horizontal draught type Kiln | 9(18.8) | 6(20.7) | - | 2(66.7) |
| Methods adopted for measuring the burning temperature | Judged by practical experience | 44(91.7) | 28(96.6) | 4(100.0) | 3(100.0) |
| | Thermocouple | 4(8.3) | 1(3.4) | - | - |
| Test adopted to check finished tiles | Water absorption test | 14(29.2) | 4(13.8) | - | 1(33.3) |
| | Breaking strength test | 7(14.6) | 7(24.1) | 3(75.0) | 1(33.3) |
| | Judgement by experienced supervisors | 27(56.3) | 18(62.1) | 1(25.0) | 1(33.3) |
| Breakage of tiles per load (in Numbers) | Below 50 | 17(35.4) | 7(24.1) | - | 2(66.7) |
| | 50-100 | 8(16.7) | 11(37.9) | 3(75.0) | 1(33.3) |
| | 100-150 | 18(37.5) | 8(27.6) | 1(25.0) | - |
| | Above 150 | 5(10.4) | 3(10.3) | - | - |
| Performance of production function | Bad | 5(10.4) | 3(10.3) | - | - |
| | Moderate | 9(18.8) | 5(17.2) | - | 2(66.7) |
| | Good | 29(60.4) | 20(69.0) | 4(100.0) | 1(33.3) |
| | Excellent | 5(10.4) | 1(3.4) | - | - |

( ) in Percentage Contingency Coefficient ≥ 0.5 P-Value < 0.01[a] Contingency Coefficient ≥ 0.5 P-Value < 0.05[b]
Contingency Coefficient ≤ 0.5 P-Value < 0.01[c] Contingency Coefficient ≤ 0.5 P-Value < 0.05[d]

- Most of the units procure clay through contractors.
- 12 units of A, 4 of B and 1 of D use China clay and terracotta; all the remaining units use only terracotta.
- One unit of A uses box feeder for storing clay, but most units store the clay in heaps.
- Manual cutting is done in 28 units, but most units do both manual cutting and automatic cutting.
- Though 75 per cent of C depends on wells for water, bore wells are the main source of water for most units.
- Manual processing and power pressing are both adopted to suit the conditions.
- 22 units of A, 17 of B, 1 of C and 3 of D use de-airing machine and the rest do not.
- Both manual trimming and mechanical trimming were adopted by most units.
- The use of light diesel is more favoured (42 units) than rice brawn oil (12) and Kerosene (30).
- 10 to 20 litres of oil per load is the norm with a majority 75 per cent of A, 65.5 per cent of B, 100 per cent of C and 100 per cent of D attaining the norm.
- 29 units use coir belt for conveyance and 20 units use chain conveyor. 12 units use rubber belt and 3 use elevators.
- The natural method of exposing the tiles to sunlight is adopted by most of the units.
- The source of firewood is outside the Panchayat, but within the District for most units.
- 23 units of A, 7 of B and 2 of C purchase firewood only in summer, but the rest purchase throughout the year.
- For 36 units, a maximum of 17units of A, 16 units of B, 2 units of C and 1 unit of D, source of firewood is 15 km away, but for the rest it is within 15 km.
- Firewood used per load is 3 to 6 tonnes in most of the units (64.6 per cent of A, 51.7 per cent of B, 50 per cent of C and 66.7 per cent of D).

- 51 units use sawdust as fuel and the rest use cashew shell.
- Downdraught kiln (34 units) and semi-continuous downdraught kiln (33units) are more used than the Hoffman kiln (17 units).
- Burning temperature is measured by practical experience than with the use of thermocouple.
- Similarly, judgement by experienced supervisors is adopted to check the finished tiles.
- 5 units of A and 3 of B break about 150 tiles per load. The rest maintain breakage below that level.
- The performance is uniformly good (60.4 per cent of A, 69 per cent of B, 100 per cent of C and 33.3 per cent of D).

Moreover, the results of the contingency co-efficient suggest that the factors of production such as methods adopted for procuring the clay, methods used for pressing the tiles and methods for transporting the clay to machines were associated with the ownership of the units and these were statistically significant at five per cent level.

Table 39 depicts the particulars of production on the basis of the qualifications of the owners. The following code is used:

A = below SSLC

B = Pre-degree

C = Technical qualification

D = Graduate

E = Post Graduate

When 5 numbers occur successively, they meanA, B, C, D and E respectively.

- Production is about 6000 tiles per day in most of the units (88.9 per cent of A, 76.5 per cent of B, 66.7 per cent of C, 62.1 per cent of D and 66.7 per cent of E).
- The source of clay tiles is from outside the Panchayat, but within the district.

**Table 39**
**Factors of Production Based on the Educational Qualifications of the Unit Owner**

| *Factors* | | *Qualification* | | | | |
|---|---|---|---|---|---|---|
| | | *Below S.S.L.C (n=9)* | *Pre-Degree (n=34)* | *Technical (n=9)* | *Graduate (n=29)* | *Post-graduate (n=3)* |
| Actual production per day(in Numbers) | Below 6000 | 8 (88.9) | 26 (76.5) | 6 (66.7) | 18 (62.1) | 2 (66.7) |
| | 6000-12000 | - | 4 (11.8) | 1 (11.1) | 7 (24.1) | - |
| | 12000-18000 | 1 (11.1) | 4 (11.8) | 2 (22.2) | 4 (13.8) | 1 (33.3) |
| Place of procurement of clay | Within the Panchayat | 7 (77.8) | 7 (20.6) | 3 (33.3) | 13 (44.8) | 2 (66.7) |
| | Outside the Panchayat but within the District | 2 (22.2) | 27 (79.4) | 6 (66.7) | 16 (55.2) | 1 (33.3) |
| Distance from the factory to procure clay (in Kms.) | 5-10 | 2 (22.2) | 11 (32.4) | 2 (22.2) | 13 (44.8) | 1 (33.3) |
| | 10-15 | 6 (66.7) | 11 (32.4) | 4 (44.4) | 11 (37.9) | 1 (33.3) |
| | Above 15 | 1 (11.1) | 12 (35.3) | 3 (33.3) | 5 (17.2) | 1 (33.3) |
| Methods adopted for procuring clay [d] | Own land/farm | - | 2 (5.9) | 1 (11.1) | 1 (3.4) | - |
| | Lease hold land/farm | 3 (33.3) | 5 (14.7) | 5 (55.6) | 5 (17.2) | 1 (33.3) |
| | Through contractors | 6 (66.7) | 26 (76.5) | 3 (33.3) | 23 (79.3) | 2 (66.7) |
| | Other agencies | - | 1 (2.9) | - | - | - |
| Clay used for production | Terracotta clay | 8 (88.9) | 29 (85.3) | 8 (88.9) | 20 (69.0) | 2 (66.7) |
| | Terracotta & China clay | 1 (11.1) | 5 (14.7) | 1 (11.1) | 9 (31.0) | 1 (33.3) |
| Methods adopted for storing clay | Heap method | 8 (88.9) | 30 (88.2) | 7 (77.8) | 20 (69.0) | 2 (66.7) |
| | Box feeder | - | - | - | 1 (3.4) | - |
| | Both | 1 (11.1) | 4 (11.8) | 2 (22.2) | 8 (27.6) | 1 (33.3) |

*Contd...*

| Factors | | Qualification | | | | |
|---|---|---|---|---|---|---|
| | | *Below S.S.L.C (n=9)* | *Pre-Degree (n=34)* | *Technical (n=9)* | *Graduate (n=29)* | *Post-graduate (n=3)* |
| Methods of cutting clay blocks | Manual cutting | 6 (66.7) | 11 (32.4) | 3 (33.3) | 7 (24.1) | 1 (33.3) |
| | Automatic cutting | 1 (11.1) | 8 (23.5) | 2 (22.2) | 10 (34.5) | 1 (33.3) |
| | Both | 2 (22.2) | 15 (44.1) | 4 (44.4) | 12 (41.4) | 1 (33.3) |
| Sources of water | Well | 4 (44.4) | 11 (32.4) | 2 (22.2) | 10 (34.5) | - |
| | Bore-Well | 3 (33.3) | 16 (47.1) | 4 (44.4) | 16 (55.2) | 2 (66.7) |
| | Outside source | 2 (22.2) | 7 (20.6) | 3 (33.3) | 3 (10.3) | 1 (33.3) |
| Methods used for pressing the tiles | Manual pressing | 4 (44.4) | 9 (26.5) | 2 (22.2) | 5 (17.2) | - |
| | Power operated pressing | 1 (11.1) | 8 (23.5) | 3 (33.3) | 10 (34.5) | 1 (33.3) |
| | Both | 4 (44.4) | 17 (50.0) | 4 (44.4) | 14 (48.3) | 2 (66.7) |
| De-airing machine used in production | Yes | 3 (33.3) | 19 (55.9) | 3 (33.3) | 15 (51.7) | 3 (100.0) |
| | No | 6 (66.7) | 15 (44.1) | 6 (66.7) | 14 (48.3) | - |
| Methods of trimming tiles | Manual trimming | 3 (33.3) | 9 (26.5) | 2 (22.2) | 4 (13.8) | - |
| | Automatic trimming | 3 (33.3) | 7 (20.6) | 3 (33.3) | 11 (37.9) | 1 (33.3) |
| | Both | 3 (33.3) | 18 (52.9) | 4 (44.4) | 14 (48.3) | 2 (66.7) |
| Oil used in production | Rice Bran oil | 2 (22.2) | 2 (5.9) | 1 (11.1) | 7 (24.1) | - |
| | Light diesel oil | 4 (44.4) | 17 (50.0) | 5 (55.6) | 14 (48.3) | 2 (66.7) |
| | Kerosene | 3 (33.3) | 15 (44.1) | 3 (33.3) | 8 (27.6) | 1 (33.3) |
| Oil used per load(in Litres) | Below 10 | - | 1 (2.9) | - | - | - |
| | 10-20 | 5 (55.6) | 24 (70.6) | 8 (88.9) | 23 (79.3) | 2 (66.7) |
| | 20-30 | 1 (11.1) | - | - | - | - |
| | 30-40 | 2 (22.2) | 5 (14.7) | - | 2 (6.9) | - |
| | 40 and Above | 1 (11.1) | 4 (11.8) | 1 (11.1) | 4 (13.8) | 1 (33.3) |

*Contd...*

| Factors | | Qualification | | | | |
|---|---|---|---|---|---|---|
| | | Below S.S.L.C (n=9) | Pre-Degree (n=34) | Technical (n=9) | Graduate (n=29) | Post-graduate (n=3) |
| Methods for transporting the clay to machines [d] | Coir belt | 2 (22.2) | 14 (41.2) | 2 (22.2) | 11 (37.9) | - |
| | Rubber belt | - | 3 (8.8) | 1 (11.1) | 6 (20.7) | 2 (66.7) |
| | Chain conveyor | 2 (22.2) | 6 (17.6) | 1 (11.1) | 10 (34.5) | 1 (33.3) |
| | Elevators | - | 2 (5.9) | 1 (11.1) | - | - |
| | Manual | 5 (55.6) | 9 (26.5) | 4 (44.4) | 2 (6.9) | - |
| Methods used todrying thetiles | Natural | 8 (88.9) | 29 (85.3) | 5 (55.6) | 22 (75.9) | 2 (66.7) |
| | Smoke drying system | - | - | - | 2 (6.9) | - |
| | Steam Heating system | - | 1 (2.9) | 2 (22.2) | - | - |
| | Natural and Smoke drying system | 1 (11.1) | 4 (11.8) | 2 (22.2) | 5 (17.2) | 1 (33.3) |
| Place of procurement of firewood | Within Panchayat | 2 (22.2) | 12 (35.3) | 3 (33.3) | 9 (31.0) | 1 (33.3) |
| | Outside the District | 1 (11.1) | 1 (2.9) | 2 (22.2) | 2 (6.9) | - |
| | Outside the Panchayat but within district | 6 (66.7) | 21 (61.8) | 4 (44.4) | 18 (62.1) | 2 (66.7) |
| Season of purchasing firewood | Summer | 4 (44.4) | 15 (44.1) | 3 (33.3) | 10 (34.5) | - |
| | All seasons | 5 (55.6) | 19 (55.9) | 6 (66.7) | 19 (65.5) | 3 (100.0) |
| Distance from the factory to procure firewood (in Kms.) | 5-10 | 2 (22.2) | 10 (29.4) | 3 (33.3) | 9 (31.0) | 1 (33.3) |
| | 10-15 | 2 (22.2) | 12 (35.3) | - | 9 (31.0) | - |
| | Above 15 | 5 (55.6) | 12 (35.3) | 6 (66.7) | 11 (37.9) | 2 (66.7) |
| Firewood used per load(in Tonnes) | Below 3 | 3 (33.3) | 4 (11.8) | 5 (55.6) | 7 (24.1) | 1 (33.3) |
| | 3-6 | 4 (44.4) | 23 (67.6) | 3 (33.3) | 19 (65.5) | 1 (33.3) |
| | 6-9 | 1 (11.1) | 7 (20.6) | 1 (11.1) | 3 (10.3) | - |
| | 9 and Above | 1 (11.1) | - | - | - | 1 (33.3) |
| Fuel used in production | Sawdust | 6 (66.7) | 20 (58.8) | 7 (77.8) | 17 (58.6) | 1 (33.3) |
| | Cashew shell | 3 (33.3) | 14 (41.2) | 2 (22.2) | 12 (41.4) | 2 (66.7) |

*Contd...*

| *Factors* | | *Qualification* | | | | |
|---|---|---|---|---|---|---|
| | | *Below S.S.L.C (n=9)* | *Pre-Degree (n=34)* | *Technical (n=9)* | *Graduate (n=29)* | *Post-graduate (n=3)* |
| Methods followed for burning the tiles | Downdraught Kiln | 6 (66.7) | 13 (38.2) | 5 (55.6) | 9 (31.0) | 1 (33.3) |
| | Semi-continuous down draught chamber type Kiln | 2 (22.2) | 15 (44.1) | 2 (22.2) | 13 (44.8) | 1 (33.3) |
| | Hoffman continuous Horizontal draught type Kiln | 1 (11.1) | 6 (17.6) | 2 (22.2) | 7 (24.1) | 1 (33.3) |
| Methods adopted for measuring the burning temperature | Judged by practical experience | 9 (100.0) | 34 (100.0) | 8 (88.9) | 25 (86.2) | 3 (100.0) |
| | Thermocouple | - | - | 1 (11.1) | 4 (13.8) | - |
| Test adopted to check finished tiles | Water absorption test | 1 (11.1) | 5 (14.7) | 2 (22.2) | 10 (34.5) | 1 (33.3) |
| | Breaking strength test | 4 (44.4) | 6 (17.6) | 1 (11.1) | 6 (20.7) | 1 (33.3) |
| | Judgement by experienced supervisors | 4 (44.4) | 23 (67.6) | 6 (66.7) | 13 (44.8) | 1 (33.3) |
| Breakage of tiles per load (in Numbers)[a] | Below 50 | 1 (11.1) | 6 (17.6) | 3 (33.3) | 15 (51.7) | 1 (33.3) |
| | 50-100 | 2 (22.2) | 16 (47.1) | - | 4 (13.8) | 1 (33.3) |
| | 100-150 | 2 (22.2) | 9 (26.5) | 5 (55.6) | 10 (34.5) | 1 (33.3) |
| | Above 150 | 4 (44.4) | 3 (8.8) | 1 (11.1) | - | - |
| Performance of production function[d] | Bad | 1 (11.1) | 3 (8.8) | 1 (11.1) | 1 (3.4) | 2 (66.7) |
| | Moderate | 2 (22.2) | 6 (17.6) | 1 (11.1) | 7 (24.1) | - |
| | Good | 6 (66.7) | 24 (70.6) | 7 (77.8) | 16 (55.2) | 1 (33.3) |
| | Excellent | - | 1 (2.9) | - | 5 (17.2) | - |

( ) in Percentage
Contingency Coefficient $\geq 0.5$ P-Value $<0.01$[a]
Contingency Coefficient $\geq 0.5$ P-Value $<0.05$[b]
Contingency Coefficient $\leq 0.5$ P-Value $<0.01$[c]
Contingency Coefficient $\leq 0.5$ P-Value $<0.05$[d]

- The source of clay is within 15 kms for 62 units and 22 units have to go beyond 15 kms.
- Clay is obtained mainly through contractors (66.7 per cent of A, 76.5 per cent of B, 33.3 per cent of C, 79.3 per cent of D and 66.7 per cent of E).
- Although terracotta and china clay are both used, terracotta is more favoured (88.9 per cent of A, 85.3 per cent of B, 88.9 per cent of C, 69 per cent of D and 66.7 per cent of E).
- Only one unit of D used box feeder for storing the clay otherwise most of the units keep the clay in heaps.
- Though 66 per cent of A and about one third in each category do only manual cutting, both manual cutting and automatic cutting are practised by most of the units.
- Bore-wells are the main suppliers of water to most of the units.
- Both manual pressing and power operated pressing is done in most units (44 per cent of A, 50 per cent of B, 44.4 per cent C, 48.3 per cent of D and 66.7 per cent of E).
- 55.9 per cent of B and 51.7 per cent of D use de-airing machine. But many units don't use it (41 units)
- Most of the units trim the tiles both manually and with the help of machines.
- Of the three oils used (rice bran, light diesel and kerosene) light diesel oil is more popular (44.4 per cent of A, 50 per cent of B, 55 per cent of C, 48 per cent of D and 66.7 per cent of E).
- The average of oil used is 10 to 20 liters per load (55.6 per cent of A, 70.6 per cent of B, 88.9 per cent of C, 79.3 per cent of D and 66.7 per cent E).
- Elevator is the least used conveyance and the coir belt is the most used conveyance (22.2 per cent of A, 41.2 per cent of B, 22.2 per cent of C and 37.9 per cent of D).

- The natural method of exposure to sunlight is adopted by most factories to dry the tiles with a maximum 88.9 per cent of A, 85.3 per cent of B, 55.6 per cent of C, 75.9 per cent of D and 66.7 per cent of E using the method.
- The source of firewood for most units lies outside the Panchayat with a majority of 66.7 per cent of A, 61.8 per cent of B, 44.4 per cent of C, 62.1 per cent of D and 66.7 per cent of E depending on this source.
- Most units (52) purchase firewood all through the year.
- Most of the units get firewood from sources 15 kms away.
- Most units (50) keep consumption of firewood at 3 to 6 tonnes per load, though one unit of A and one of E exceed 9 tonnes.
- Sawdust is more favoured as fuel than cashew shell.
- Downdraught kiln and semi-continuous downdraught kiln are more used than Hoffman kiln.
- The method adopted for measuring burning temperature is judgement by practical experience.
- 47 units accept judgement passed by experienced supervisors on the finished tiles, though the remaining units use water absorption test as breaking strength test.
- The normal breakage is between 50 and 150 tiles per load (4 units of A, 25 units of B, 5 units of C, 14 units of D and 2 units of E).
- 1 unit of B and 5 of D have registered excellent performance, and 8 units recorded bad performance. Otherwise, the performance is good. (66.7 per cent of A, 70.6 per cent of B, 77.8 per cent of C, 55.2 per cent of D and 33.3 per cent of E).

Moreover, the results of the contingency co-efficient suggest that the factors of production namely methods adopted for procuring the clay, methods for transporting the clay to machines, firewood used per load, breakage of tiles per load and performance of production function were associated with the qualification of the units owner and these were statistically significant at five per cent and one per cent level.

Table 40 gives particulars of production on the basis of units' capacity. The following code is used:

A = below 8000 tiles

B = 8000 to 16000 tiles

C = 16000 to 24000 tiles

When three numbers appear successively, they refer to A, B and C.

- Though 70 per cent of C exceeds 12,000 tiles a day, the normal production is about 6000 tiles a day, 100 per cent of A and 78.8 per cent of B.
- The source of clay lies outside the Panchayat for most units.
- 62 units have their source of clay within 15 km and the rest beyond.
- Most units get the help of contractors to obtain clay.
- Though china clay is used, 97.1 per cent of A, 87.9 per cent of B and 29.4 per cent of C prefer terracotta.
- Even though one unit used box feeder to store clay, most of the units store clay in heaps.
- Most units adopt both manual cutting of clay and mechanical cutting.
- Bore-wells are the main suppliers of water to the units (41.2 per cent of A, 54.5 per cent of B and 52.9 per cent of C).
- Manual pressing and power operated pressing are used in majority of the units.
- A majority of 88.2 per cent of A and one third of B do not use de-aired vacuum pumps. Others do use it.
- Manual trimming of clay and automatic trimming are both practiced.
- 50 per cent of A, 60 per cent of B and 29.4 per cent of C uses light diesel oil.

**Table 40**

**Factors of Production Based on Installed Production Capacity Per Day**

| Factors | | Capacity (in tiles) | | |
|---|---|---|---|---|
| | | *Below 8000 tiles (n=34)* | *8000-16000 tiles (n=33)* | *16000-24000 tiles (n=17)* |
| Actual production per day (in Numbers) [a] | Below 6000 | 34 (100.0) | 26 (78.8) | - |
| | 6000-12000 | - | 7 (21.2) | 5 (29.4) |
| | 12000-18000 | - | - | 12 (70.6) |
| Place of procurement of clay | Within the Panchayat | 10 (29.4) | 15 (45.5) | 7 (41.2) |
| | Outside the Panchayatbut within the District | 24 (70.6) | 18 (54.5) | 10 (58.8) |
| Distance from the factory to procure clay (in Kms.) | 5-10 | 8 (23.5) | 15 (45.5) | 6 (35.3) |
| | 10-15 | 16 (47.1) | 11 (33.3) | 6 (35.3) |
| | Above 15 | 10 (29.4) | 7 (21.2) | 5 (29.4) |
| Methods adopted for procuring cay | Own land/farm | 2 (5.9) | 2 (6.1) | - |
| | Lease hold land/farm | 8 (23.5) | 6 (18.2) | 5 (29.4) |
| | Through contractors | 23 (67.6) | 25 (75.8) | 12 (70.6) |
| | Other agencies | 1 (2.9) | - | - |
| Clay used for production [a] | Terracotta clay | 33 (97.1) | 29 (87.9) | 5 (29.4) |
| | Terracotta & China clay | 1 (2.9) | 4 (12.1) | 12 (70.6) |
| Methods adopted for storing clay [a] | Heap method | 34 (100.0) | 29 (87.9) | 4 (23.5) |
| | Box feeder | - | - | 1 (5.9) |
| | Both | - | 4 (12.1) | 12 (70.6) |

*Contd...*

| Factors | | Capacity (in tiles) | | |
|---|---|---|---|---|
| | | Below 8000 tiles (n=34) | 8000-16000 tiles (n=33) | 16000-24000 tiles (n=17) |
| Methods of cutting clay blocks[a] | Manual cutting | 23 (67.6) | 5 (15.2) | - |
| | Automatic cutting | 2 (5.9) | 3 (9.1) | 17 (100.0) |
| | Both | 9 (26.5) | 25 (75.8) | - |
| Sources of water | Well | 11 (32.4) | 11 (33.3) | 5 (29.4) |
| | Bore-Well | 14 (41.2) | 18 (54.5) | 9 (52.9) |
| | Outside source | 9 (26.5) | 4 (12.1) | 3 (17.6) |
| Methods used for pressing the tiles[a] | Manual pressing | 18 (52.9) | 2 (6.1) | - |
| | Power operated pressing | 2 (5.9) | 4 (12.1) | 17 (100.0) |
| | Both | 14 (41.2) | 27 (81.8) | - |
| De-airing machine used in production[a] | Yes | 4 (11.8) | 22 (66.7) | 17 (100.0) |
| | No | 30 (88.2) | 11 (33.3) | - |
| Methods of trimming tiles[a] | Manual trimming | 18 (52.9) | - | - |
| | Automatic trimming | 3 (8.8) | 5 (15.2) | 17 (100.0) |
| | Both | 13 (38.2) | 28 (84.8) | - |
| Oil used in production | Rice Bran oil | 5 (14.7) | 2 (6.1) | 5 (29.4) |
| | Light diesel oil | 17 (50.0) | 20 (60.6) | 5 (29.4) |
| | Kerosene | 12 (35.3) | 11 (33.3) | 7 (41.2) |
| Oil used per load(in Litres) | Below 10 | - | - | 1 (5.9) |
| | 10-20 | 24 (70.6) | 25 (75.8) | 13 (76.5) |
| | 20-30 | 1 (2.9) | - | - |
| | 30-40 | 4 (11.8) | 3 (9.1) | 2 (11.8) |
| | 40 and Above | 5 (14.7) | 5 (15.2) | 1 (5.9) |

Contd...

| Factors | | Capacity (in tiles) | | |
|---|---|---|---|---|
| | | Below 8000 tiles (n=34) | 8000-16000 tiles (n=33) | 16000-24000 tiles (n=17) |
| Methods for transporting the clay to machines [a] | Coir belt | 11 (32.4) | 18 (54.5) | - |
| | Rubber belt | 5 (14.7) | 5 (15.2) | 2 (11.8) |
| | Chain conveyor | 2 (5.9) | 6 (18.2) | 12 (70.6) |
| | Elevators | - | - | 3 (17.6) |
| | Manual | 16 (47.1) | 4 (12.1) | - |
| Methods used to dry tiles [a] | Natural | 32 (94.1) | 31 (93.9) | 3 (17.6) |
| | Smoke drying system | - | 1 (3.0) | 1 (5.9) |
| | Steam Heating system | 2 (5.9) | 1 (3.0) | - |
| | Natural and Smoke drying system | - | - | 13 (76.5) |
| Place of procurement of firewood | Within Panchayat | 9 (26.5) | 8 (24.2) | 10 (58.8) |
| | Outside the District | 2 (5.9) | 4 (12.1) | - |
| | Outside the Panchayat but within district | 23 (67.6) | 21 (63.6) | 7 (41.2) |
| Season of purchasing firewood [c] | Summer | 19 (55.9) | 13 (39.4) | - |
| | All seasons | 15 (44.1) | 20 (60.6) | 17 (100.0) |
| Distance from the factory to procure firewood (in Kms.) [c] | 5-10 | 7 (20.6) | 7 (21.2) | 11 (64.7) |
| | 10-15 | 11 (32.4) | 8 (24.2) | 4 (23.5) |
| | Above 15 | 16 (47.1) | 18 (54.5) | 2 (11.8) |
| Firewood used per load(in Tonnes) | Below 3 | 7 (20.6) | 7 (21.2) | 6 (35.3) |
| | 3-6 | 20 (58.8) | 22 (66.7) | 8 (47.1) |
| | 6-9 | 6 (17.6) | 4 (12.1) | 2 (11.8) |
| | 9 and Above | 1 (2.9) | - | 1 (5.9) |

| Factors | | Capacity (in tiles) | | |
|---|---|---|---|---|
| | | *Below 8000 tiles (n=34)* | *8000-16000 tiles (n=33)* | *16000-24000 tiles (n=17)* |
| Fuel used in production | Sawdust | 17 (50.0) | 22 (66.7) | 12 (70.6) |
| | Cashew shell | 17 (50.0) | 11 (33.3) | 5 (29.4) |
| Method followedfor burning the tiles [a] | Down draught Kiln | 32 (94.1) | 2 (6.1) | - |
| | Semi-continuous down draught chamber type Kiln | 2 (5.9) | 31 (93.9) | - |
| | Hoffman continuous Horizontal draught type Kiln | - | - | 17 (100.0) |
| Methods adopted for measuring the burning temperature [c] | Judged by practical experience | 34 (100.0) | 33 (100.0) | 12 (70.6) |
| | Thermocouple | - | - | 5 (29.4) |
| Test adopted to check finished tiles [d] | Water absorption test | 2 (5.9) | 9 (27.3) | 8 (47.1) |
| | Breaking strength test | 9 (26.5) | 7 (21.2) | 2 (11.8) |
| | Judgement by experienced supervisors | 23 (67.6) | 17 (51.5) | 7 (41.2) |
| Breakage of tiles per load(in Numbers) [a] | Below 50 | 2 (5.9) | 11 (33.3) | 13 (76.5) |
| | 50-100 | 10 (29.4) | 9 (27.3) | 4 (23.5) |
| | 100-150 | 17 (50.0) | 10 (30.3) | - |
| | Above 150 | 5 (14.7) | 3 (9.1) | - |
| Performance of production function | Bad | 6 (17.6) | 2 (6.1) | - |
| | Moderate | 9 (26.5) | 5 (15.2) | 2 (11.8) |
| | Good | 18 (52.9) | 23 (69.7) | 13 (76.5) |
| | Excellent | 1 (2.9) | 3 (9.1) | 2 (11.8) |

( ) in Percentage Contingency Coefficient ≥ 0.5 P-Value <0.01[a] Contingency Coefficient ≥ 0.5 P-Value <0.05[b]
Contingency Coefficient ≤ 0.5 P-Value <0.01[c] Contingency Coefficient ≤ 0.5 P-Value <0.05[d]

- Most units use 10 to 20 litres of oil on each load (24 units of A, 25 units of B and 13 units of C).
- Coir belt and chain conveyors are more used than rubber belt and elevator. Most of the units in A do not adopt any method.
- The natural method of exposure to sunlight best suits most of the factories a majority of 94.1 per cent of A, 93.9 per cent B, 76.5 per cent C.
- For most units, a maximum 67.6 per cent of A, 63.6 per cent of B and 41.2 per cent, the source of firewood lies outside the Panchayat, but within district.
- Though 19 units of A and 13 units of B limit their purchasing of firewood to summer, other units procure firewood any time of the year.
- The source of firewood is beyond 15 km for 36 units and within 15 km for other units.
- Most units use 3 to 6 tonnes of firewood for each load with a majority of 58.8 per cent of A, 66.7 per cent of B and 47.1 per cent of C using the same.
- Sawdust is more used than cashew shell registering a maximum of 50 per cent of A, 66.7 per cent of B and 70 per cent of C.
- Downdraught kiln and semi-continuous downdraught kiln are more used than Hoffman kiln for burning the tiles.
- Burning temperature is measured by practical experience.
- Judgement by experienced supervisors is accepted to check the finished tiles.
- Abnormal breakage (above 150 per load) occurs in 5 units of A and 3 of B, 2 units of A, 11 units of B and 13 units of C manage breakage at less than 50 tiles per load. Other units have a breakage of 50 to 150 tiles per load.
- The production performance of most of the units is good, recording a maximum 52.9 per cent of A, 69.7 per cent of B and 76.5 per cent of C.

Moreover, the results of the contingency co-efficient suggest that the factors of production namely actual production per day, clay used for production, methods adopted for storing the clay, methods of cutting the clay blocks, methods used for pressing the tiles, de-airing machine used in production, methods of trimming the tiles, methods for transporting the clay to machines, methods used for drying the tiles, season of purchasing firewood, distance from the factory to procure the firewood, methods followed for burning the tiles, methods adopted for measuring the burning temperature, test adopted to check finished tiles and breakage of tiles per load were associated with installed production capacity of the units and these were statistically significant at five per cent and one per cent level.

**Table 41**
**Neural Classification Analysis–The Contribution of Various Production Factors to the Performance of Production Function in Alagappanagar**

| *Dependent variable: Performance of Production function* | | |
|---|---|---|
| *Independent Variables* | *Importance Co-efficient* | *Normalised Weights* |
| Sources of water | 0.1667 | 16.667 |
| Season of purchasing firewood | 0.667 | 66.667 |
| Methods adopted for measuring the burning temperature | 0.0833 | 8.333 |
| Average number of breakage of tiles per load | 0.0833 | 8.333 |

No. of hidden layers = 0 | Estimation = Sequential Algorithm
Correct classification rate = 86.96%

Table 41 depicts the important co-efficients and normalised weights for the various factors of production contributed to the performance of production in Alagappanagar. The results of the neural classification analysis confirmed that the factors of production such as season of purchasing firewood, sources of procuring water, methods adopted for measuring the burning temperature and average number of breakage of tiles per load achieved a normalized weight of 66.667 per cent, 16.667 per cent, 8.333 per cent and 8.333 per cent respectively.

Moreover the number of hidden layers between the performance of production and various factors of production was 0. This shows the various factors of production were linearly related with the performance of production. Finally, the above factors of production correctly signified the level of performance of production at the rate of 86.96 per cent.

Hence, the season of purchasing firewood emerged as a best predictor which contributed to the level of performance of production followed by the factors such as sources of water, methods adopted for measuring the burning temperature and average breakage of tiles per load also contributed to the level of performance of production function in Alagappanagar.

**Table 42**
**Neural Classification Analysis–The Contribution of Various Production Factors to the Performance of Production Function in Chittissery**

*Dependent variable: Performance of Production function*

| *Independent Variables* | *Importance Co-efficient* | *Normalised Weights* |
|---|---|---|
| Methods of cutting clay blocks | 0.5714 | 57.143 |
| Methods of trimming tiles | 0.0476 | 4.762 |
| Oil used in production | 0.0476 | 4.762 |
| Methods adopted for transporting clay to machines | 0.0952 | 9.524 |
| Place of procuring firewood | 0.0952 | 9.524 |
| Season of purchasing firewood | 0.0476 | 4.762 |
| Firewood used per load | 0.0476 | 4.762 |
| Average number of breakage of tiles per load | 0.0476 | 4.762 |

No. of hidden layers = 0 | Estimation = Sequential Algorithm
Correct classification rate = 84.62%

Table 42 shows the important co-efficients and normalised weights for the various factors of production contributed to the production performance of the units in Chittissery. The results of the neural classification analysis confirmed that the factors of production such as methods of cutting clay blocks, methods adopted for transporting clay to machines, place of procuring firewood and methods of trimming the tiles attained a normalized weight of 57.143 per cent, 9.524 per cent and 4.762

per cent respectively. Moreover the number of hidden layers between the performance of production and various factors of production was 0. This shows the various factors of production were linearly related with the performance of production. Finally, the above factors of production correctly signified the level of performance of production at the rate of 84.62 per cent.

Hence, the methods of cutting clay blocks emerged as the best predictor which contributed to the level of performance of production followed by the factors such as methods adopted for transporting clay to machines and methods of trimming the tiles also contributed to the level of production performance in Chittissery.

**Table 43**
**Neural Classification Analysis–The Contribution of Various Production Factors to the Performance of Production Function in Pudukad**

| *Dependent variable: Performance of Production function* | | |
|---|---|---|
| *Independent variables* | *Importance Co-efficient* | *Normalised Weights* |
| Place of procuring clay | 0.0769 | 7.692 |
| De-airing machine used in production | 0.0769 | 7.692 |
| Type of oil used to pressing the tiles | 0.0769 | 7.692 |
| Oil used per load | 0.0769 | 7.692 |
| Methods adopted for transportation of clay to machines | 0.0769 | 7.692 |
| Firewood used per load | 0.0769 | 7.692 |
| Fuels used in production | 0.0769 | 7.692 |
| Test adopted to check finished tiles | 0.0769 | 7.692 |
| Average number of breakage of tiles per load | 0.3846 | 38.462 |

No. of hidden layers = 0 Estimation = Sequential Algorithm
Correct classification rate = 90.91%

Table 43 shows the important co-efficients and normalised weights for the various factors of production contributed to the performance of production of the units in Pudukad. The results of the neural classification analysis confirmed that the production factors such as average number of breakage of tiles, place of procuring of clay, de-airing machine used in production and type of oil used to pressing the tiles were achieved at a normalized weight of 38.462 per cent and 7.69 per cent respectively. Moreover the number of hidden layers between the performance of production and various factors of production was 0. This shows the various factors of production were linearly related with the performance of production. Finally, the above factors of production correctly signified the level of performance of production function at the rate of 90.91 per cent.

Hence, the average breakage of tiles per load emerged as the best predictor which contributed to the level of performance of production in Pudukad followed by an equal contribution made by the factors such as place of procuring of clay, de-airing machine used in production and the type of oil used for pressing the tiles.

**Table 44**

**Neural Classification Analysis–The Contribution of Various Production Factors to the Performance of Production Function in Thrissur District**

*Dependent variable: Performance of Production function*

| *Independent variables* | *Importance Co-efficient* | *Normalised Weights* |
|---|---|---|
| Actual production capacity (tiles per day) | 0.0412 | 4.124 |
| Principal method of procuring clay | 0.0618 | 6.186 |
| Clay used for production | 0.0412 | 4.124 |
| Methods of clay storage | 0.0309 | 3.093 |
| Methods of cutting blocks of clay | 0.1958 | 19.588 |
| Sources of water | 0.0206 | 2.062 |
| Methods of pressing the tiles | 0.0103 | 1.031 |
| Follow of de-airing machine | 0.0206 | 2.062 |
| Methods of trimming tiles | 0.0721 | 7.216 |
| Type of oil used for pressing the tiles | 0.0103 | 1.031 |
| Oil used per 6000 tiles (in litres) | 0.0103 | 1.031 |
| Transportation of clay to machines | 0.0206 | 2.062 |
| Methods of drying tiles | 0.0721 | 7.216 |
| Major sources of procuring firewood | 0.0412 | 4.124 |
| Season of purchasing firewood | 0.0206 | 2.062 |
| Distance from factory to procure firewood (in kms) | 0.0206 | 2.062 |
| Firewood used per 6000 tiles(in tonnes) | 0.1134 | 11.34 |
| Fuels used in production | 0.0206 | 2.062 |
| Methods followed to burn tiles | 0.0412 | 4.124 |
| Quality test used to check finished products | 0.0103 | 1.031 |
| Average number of breakage of tiles per load | 0.1237 | 12.371 |

No. of hidden layers = 1 Estimation = Sequential Algorithm
Correct classification rate = 89.29%

Table 44 portrays the important co-efficients and normalised weights for the various factors of production contributed to the performance of production of the units in Thrissur District. The results of the neural classification analysis confirmed that the production factors such as methods of cutting blocks of clay, average number of breakage of tiles per load, firewood used per 6000 tiles, methods of drying the tiles, methods of trimming the tiles and principal method of procuring clay attained a normalized weight of 19.588 per cent, 12.371 per cent, 11.34 per cent, 7.216 per cent and 6.186 per cent respectively. Moreover the number of hidden layers between the performance of production and various factors of production was 1. This shows the various factors of production were non-linearly related with the performance of production function. Finally, the above said factors of production correctly signified the level of the performance of production at the rate of 89.29 per cent.

Hence, the methods of cutting blocks of clay, average breakage of tiles per load and firewood used per 6000 tiles emerged as a best predictor which contributed to the level of performance of production. Similarly the factors such as methods of drying the tiles, methods of trimming the tiles and principal method of procuring clay contributed to the performance of production of the clay tiles manufacturing units in Thrissur District.

Table 45 visualises the various problems in production function based on the location of the units. The locations of the units were classified into three major areas such as Alagappanagar, Chittissery and Pudukad.

From the total of 23 units located in Alagappanagar, 47.8 per cent of them expressed that they were facing a problem of price hike in the clay procurement from the market. Similarly, 43.5 per cent, 47.8 per cent, 56.5 per cent, 47.8 per cent, 60.9 per cent and 39.1 per cent of the units revealed that the problems such as shortage of clay, procurement of clay, possibility of pollution created by kiln, high cost of firewood, shortage of firewood and fulfillment of the legal formalities in procuring the firewood were faced by the units respectively. More over,

**Table 45**
**Problems in Production Function Based on the Location of the Units**

| *Problems* | | *Location* | | |
|---|---|---|---|---|
| | | *Alagappanagar (n=23)* | *Chittissery (n=39)* | *Pudukad (n=22)* |
| High price for clay in the market | Strongly Disagree | 1 (4.3) | - | - |
| | Disagree | - | 1 (2.6) | - |
| | Neutral | 1 (4.3) | 2 (5.1) | 2 (9.1) |
| | Agree | 10 (43.5) | 19 (48.7) | 12 (54.5) |
| | Strongly Agree | 11 (47.8) | 17 (43.6) | 8 (36.4) |
| Shortage of clay | Strongly Disagree | 1 (4.3) | 7 (17.9) | 2 (9.1) |
| | Disagree | 10 (43.5) | 12 (30.8) | 8 (36.4) |
| | Neutral | 8 (34.8) | 9 (23.1) | 6 (27.3) |
| | Agree | 2 (8.7) | 7 (17.9) | 3 (13.6) |
| | Strongly Agree | 2 (8.7) | 4 (10.3) | 3 (13.6) |
| Delay in delivery of clay | Strongly Disagree | - | 1 (2.6) | - |
| | Disagree | 4 (17.4) | 5 (12.8) | 4 (18.2) |
| | Neutral | 8 (34.8) | 8 (20.5) | 6 (27.3) |
| | Agree | 4 (17.4) | 19 (48.7) | 8 (36.4) |
| | Strongly Agree | 7 (30.4) | 6 (15.4) | 4 (18.2) |
| Procurement of clay without objection | Strongly Disagree | 5 (21.7) | 15 (38.5) | 6 (27.3) |
| | Disagree | 11 (47.8) | 20 (51.3) | 10 (45.5) |
| | Neutral | 7 (30.4) | 2 (5.1) | 6 (27.3) |
| | Agree | - | 1 (2.6) | - |
| | Strongly Agree | - | 1 (2.6) | -- |
| Possibility of pollution created by kiln | Strongly Disagree | 5 (21.7) | 12 (30.8) | 5 (22.7) |
| | Disagree | 13 (56.5) | 20 (51.3) | 14 (63.6) |
| | Neutral | 4 (17.4) | 5 (12.8) | 3 (13.6) |
| | Agree | 1 (4.3) | 2 (5.1) | - |
| | Strongly Agree | 1 (4.3) | - | - |
| High cost of firewood | Strongly Disagree | 2 (8.7) | 3 (7.7) | 5 (22.7) |
| | Disagree | 11 (47.8) | 21 (53.8) | 9 (40.9) |
| | Neutral | 9 (39.1) | 15 (38.5) | 8 (36.4) |
| | Agree | 2 (8.7) | 5 (12.8) | 2 (9.1) |
| | Strongly Agree | 2 (8.7) | 14 (35.9) | 4 (18.2) |
| Shortage of firewood | Strongly Disagree | 14 (60.9) | 12 (30.8) | 10 (45.5) |
| | Disagree | 5 (21.7) | 8 (20.5) | 5 (22.7) |
| | Neutral | - | - | 1 (4.5) |
| | Agree | 2 (8.7) | 5 (12.8) | 2 (9.1) |
| Strongly Agree | 5(21.7) | 12 (30.8) | 6 (27.3) | |
| Fulfillment of legal formalities to procure firewood | Strongly Disagree | 9 (39.1) | 8 (20.5) | 5 (22.7) |
| | Disagree | 5 (21.7) | 7 (17.9) | 8 (36.4) |
| | Neutral | 2 (8.7) | 7 (17.9) | 1 (4.5) |
| | Agree | 1 (4.3) | - | - |
| | Strongly Agree | - | 1 (2.6) | - |

( ) in Percentage.

34.8 per cent of the units were neutral in their responses about the problem of delay in delivery of the clay.

As far as Chittissery is concerned, 48.7 per cent of the units agreed that the problems of high price of clay as well as delay in delivery of clay existed in their units in the course of production. Similarly, 30.8 per cent, 51.3 per cent, 53.8 per cent, 30.8 per cent and 20.5 per cent of the units proclaimed that they encountered problems like shortage of clay, procurement of clay, possibility of pollution by kiln, shortage of high cost of firewood and fulfillment of legal formalities in procuring the firewood in their units respectively.

Finally, from the total of 22 units located in Pudukad, 54.5 per cent and 36.4 per cent of them agreed that they were also suffering with the problems such as high price of clay and delay in delivery of clay respectively. Similarly, 36.4 per cent, 45.5 per cent, 63.6 per cent, 40.9 per cent, 45.5 per cent and 36.4 per cent of the units revealed that the problems such as delay in delivery of clay, procurement of clay, possibility of pollution by kiln, high cost of firewood, shortage of firewood and fulfillment of legal formalities in procuring the firewood existed in their units respectively.

**Table 46**

**Stepwise Multiple Regression Analysis–The Impact of Various Production Problems on the Performance of Production Function in Alagappanagar**

| *Dependent variable: Performance of Production function (Y)* | | | | | |
|---|---|---|---|---|---|
| *Independent variable* | *Unstandardised Co-efficient* | *Standard Error* | *Standardised Co-efficient* | *t-value* | *p-value* |
| Constant | 2.118 | 0.406 | - | 5.222 | 0.000 |
| Procurement of clay without objection ($X_1$) | 0.673 | 0.184 | 0.624 | 3.661 | 0.001 |

Multiple R = 0.624 F- value = 13.405 d.f. (1,21) P-value < 0.01

R square = 0.39

$$\hat{Y} = 2.118 + 0.673\, X_1$$

Where $\hat{Y}$ is the estimated performance of production.

Table 46 explains the impact of various problems of production on its performance. The equation describes that, on an average if "Procurement of clay without objection" changes by one unit, there will be an increase of 0.673 units in the performance of production function.

The result of t-test confirms that, the estimated regression coefficient (0.673) is highly significant at one percent level. The multiple R of 0.624 shows that there exists a relationship of 62.4 per cent between "Procurement of clay without objection" and performance of production. Moreover, the $R^2$ of 0.39 confirms that there exists 39 per cent of variation in the performance of production. Finally, the result of f-test signifies that the variation was statistically significant at one per cent level.

Hence, it can be concluded that the problem of procurement of clay without objection existed in Alagappanagar; it has not significantly weakened the production performance of the units.

**Table 47**

**Stepwise Multiple Regression Analysis–The Impact of Various Production Problems on the Performance of Production Function in Chittissery**

*Dependent variable: Performance of Production function (Y)*

| *Independent variables* | *Unstandardised Co-efficient* | *Standard Error* | *Standardised Co-efficient* | *t-value* | *p-value* |
|---|---|---|---|---|---|
| Constant | 3.785 | 0.331 | - | 11.430 | 0.000 |
| Fulfillment of legal formalities to procure firewood ($X_1$) | 0.201 | 0.079 | 0.383 | 2.557 | 0.015 |
| Possibility of pollution created by kiln ($X_2$) | -0.265 | 0.129 | -0.308 | -2.056 | 0.047 |

Multiple R = 0.456 F- value = 4.790 d.f. (1,37) P-value < 0.05
R square = 0.208

$$\hat{Y} = 3.785+0.201X_1-0.265X_2$$

Where $\hat{Y}$ is the estimated performance of production.

Table 3.47 exhibits the impact of various problems of production on its performance. The equation describes that, on an average if the problem "Possibility of pollution created by Kiln" changes by one unit, there will be a decline of 0.265 units in the performance of production when the other problem

"Fulfillment of legal formalities in procuring the firewood" is kept constant and vice versa.

The result of t-test confirms that, the estimated regression coefficients (0.201) and (-0.265) is significant at five percent level. The multiple R of 0.456 shows that there exists a relationship of 45.6 per cent between the above problem and the performance of production. Moreover, the $R^2$ of 0.208 confirms that these problems only explained 20.8 per cent of variation in the performance of production function. Finally, the result of f-test signifies that the variation was statistically significant at five per cent level.

Hence, it can be concluded that, among the eight production problems identified by the researcher, only two problems namely "Possibility of pollution created by Kiln" and "Fulfillment of legal formalities in procuring the firewood" have significant impact on the production performance. Among these, "Possibility of pollution created by Kiln" emerged as the significant problem reducing the production performance of the units located in Chittissery.

**Table 48**

**Stepwise Multiple Regression Analysis–The Impact of Various Production Problems on the Performance of Production Function in Pudukad**

| *Dependent variable: Performance of Production function (Y)* | | | | | |
|---|---|---|---|---|---|
| *Independent variables* | *Unstandardised Co-efficient* | *Standard Error* | *Standardised Co-efficient* | *t-value* | *p-value* |
| Constant | 2.809 | 0.990 | - | 2.837 | 0.011 |
| Delay in delivery of clay ($X_1$) | -0.368 | 0.130 | -0.503 | -2.824 | 0.011 |
| High price of clay in the market ($X_2$) | 0.478 | 0.209 | 0.408 | 2.289 | 0.034 |

Multiple R = 0.631 F- value = 6.274 d.f. (2,19) P-value < 0.01
R square = 0.398

$$\hat{Y} = 2.809 - 0.368X_1 + 0.478X_2$$

Where $\hat{Y}$ is the estimated performance of production.

Table 48 portrays the impact of various problems of production on its performance. The equation describes that, on an average if the problem "Delay in delivery of clay" changes by one unit, there will be a decline of 0.368 units in the performance of production when the other problem "High price of clay in the market" is kept constant and vice versa.

The results of t-test indicate that, the estimated regression coefficients (-0.368) and (0.478) are significant at five percent level. The multiple R of 0.631 shows that there exists a relationship of 63.1 per cent between the above problems and the performance of production function. Moreover, the $R^2$ of 0.398 confirms that these problems only explained 39.8 per cent of variation in the performance of production. Finally, the result of f-test signifies that the explained variation was statistically significant at one per cent level.

Hence, it can be concluded that, among the eight production problems identified by the researcher, only two problems namely "Delay in delivery of clay" and "High price of clay in the market" have significant impact on the production performance. Among these, "Delay in delivery of clay" emerged as significant problem decreasing the production performance of the units located in Pudukad.

**Table 49**

**Stepwise Multiple Regression Analysis-The Impact of Various Production Problems on the Performance of Production Function in Thrissur District**

*Dependent variable: Performance of Production function (Y)*

| *Independent variables* | *Unstandardised Co-efficient* | *Standard Error* | *Standardised Co-efficient* | *t-value* | *p-value* |
|---|---|---|---|---|---|
| Constant | 1.860 | 0.505 | - | 3.681 | 0.000 |
| Procurement of clay without objection ($X_1$) | 0.280 | 0.095 | 0.302 | 2.940 | 0.004 |
| High price for clay in the market ($X_2$) | 0.300 | 0.103 | 0.300 | 2.916 | 0.005 |

Multiple R = 0.398 F- value = 7.630 d.f. (2,81) P-value < 0.01
R square = 0.159

$$\hat{Y} = 1.860 + 0.280X_1 + 0.300X_2$$

Where $\hat{Y}$ is the estimated performance of production.

Table 49 shows the impact of various problems of production on its performance. The equation describes that, on an average if the problem "Procurement of clay without objection" changes by one unit, there will be an increase of 0.280 units in the performance of production when the other problem "High price for clay in the market" is kept constant and vice versa.

The results of t-test confirm that, the estimated regression coefficients (0.280) and (0.300) are significant at one percent level. The multiple R of 0.398 shows that there exists a relationship of 39.8 per cent between the above problems and the performance of production. Moreover, the $R^2$ of 0.159 confirms that these problems only explained 15.9 per cent of variation in the performance of production function. Finally, the result of f-test signifies that the variation was statistically significant at one per cent level.

Hence, it can be concluded that, the problems such as "Procurement of clay without objection" and "High price for clay in the market" positively contributed to the production performance. This shows these two problems existed in the production function of the units located in Thrissur District and these do not significantly reduce the performance of production.

**Table 50**
**Mode of Getting Orders**

| *Mode* | *No. of Units* | *Per cent* |
|---|---|---|
| Regular customers within the State | 5 | 6.0 |
| Through Agents | 11 | 13.1 |
| Regular customers outside the State | 7 | 8.3 |
| Through Govt. contractors | 58 | 69.0 |
| Customers within the State and Through Agents | 3 | 3.6 |
| Total | 84 | 100.0 |

*Source:* Primary Data.

Table 50 shows the various modes of getting orders. From the total of 84 units, 69 per cent (58) of the units get orders through Government contractors; 13.1 per cent (11) from agents and 8.3 per cent (7) from regular customers outside the state.

Hence, the maximum of 69 per cent of the units were getting the orders through the Government contractors.

**Table 51**
**Supply of Tiles to Other States**

| *State* | *No. of Units* | *Per cent* |
|---|---|---|
| Tamilnadu | 62 | 73.8 |
| Pondicherry | 5 | 6.0 |
| Andhra Pradesh | 11 | 13.1 |
| Karnataka | 6 | 7.1 |
| Total | 84 | 100.0 |

*Source:* Primary Data.

Table 51 shows the supply of tiles to other States. Out of 84 units, 73.8 per cent (62) of the units supplied the tiles to Tamilnadu, 13.1 per cent (11) to Andhra Pradesh and 7.1 per cent (6) to Karnataka.

Hence, the majority of 73.8 per cent of the units supplied clay tiles to Tamilnadu.

**Table 52**
**Methods Adopted for Price Fixation**

| *Methods* | *No. of Units* | *Per cent* |
|---|---|---|
| Cost-based | 35 | 41.6 |
| Demand-based | 1 | 1.2 |
| Cost and demand-based | 47 | 56.0 |
| Competition-based | 1 | 1.2 |
| Total | 84 | 100.0 |

*Source:* Primary Data.

Table 52 explains the various methods of fixing the price of a clay tile. 56 per cent (47) of the units followed the cost and demand based pricing and 41.7 per cent purely depend on the cost-based pricing method.

Hence, the majority of 56 per cent of the units adopted the cost- and demand-based method of pricing.

**Table 53**
**Nature of Sales**

| *Nature* | *No. of Units* | *Per cent* |
|---|---|---|
| Cash | 18 | 21.4 |
| Credit | 8 | 9.6 |
| Both | 58 | 69.0 |
| Total | 84 | 100.0 |

*Source:* Primary Data.

Table 53 shows the nature of sales. It is inferred from the table that nearly three fourths of the units sold the clay tiles on the basis of cash and credit; 21.4 per cent (18) on cash and the remaining of 9.6 per cent (8) on credit.

Hence, the maximum 69 per cent of the units sold their clay tiles both for cash and on credit.

**Table 54**
**Mode of Sales**

| *Methods* | *No. of Units* | *Per cent* |
|---|---|---|
| Direct sale | 31 | 36.9 |
| Through agents | 8 | 9.5 |
| Both | 45 | 53.6 |
| Total | 84 | 100.0 |

*Source:* Primary Data.

Table 54 exhibits the methods adopted for selling the tiles. More than 50 per cent (45) of the units were selling their tiles directly to their customers and through the agents; 36.9 per cent (31) direct sale and 9.5 per cent (8) through agents.

Hence, the maximum 53.6 per cent of the units were selling their tiles directly and through the agents.

**Table 55**
**Credit Period Allowed to Customers**

| *Period* | *No. of Units* | *Per cent* |
|---|---|---|
| Less than 1 week | 30 | 35.7 |
| 1 to 2 weeks | 19 | 22.6 |
| 2 to 3 weeks | 26 | 31.0 |
| More than 1 month | 9 | 10.7 |
| Total | 84 | 100.0 |

*Source:* Primary Data.

Table 55 shows the period of credit allowed to the customers. From the total of 84 units, 35.7 per cent (30) of the units allowed a credit period of less than one week, 31 per cent (26) 2 to 3 weeks and 22.6 per cent (19) 1 to 2 weeks.

Hence, the maximum 35.7 per cent of the units allowed a credit period of one week to their customers.

**Table 56**
**Location of Major Competitors**

| *Location* | *No. of Units* | *Per cent* |
|---|---|---|
| Nearby units | 43 | 51.1 |
| Within the district | 36 | 42.9 |
| Outside the district | 5 | 6.0 |
| Total | 84 | 100.0 |

*Source:* Primary Data.

Table 56 explains the location of the major competitors for the units. It is inferred from the table, 51.1 per cent (43) of the clay tiles manufacturing units are competing with the nearby units; 42.9 per cent (36) faced competition within the district and the remaining 6 per cent (5) outside the district.

Hence, the majority 51.1 per cent of the units faced competition from the nearby units in the Thrissur District.

**Table 57**
**Average Sales in a Year**

| *Numbers (in Load)* | *No. of Units* | *Per cent* |
|---|---|---|
| Below 200 | 7 | 8.3 |
| 200–400 | 65 | 77.4 |
| 400 and above | 12 | 14.3 |
| Total | 84 | 100.0 |

*Source:* Primary Data.

Table 57 shows the average number of loads of tiles sold in a year. More than 75 per cent of the units sold 200 to 400 loads in a year; 14.3 per cent (12) 400 and above and 8.3 per cent (7) of 200 or less.

Hence, the maximum 77.4 per cent of the units were selling 200 to 400 loads of tiles a year.

Table 3.58 gives the promotional techniques adopted by the units. 72.6 per cent (61) of the clay tiles manufacturing units do not follow any promotional techniques and the remaining 27.4 per cent (23) of them increased the sales volume by appointing agents.

Hence, the majority of 72.6 per cent of the units did not follow any promotional techniques for increasing their sales.

**Table 58**
**Promotional Techniques Followed**

| *Techniques* | *No. of Units* | *Per cent* |
|---|---|---|
| Appointment of agents | 23 | 27.4 |
| Discount allowed | - | - |
| Compensation for breakage | - | - |
| Arranging transport facilities for local sales | - | - |
| None of the above | 61 | 72.6 |
| Total | 84 | 100.0 |

*Source:* Primary Data.

**Table 59**
**Strategy Adopted For Maintaining the Sales**

| *Strategies* | *No. of Units* | *Per cent* |
|---|---|---|
| **Timely supply** | 48 | 57.1 |
| **Giving quality product** | 36 | 42.9 |
| **Extending credit period** | - | - |
| **Replacement of broken tiles** | - | - |
| Total | 84 | 100. |

*Source:* Primary Data.

Table 59 describes the various strategies adopted for maintaining a sustained sale. More than 55 per cent (48) of the units depend upon timely supply and the remaining 42.9 per cent (36) supply quality tiles to maintain sales.

Hence, the maximum of 57.1 per cent of the units adopted a strategy of timely supply to their customers in order to maintain sales.

**Table 60**
**Performance of Marketing Function**

| *Level* | *No. of Units* | *Per cent* |
|---|---|---|
| Bad | 4 | 4.8 |
| Moderate | 18 | 21.4 |
| Good | 55 | 65.5 |
| Excellent | 7 | 8.3 |
| Total | 84 | 100.0 |

*Source:* Primary Data.

Table 60 shows the performance of the marketing function. 65.5 per cent (55) of the units agreed that the performance of

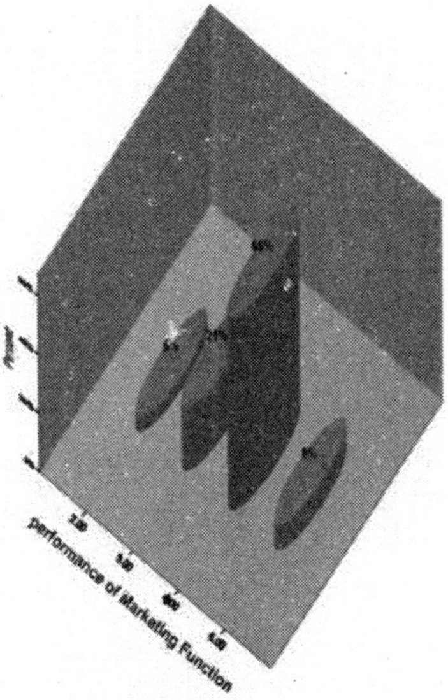


**Diagram 2**

marketing was good; 21.4 per cent (18) stated that their marketing performance was moderate and 8.3 per cent (7) excellent.

Hence, a majority of 65.5 per cent of the units had stated that their marketing performance was good.

Table 61 gives particulars of marketing based on location of the units. The following code is used.

A = Alagappanagar

B = Chittissery

C = Pudukad

When three numbers occur successively, they refer to A, B and C respectively.

- Most of the units get orders through Government contractors, a majority of 73.9 per cent of A, 64.1 per cent of B and 72.7 per cent of C.
- Maximum of 73.9 per cent of A 69.2 per cent of B and 81.8 per cent of C supply their tiles to the State of Tamilnadu.

**Table 61**
**Factors of Marketing Based on the Location of the Units**

| Factors | | Location | | |
|---|---|---|---|---|
| | | *Alagappanagar (n=23)* | *Chittissery (n=39)* | *Pudukad (n=22)* |
| Mode of Getting orders | Regular customers within the state | - | 3 (7.7) | 2 (9.1) |
| | Through agents | 4 (17.4) | 6 (15.4) | 1 (4.5) |
| | Regular customers outside the state | 1 (4.3) | 5 (12.8) | 1 (4.5) |
| | Through Govt. Contractors | 17 (73.9) | 25 (64.1) | 16 (72.7) |
| | 1 and 2 | 1 (4.3) | - | 2 (9.1) |
| Supply of tiles to other states | Tamilnadu | 17 (73.9) | 27 (69.2) | 18 (81.8) |
| | Pondicherry | 3 (13.0) | 2 (5.1) | - |
| | Andhra Pradesh | 1 (4.3) | 7 (17.9) | 3 (13.6) |
| | Karnataka | 2 (8.7) | 3 (7.7) | 1 (4.5) |
| Methods of Price fixation | Cost-based | 12 (52.2) | 14 (35.9) | 9 (40.9) |
| | Demand-based | - | - | 1 (4.5) |
| | Cost and Demand-based | 11 (47.8) | 24 (61.5) | 12 (54.5) |
| | Competition-based | - | 1 (2.6) | - |
| Nature of sales | Cash | 6 (26.1) | 8 (20.5) | 4 (18.2) |
| | Credit | 5 (21.7) | - | 3 (13.6) |
| | Both | 12 (52.2) | 31 (79.5) | 15 (68.2) |
| Mode of sales | Direct sale | 7 (30.4) | 18 (46.2) | 6 (27.3) |
| | Through agents | 3 (13.0) | 3 (7.7) | 2 (9.1) |
| | Both | 13 (56.5) | 18 (46.2) | 14 (63.6) |

*Contd...*

| Factors | | Location | | |
|---|---|---|---|---|
| | | Alagappanagar (n=23) | Chittissery (n=39) | Pudukad (n=22) |
| Period of credit allowed to customers | Less than 1 week | 7 (30.4) | 18 (46.2) | 5 (22.7) |
| | 1 to 2 weeks | 5 (21.7) | 7 (17.9) | 7 (31.8) |
| | 2 to 3 weeks | 10 (43.5) | 9 (23.1) | 7 (31.8) |
| | Above 1 month | 1 (4.3) | 5 (12.8) | 3 (13.6) |
| Location of major competitors | Nearby units | 9 (39.1) | 24 (61.5) | 10 (45.5) |
| | Within the district | 13 (56.5) | 13 (33.3) | 10 (45.5) |
| | Outside the district | 1 (4.3) | 2 (5.1) | 2 (9.1) |
| Average sales in a year (in loads) | Below 200 | 4 (17.4) | 2 (5.1) | 1 (4.5) |
| | 200-400 | 16 (69.6) | 31 (79.5) | 18 (81.8) |
| | 400 and Above | 3 (13.0) | 6 (15.4) | 3 (13.6) |
| Promotional techniques adopted | Appointment of agents | 8 (34.8) | 8 (20.5) | 7 (31.8) |
| | None of the Above | 15 (65.2) | 31 (79.5) | 15 (68.2) |
| Strategy adopted to maintain the sales | Timely supply | 14 (60.9) | 22 (56.4) | 12 (54.5) |
| | Giving Quality product | 9 (39.1) | 17 (43.6) | 10 (45.5) |
| Performance of marketing function | Bad | 2 (8.7) | - | 2 (9.1) |
| | Moderate | 7 (30.4) | 7 (17.9) | 4 (18.2) |
| | Good | 13 (56.5) | 27 (69.2) | 15 (68.2) |
| | Excellent | 1 (4.3) | 5 (12.8) | 1 (4.5) |

( ) in Percentage

- Cost and demand-based method of fixing the price is found to be most suitable, one for 11 units of A, 24 units of B and 12 units of C.
- Sale on cash and sale on credit are the only two modes of modern marketing. Most of the units have both.
- Though some units do direct selling and some sell through agents, most units adopt both the modes, a majority of 56.5 per cent of A, 46.2 per cent of B and 63.6 per cent of C.
- Only a few units - one unit of A, five units of B and three units of C allow a month or more for collection. All other units keep the period of collection within a month.
- Competition from outside the state is negligible, but competition from nearby units or units within the district is keen.
- 200 to 400 loads are sold in a year by 69.6 per cent of A, 79.5 per cent of B and 81.8 per cent of C.
- Most of the units have no need to adopt promotional techniques, a maximum 65.2 per cent of A, 79.5 per cent of B and 68.2 per cent of C don't adopt any promotional techniques.
- Timely supply is the strength of most of the units, a majority 60.9 per cent of A, 56.4 per cent of B and 54.5 per cent of C.
- One unit of A, five units of B and 1 unit of C have recorded excellent performance, and the marketing is good for 56.5 per cent of A, 70 per cent of B and 68 per cent of C.

Table 64 gives particulars of marketing on the basis of the year of establishment. The following code is adopted.

A = units established before 1981

B = units established between 1981 and 1985

C = units established between 1985 and 1990

D = units established 1990 and after

**Table 62**
**Factors of Marketing Based on the Year of Establishment**

| *Factors* | | *Year* | | | |
|---|---|---|---|---|---|
| | | *Before 1981 (n=5)* | *1981-1985 (n=7)* | *1985-1990 (n=30)* | *1990 and After (n=42)* |
| Mode of Getting orders | Regular customers within the state | - | - | 3 (10.0) | 2 (4.8) |
| | Through agents | 3 (60.0) | 1 (14.3) | 3 (10.0) | 4 (9.5) |
| | Regular customers outside the state | - | 2 (28.6) | 1 (3.3) | 4 (9.5) |
| | Through Govt. Contractors | 2 (40.0) | 4 (57.1) | 22 (73.3) | 30 (71.4) |
| | 1 and 2 | - | - | 1 (3.3) | 2 (4.8) |
| Supply of tiles to other states | Tamilnadu | 4 (80.0) | 5 (71.4) | 22 (73.3) | 31 (73.8) |
| | Pondicherry | 1 (20.0) | - | 3 (10.0) | 1 (2.4) |
| | Andhra Pradesh | - | 2 (28.6) | 3 (10.0) | 6 (14.3) |
| | Karnataka | - | - | 2 (6.7) | 4 (9.5) |
| Methods of Price fixation | Cost-based | - | 3 (42.9) | 11 (36.7) | 21 (50.0) |
| | Demand-based | - | - | 1 (3.3) | - |
| | Cost and Demand-based | 5 (100.0) | 4 (57.1) | 18 (60.0) | 20 (47.6) |
| | Competition-based | - | - | - | 1 (2.4) |
| Nature of sales [d] | Cash | - | 2 (28.6) | 9 (30.0) | 7 (16.7) |
| | Credit | - | - | 4 (13.3) | 4 (9.5) |
| | Both | 5 (100.0) | 5 (71.4) | 17 (56.7) | 31 (73.8) |
| Mode of sales | Direct sale | - | 3 (42.9) | 11 (36.7) | 17 (40.5) |
| | Through agents | - | 2 (28.6) | 2 (6.7) | 4 (9.5) |
| | Both | 5 (100.0) | 2 (28.6) | 17 (56.7) | 21 (50.0) |

*Contd...*

| Factors | | Year | | | |
|---|---|---|---|---|---|
| | | *Before 1981 (n=5)* | *1981-1985 (n=7)* | *1985-1990 (n=30)* | *1990 and After (n=42)* |
| Period of credit allowed to customers | Less than 1 week | 1 (20.0) | 2 (28.6) | 14 (46.7) | 13 (31.0) |
| | 1 to 2 weeks | 1 (20.0) | 1 (14.3) | 4 (13.3) | 13 (31.0) |
| | 2 to 3 weeks | 2 (40.0) | 2 (28.6) | 12 (40.0) | 10 (23.8) |
| | Above 1 month | 1 (20.0) | 2 (28.6) | - | 6 (14.3) |
| Location of major competitors | Nearby units | 2 (40.0) | 4 (57.1) | 9 (30.0) | 28 (66.7) |
| | Within the district | 3 (60.0) | 3 (42.9) | 18 (60.0) | 12 (28.6) |
| | Outside the district | - | - | 3 (10.0) | 2 (4.8) |
| Average sales in a year (in loads) | Below 200 | - | - | 3 (10.0) | 4 (9.5) |
| | 200-400 | 4 (80.0) | 7 (100.0) | 22 (73.3) | 32 (76.2) |
| | 400 and Above | 1 (20.0) | - | 5 (16.7) | 6 (14.3) |
| Promotional techniques adopted | Appointment of agents | 2 (40.0) | 3 (42.9) | 9 (30.0) | 9 (21.4) |
| | None of the Above | 3 (60.0) | 4 (57.1) | 21 (70.0) | 33 (78.6) |
| Strategy adopted to maintain the sales | Timely supply | 2 (40.0) | 2 (28.6) | 19 (63.3) | 25 (59.5) |
| | Giving Quality product | 3 (60.0) | 5 (71.4) | 11 (36.7) | 17 (40.5) |
| Performance of marketing | Bad | - | 1 (14.3) | 1 (3.3) | 2 (4.8) |
| | Moderate | 2 (40.0) | 1 (14.3) | 6 (20.0) | 9 (21.4) |
| | Good | 2 (40.0) | 3 (42.9) | 21 (70.0) | 29 (69.0) |
| | Excellent | 1 (20.0) | 2 (28.6) | 2 (6.7) | 2 (4.8) |

( ) in Percentage
Contingency Coefficient $\geq 0.5$ P-Value $<0.01$[a]
Contingency Coefficient $\geq 0.5$ P-Value $<0.05$[b]
Contingency Coefficient $\leq 0.5$ P-Value $<0.01$[c]
Contingency Coefficient $\leq 0.5$ P-Value $<0.05$[d]

- Except that 60 per cent of A get orders through agents, most of the units get order through Government contractors.
- Tamilnadu tops the list of customers from other states.
- Cost and demand-based mode is the most obvious and acceptable mode of fixing the price, maximum 100 per cent of A, 57.1 per cent of B, 60 per cent of C and 47.6 per cent of D adopt this method.
- Of course, sale must be either on cash or on credit and it cannot be otherwise in modern marketing. So most units follow both the practices.
- Though some units sell directly, and some through agents but 45 units adopt both the modes.
- 20 per cent of A, 28.6 per cent of B, 46.7 per cent of C and 31 per cent of D allow only one week to customers for collection and only 9 units allow one month. The rest of the units (45) fix the period between 1 week and 3 weeks.
- Competition from outside the district is negligible, but that from nearby units and units within the district is considerable, and it cannot be avoided, as all the units are situated within one district.
- 200 to 400 loads are normally sold in a year, though 12 units exceed 400.
- Promotional techniques are not adopted by the majority of the units.
- Timely supply (48 units) and quality product (36 units) are the two main stays of retaining the customers.
- Marketing performance, though bad in 4 units is good in 55 units, and it is excellent in 7 units.

Moreover, the results of the contingency co-efficient suggest that the marketing factor-nature of sales was associated with the year of establishment of the units and this was statistically significant at five per cent level.

Table 63 gives particulars of marketing on the basis of the jurisdiction of the units. The code is:

**Table 63**
**Factors of Marketing Based on the Jurisdiction of the Units**

| Factors | | Jurisdiction | | |
|---|---|---|---|---|
| | | *Panchayat (n=74)* | *Municipality (n=9)* | *Corporation (n=1)* |
| Mode of Getting orders | Regular customers within the state | 3 (4.1) | 2 (22.2) | - |
| | Through agents | 11 (14.9) | - | - |
| | Regular customers outside the state | 7 (9.5) | - | - |
| | Through Govt. Contractors | 51 (68.9) | 6 (66.7) | 1 (100.0) |
| | 1 and 2 | 2 (2.7) | 1 (11.1) | - |
| Supply of tiles to other states | Tamilnadu | 56 (75.7) | 5 (55.6) | 1 (100.0) |
| | Pondicherry | 4 (5.4) | 1 (11.1) | - |
| | Andhra Pradesh | 9 (12.2) | 2 (22.2) | - |
| | Karnataka | 5 (6.8) | 1 (11.1) | - |
| Methods of Price fixation [a] | Cost-based | 34 (45.9) | 1 (11.1) | - |
| | Demand-based | - | - | 1 (100.0) |
| | Cost and Demand-based | 39 (52.7) | 8 (88.9) | - |
| | Competition-based | 1 (1.4) | - | - |
| Nature of sales [d] | Cash | 15 (20.3) | 3 (33.3) | - |
| | Credit | 7 (9.5) | - | 1 (100.0) |
| | Both | 52 (70.3) | 6 (66.7) | - |
| Mode of sales | Direct sale | 26 (35.1) | 5 (55.6) | - |
| | Through agents | 6 (8.1) | 2 (22.2) | - |
| | Both | 42 (56.8) | 2 (22.2) | 1 (100.0) |

*Contd...*

| Factors | | Jurisdiction | | |
|---|---|---|---|---|
| | | *Panchayat (n=74)* | *Municipality (n=9)* | *Corporation (n=1)* |
| Period of credit allowed to customers | Less than 1 week | 26 (35.1) | 4 (44.4) | - |
| | 1 to 2 weeks | 17 (23.0) | 2 (22.2) | - |
| | 2 to 3 weeks | 22 (29.7) | 3 (33.3) | 1 (100.0) |
| | Above 1 month | 9 (12.2) | - | - |
| Location of major competitors | Nearby units | 40 (54.1) | 3 (33.3) | - |
| | Within the district | 30 (40.5) | 5 (55.6) | 1 (100.0) |
| | Outside the district | 4 (5.4) | 1 (11.1) | - |
| Average sales in a year (in loads) | Below 200 | 7 (9.5) | - | - |
| | 200-400 | 58 (78.4) | 6 (66.7) | 1 (100.0) |
| | 400 and Above | 9 (12.2) | 3 (33.3) | - |
| Promotional techniques adopted | Appointment of agents | 19 (25.7) | 4 (44.4) | - |
| | None of the Above | 55 (74.3) | 5 (55.6) | 1 (100.0) |
| Strategy adopted to maintain the sales | Timely supply | 42 (56.8) | 5 (55.6) | 1 (100.0) |
| | Giving Quality product | 32 (43.2) | 4 (44.4) | - |
| Performance of marketing function | Bad | 4 (5.4) | - | - |
| | Moderate | 17 (23.0) | 1 (11.1) | - |
| | Good | 47 (63.5) | 7 (77.8) | 1 (100.0) |
| | Excellent | 6 (8.1) | 1 (11.1) | - |

( ) in Percentage Contingency Coefficient $\geq$ 0.5 P-Value <0.01[a]
Contingency Coefficient $\geq$ 0.5 P-Value <0.05[b]
Contingency Coefficient $\leq$ 0.5 P-Value <0.01[c]
Contingency Coefficient $\leq$ 0.5 P-Value <0.05[d]

A = Panchayat

B = Municipality

C = Corporation

When three figures occur in succession, they refer to A, B and C.

- Except 23 units, all the other units get orders through Government contractors.
- Though the units supply tiles to Karnataka, Pondicherry and Andhra Pradesh, the most viable customer is Tamilnadu, a majority 75.7 per cent of A, 55.6 per cent of B and 100 per cent of C.
- Cost and demand-based fixing of price is the most acceptable mode in majority of the units, 52.7 per cent of A, 88.9 per cent of B, while the one unit of C fixes the price on demand only.
- Though C allows sale on credit. Sale on cash and credit is done by most of the units (70.3 per cent of A and 66.7 per cent of B).
- Direct sale and sale through agents are undertaken by 56.8 per cent of A, 56.8 per cent of B and 100 per cent of C.
- 35 per cent of A and 44.4 per cent of B allow only one week to the customers. 45 units allow between one week and one month for collection.
- Naturally, competition from the nearby units and the units in the district is keen, whereas competition outside the district is negligible.
- Though 9 units of A and 3 units of B exceed 400 loads a year, the average sale is 200 to 400, a maximum of 78.4 per cent A and 66.7 per cent of B and one unit of C.
- Promotional techniques are not adopted by the majority of the units (74.3 per cent of A, 55.6 per cent of B and one unit of C).
- Timely supply helps to maintain the sales adopted by 56.8 per cent of A, 55.6 per cent of B and one unit of C.

- 4 units of A have fared badly and 6 of A and 1 of B excellently. Otherwise the performance is good.

Moreover, the results of the contingency co-efficient suggest that the factors of marketing such as methods of price fixation, nature of sales were associated with the jurisdiction of the units and these were statistically significant at one per cent and five per cent level respectively.

Table 64 provides particulars of marketing based on the type of clay manufactured in the units, the code is:

A = Roofing tiles

B = Flooring tiles

C = Other tiles

D = Roofing and flooring tiles

E = Flooring and decorative tiles

F = Decorative and other tiles

- 50 per cent of A and 33.3 per cent of C get orders from customers outside the State. But for this exception, most of the units get orders through Government contractors.
- The largest supply of tiles outside Kerala is to Tamilnadu. Majority 3 units of A, 33 units of B, 6 units of C and D, 13 units of E and 1 of F supply to Tamilnadu.
- Though cost-based fixation of price is followed by 35 units, cost and demand-based fixation is adopted by 3 units of A, 21 units of B, 4 units of C, 5 units of D, 13 units of E and 1 of F.
- The sale on cash and on credit is made by 3 units of A, 30 units of B, 6 units of C, 5 units of D, 13 units of E and 1 of F.
- Though 62.5 per cent of D believe in direct sale and totally 8 units sale through agents, both the methods are adopted by 3 units of A, 20 units of B, 7 units of C, 2 units of D, 12 units of E and 1 of F.
- As regards the period allowed for payment, 42.9 per cent of B and a few units of other categories allow only one week. On the other hand, 9 units allow more than

**Table 64**

**Factors of Marketing Based on Type of Clay Tiles Manufactured by the Units**

| Factors | | *Types of Clay Tiles* | | | | | |
|---|---|---|---|---|---|---|---|
| | | *Roofing (n=4)* | *Flooring (n=42)* | *Other tiles (n=9)* | *Roofing & Flooring (n=8)* | *Flooring & Decorative (n=20)* | *Decorative & other tiles (n=1)* |
| Mode of Getting orders [a] | Regular customers within the state | - | 2 (4.8) | 1 (11.1) | - | 2 (10.0) | - |
| | Through agents | - | 6 (14.3) | 2 (22.2) | 2 (25.0) | 1 (5.0) | - |
| | Regular customers outside the state | 2 (50.0) | 2 (4.8) | 3 (33.3) | - | - | - |
| | Through Govt. Contractors | 2 (50.0) | 31 (73.8) | 3 (33.3) | 5 (62.5) | 17 (85.0) | - |
| | 1 and 2 | - | 1 (2.4) | - | 1 (12.5) | - | 1 (100.0) |
| Supply of tiles to other states | Tamilnadu | 3 (75.0) | 33 (78.6) | 6 (66.7) | 6 (75.0) | 13 (65.0) | 1 (100.0) |
| | Pondicherry | - | 3 (7.1) | 1 (11.1) | - | 1 (5.0) | - |
| | Andhra Pradesh | 1 (25.0) | 5 (11.9) | 2 (22.2) | 1 (12.5) | 2 (10.0) | - |
| | Karnataka | - | 1 (2.4) | - | 1 (12.5) | 4 (20.0) | - |
| Methods of Price fixation | Cost-based | 1 (25.0) | 19 (45.2) | 5 (55.6) | 3 (37.5) | 7 (35.0) | - |
| | Demand-based | - | 1 (2.4) | - | - | - | - |
| | Cost and Demand-based | 3 (75.0) | 21 (50.0) | 4 (44.4) | 5 (62.5) | 13 (65.0) | 1 (100.0) |
| | Competition-based | - | 1 (2.4) | - | - | - | - |
| Nature of sales | Cash | 1 (25.0) | 8 (19.0) | 1 (11.1) | 2 (25.0) | 6 (30.0) | - |
| | Credit | - | 4 (9.5) | 2 (22.2) | 1 (12.5) | 1 (5.0) | - |
| | Both | 3 (75.0) | 30 (71.4) | 6 (66.7) | 5 (62.5) | 13 (65.0) | 1 (100.0) |
| Mode of sales | Direct sale | 1 (25.0) | 17 (40.5) | 1 (11.1) | 5 (62.5) | 7 (35.0) | - |
| | Through agents | - | 5 (11.9) | 1 (11.1) | 1 (12.5) | 1 (5.0) | - |
| | Both | 3 (75.0) | 20 (47.6) | 7 (77.8) | 2 (25.0) | 12 (60.0) | 1 (100.0) |

*Contd...*

| Factors | | Types of Clay Tiles | | | | | |
|---|---|---|---|---|---|---|---|
| | | Roofing (n=4) | Flooring (n=42) | Other tiles (n=9) | Roofing & Flooring (n=8) | Flooring & Decorative (n=20) | Decorative & other tiles (n=1) |
| Period of credit allowed to customers | Less than 1 week | 1 (25.0) | 18 (42.9) | 2 (22.2) | 2 (25.0) | 7 (35.0) | - |
| | 1 to 2 weeks | - | 11 (26.2) | 2 (22.2) | 3 (37.5) | 3 (15.0) | - |
| | 2 to 3 weeks | 2 (50.0) | 10 (23.8) | 3 (33.3) | 1 (12.5) | 9 (45.0) | 1 (100.0) |
| | Above 1 month | 1 (25.0) | 3 (7.1) | 2 (22.2) | 2 (25.0) | 1 (5.0) | - |
| Major competitors faced | Nearby units | 3 (75.0) | 20 (47.6) | 4 (44.4) | 4 (50.0) | 12 (60.0) | - |
| | Within the district | 1 (25.0) | 18 (42.9) | 5 (55.6) | 4 (50.0) | 7 (35.0) | 1 (100.0) |
| | Outside the district | - | 4 (9.5) | - | - | 1 (5.0) | - |
| Average sales in a year (in loads)[a] | Below 200 | - | - | 2 (22.2) | 5 (62.5) | - | - |
| | 200-400 | 4 (100.0) | 33 (78.6) | 7 (77.8) | 3 (37.5) | 17 (85.0) | 1 (100.0) |
| | 400 and Above | - | 9 (21.4) | - | - | 3 (15.0) | - |
| Promotional techniques adopted | Appointment of agents | - | 12 (28.6) | 5 (55.6) | 1 (12.5) | 5 (25.0) | - |
| | None of the Above | 4 (100.0) | 30 (71.4) | 4 (44.4) | 7 (87.5) | 15 (75.0) | 1 (100.0) |
| Strategy adopted to maintain the sales | Timely supply | 2 (50.0) | 26 (61.9) | 4 (44.4) | 4 (50.0) | 12 (60.0) | - |
| | Giving Quality product | 2 (50.0) | 16 (38.1) | 5 (55.6) | 4 (50.0) | 8 (40.0) | 1 (100.0) |
| Performance of marketing | Bad | - | 1 (2.4) | - | 2 (25.0) | 1 (5.0) | - |
| | Moderate | 1 (25.0) | 7 (16.7) | 4 (44.4) | - | 6 (30.0) | - |
| | Good | 3 (75.0) | 31 (73.8) | 3 (33.3) | 5 (62.5) | 12 (60.0) | 1 (100.0) |
| | Excellent | - | 3 (7.1) | 2 (22.2) | 1 (12.5) | 1 (5.0) | - |

( ) in Percentage Contingency Coefficient ≥ 0.5 P-Value <0.01[a]
Contingency Coefficient ≥ 0.5 P-Value <0.05[b]
Contingency Coefficient ≤ 0.5 P-Value <0.01[c]
Contingency Coefficient ≤ 0.5 P-Value <0.05[d]

one month. The rest (45 units) allow between one week and one month.

- Only 4 units of B and 1 of E face competition from outside the district. As all the units are situated within Thrissur district, they face stiff competition among themselves.
- The average sale in a year is 200 to 400 loads in majority of the units.
- Though 23 units adopt promotional techniques (like appointment of agents), 61 units do not adopt any.
- Needless to say, timely supply, coupled with the quality of the product, helps to maintain the sales.
- Performance of marketing is good in majority of the units.

Moreover, the results of the contingency co-efficient suggest that the factors of marketing such as mode of getting orders and average sales in a year were associated with the type of clay tiles manufactured by the units and these were statistically significant at one per cent level.

Table 65 gives particulars of marketing on the basis of the ownership of the units. The code is:

A = Sole proprietorship

B = Partnership

C = Co-operative society

D = Private company

Where 4 figures appear in succession, they point to A, B, C and D respectively.

- Most of the units get orders through Government contractors with a majority 36 units of A, 17 units of B, 3 units of C and 2 units of D.
- Though tiles are supplied to all the three southern States and Pondichery, the largest supply is to Tamilnadu (36 units of A, 21 units of B, 3 units of C and 2 of D).
- Cost and demand-based fixation of price is most accepted method of pricing for 54.2 per cent of A, 55.2 per cent of B, 75 per cent of C and 66.7 per cent of D.

## Table 65
## Factors of Marketing Based on Ownership of the Units

| *Factors* | | *Ownership* | | | |
|---|---|---|---|---|---|
| | | *Sole Proprietor (n=48)* | *Partnership (n=29)* | *Co-op. Society (n=4)* | *Private company (n=3)* |
| Mode of Getting orders | Regular customers within the state | 2 (4.2) | 3 (10.3) | - | - |
| | Through agents | 3 (6.3) | 6 (20.7) | 1 (25.0) | 1 (33.3) |
| | Regular customers outside the state | 4 (8.3) | 3 (10.3) | - | - |
| | Through Govt. Contractors | 36 (75.0) | 17 (58.6) | 3 (75.0) | 2 (66.7) |
| | 1 and 2 | 3 (6.3) | - | - | - |
| Supply of tiles to other states | Tamilnadu | 36 (75.0) | 21 (72.4) | 3 (75.0) | 2 (66.7) |
| | Pondicherry | 3 (6.3) | - | 1 (25.0) | 1 (33.3) |
| | Andhra Pradesh | 5 (10.4) | 6 (20.7) | - | - |
| | Karnataka | 4 (8.3) | 2 (6.9) | - | - |
| Methods of Price fixation | Cost-based | 22 (45.8) | 12 (41.4) | - | 1 (33.3) |
| | Demand-based | - | - | 1 (25.0) | - |
| | Cost and Demand-based | 26 (54.2) | 16 (55.2) | 3 (75.0) | 2 (66.7) |
| | Competition-based | - | 1 (3.4) | - | - |
| Nature of sales | Cash | 11 (22.9) | 5 (17.2) | 1 (25.0) | 1 (33.3) |
| | Credit | 3 (6.3) | 4 (13.8) | 1 (25.0) | - |
| | Both | 34 (70.8) | 20 (69.0) | 2 (50.0) | 2 (66.7) |
| Mode of sales | Direct sale | 21 (43.8) | 8 (27.6) | 1 (25.0) | 1 (33.3) |
| | Through agents | 3 (6.3) | 5 (17.2) | - | - |
| | Both | 24 (50.0) | 16 (55.2) | 3 (75.0) | 2 (66.7) |

*Contd...*

| *Factors* | | *Ownership* | | | |
|---|---|---|---|---|---|
| | | *Sole Proprietor (n=48)* | *Partnership (n=29)* | *Co-op. Society (n=4)* | *Private company (n=3)* |
| Period of credit allowed to customers | Less than 1 week | 16 (33.3) | 10 (34.5) | 1 (25.0) | 3 (100.0) |
| | 1 to 2 weeks | 12 (25.0) | 7 (24.1) | - | - |
| | 2 to 3 weeks | 16 (33.3) | 8 (27.6) | 2 (50.0) | - |
| | Above 1 month | 4 (8.3) | 4 (13.8) | 1 (25.0) | - |
| Location of major competitors | Nearby units | 25 (52.1) | 16 (55.2) | 1 (25.0) | 1 (33.3) |
| | Within the district | 19 (39.6) | 12 (41.4) | 3 (75.0) | 2 (66.7) |
| | Outside the district | 4 (8.3) | 1 (3.4) | - | - |
| Average sales in a year (in loads) | Below 200 | 5 (10.4) | 2 (6.9) | - | - |
| | 200-400 | 36 (75.0) | 23 (79.3) | 4 (100.0) | 2 (66.7) |
| | 400 and Above | 7 (14.6) | 4 (13.8) | - | 1 (33.3) |
| Promotional techniques adopted | Appointment of agents | 11 (22.9) | 10 (34.5) | - | 2 (66.7) |
| | None of the Above | 37 (77.1) | 19 (65.5) | 4 (100.0) | 1 (33.3) |
| Strategy adopted to maintain the sales | Timely supply | 29 (60.4) | 15 (51.7) | 3 (75.0) | 1 (33.3) |
| | Giving Quality product | 19 (39.6) | 14 (48.3) | 1 (25.0) | 2 (66.7) |
| Performance of marketing function | Bad | 1 (2.1) | 2 (6.9) | 1 (25.0) | - |
| | Moderate | 12 (25.0) | 5 (17.2) | 1 (25.0) | - |
| | Good | 29 (60.4) | 21 (72.4) | 2 (50.0) | 3 (100.0) |
| | Excellent | 6 (12.5) | 1 (3.4) | - | - |

( ) in Percentage Contingency Coefficient $\geq 0.5$ P-Value $<0.01^{a}$
Contingency Coefficient $\geq 0.5$ P-Value $<0.05^{b}$
Contingency Coefficient $\leq 0.5$ P-Value $<0.01^{c}$
Contingency Coefficient $\leq 0.5$ P-Value $<0.05^{d}$

- Most units sell tiles on cash and on credit (70.8 per cent of A, 69 per cent of B, 50 per cent of C and 66.7 per cent of D).
- Direct sale is suitable for 31 units; sale through agents is done by 8 units. But most units adopt both methods for sale of their products (50 per cent of A, 55 per cent of B, 75 per cent of C and 66.7 per cent of D).
- 16 units of A, 10 units of B and 3 units of D are strict regarding the period allowed to the customers for payment- just a week. On the contrary each 4 units of A and B, 1 of C are generous granting a month or more. But 45 units allowed a period between one week and one month.
- As competition from outside the district is not much, the units face stiff competition from nearby units and other units in the same district.
- Average sale ranges between 200 and 400 loads in a year by 36 units of A, 23 units of B, 4 units of C and 2 units of D.
- Most of the units don't adopt any promotional techniques for selling their products.
- Timely supply is the backbone in any industry. It is so with the units 60.4 per cent of A, 51.7 per cent of B, 75 per cent of C and 33.3 per cent of D, but quality has not be ignored some of the units.
- The marketing performance of most of the units is good, a maximum of 60.4 per cent of A, 72.4 per cent of B, 50 per cent of C and 100 per cent of D.

Moreover, the results of the contingency co-efficient suggest that the factor of marketing namely methods of price fixation was associated with the ownership of the units and this was statistically significant at one per cent level.

Table 66 gives particulars of marketing based on the educational qualifications of the owners. The following code is used.

**Table 66**

**Factors of Marketing Based on the Educational Qualifications of the Unit Owner**

| *Factors* | | *Qualification* | | | | |
|---|---|---|---|---|---|---|
| | | *Below S.S.L.C (n=9)* | *Pre-Degree (n=34)* | *Technical (n=9)* | *Graduate (n=29)* | *Post-graduate (n=3)* |
| Mode of Getting orders | Regular customers within the state | - | 2 (5.9) | - | 2 (6.9) | 1 (33.3) |
| | Through agents | - | 4 (11.8) | 2 (22.2) | 5 (17.2) | - |
| | Regular customers outside the state | 1 (11.1) | 4 (11.8) | 1 (11.1) | 1 (3.4) | - |
| | Through Govt. Contractors | 8 (88.9) | 23 (67.6) | 6 (66.7) | 19 (65.5) | 2 (66.7) |
| | 1 and 2 | - | 1 (2.9) | - | 2 (6.9) | - |
| Supply of tiles to other states | Tamilnadu | 7 (77.8) | 24 (70.6) | 5 (55.6) | 23 (79.3) | 3 (100.0) |
| | Pondicherry | - | 2 (5.9) | 1 (11.1) | 2 (6.9) | - |
| | Andhra Pradesh | 1 (11.1) | 6 (17.6) | 1 (11.1) | 3 (10.3) | - |
| | Karnataka | 1 (11.1) | 2 (5.9) | 2 (22.2) | 1 (3.4) | - |
| Methods of Price fixation | Cost-based | 2 (22.2) | 17 (50.0) | 6 (66.7) | 10 (34.5) | - |
| | Demand-based | 1 (11.1) | - | - | - | - |
| | Cost and Demand-based | 6 (66.7) | 16 (47.1) | 3 (33.3) | 19 (65.5) | 3 (100.0) |
| | Competition-based | - | 1 (2.9) | - | - | - |
| Nature of sales | Cash | 4 (44.4) | 7 (20.6) | 2 (22.2) | 5 (17.2) | - |
| | Credit | 1 (11.1) | 4 (11.8) | - | 2 (6.9) | 1 (33.3) |
| | Both | 4 (44.4) | 23 (67.6) | 7 (77.8) | 22 (75.9) | 2 (66.7) |

*Contd...*

| *Factors* | | *Qualification* | | | | |
|---|---|---|---|---|---|---|
| | | *Below S.S.L.C (n=9)* | *Pre-Degree (n=34)* | *Technical (n=9)* | *Graduate (n=29)* | *Post-graduate (n=3)* |
| Mode of sales | Direct sale | 4 (44.4) | 11 (32.4) | 6 (66.7) | 9 (31.0) | 1 (33.3) |
| | Through agents | - | 4 (11.8) | 1 (11.1) | 3 (10.3) | - |
| | Both | 5 (55.6) | 19 (55.9) | 2 (22.2) | 17 (58.6) | 2 (66.7) |
| Period of credit allowed to customers | Less than 1 week | 5 (55.6) | 11 (32.4) | 5 (55.6) | 9 (31.0) | - |
| | 1 to 2 weeks | 1 (11.1) | 7 (20.6) | - | 10 (34.5) | 1 (33.3) |
| | 2 to 3 weeks | 2 (22.2) | 14 (41.2) | 1 (11.1) | 8 (27.6) | 1 (33.3) |
| | Above 1 month | 1 (11.1) | 2 (5.9) | 3 (33.3) | 2 (6.9) | 1 (33.3) |
| Location of major competitors | Nearby units | 4 (44.4) | 20 (58.8) | 6 (66.7) | 12 (41.4) | 1 (33.3) |
| | Within the district | 5 (55.6) | 13 (38.2) | 2 (22.2) | 14 (48.3) | 2 (66.7) |
| | Outside the district | - | 1 (2.9) | 1 (11.1) | 3 (10.3) | - |
| Average sales in a year (in loads) | Below 200 | 1 (11.1) | 4 (11.8) | - | 1 (3.4) | 1 (33.3) |
| | 200-400 | 8 (88.9) | 28 (82.4) | 7 (77.8) | 21 (72.4) | 1 (33.3) |
| | 400 and Above | - | 2 (5.9) | 2 (22.2) | 7 (24.1) | 1 (33.3) |
| Promotional techniques adopted | Appointment of agents | 1 (11.1) | 11 (32.4) | 2 (22.2) | 9 (31.0) | - |
| | None of the Above | 8 (88.9) | 23 (67.6) | 7 (77.8) | 20 (69.0) | 3 (100.0) |
| Strategy adopted to maintain the sales | Timely supply | 5 (55.6) | 20 (58.8) | 7 (77.8) | 16 (55.2) | - |
| | Giving Quality product | 4 (44.4) | 14 (41.2) | 2 (22.2) | 13 (44.8) | 3 (100.0) |
| Performance of marketing function | Bad | - | 2 (5.9) | - | 2 (6.9) | - |
| | Moderate | 1 (11.1) | 8 (23.5) | 3 (33.3) | 5 (17.2) | 1 (33.3) |
| | Good | 8 (88.9) | 23 (67.6) | 6 (66.7) | 16 (55.2) | 2 (66.7) |
| | Excellent | - | 1 (2.9) | - | 6 (20.7) | - |

( ) in Percentage

A = below SSLC

B = Pre-degree

C = Technical qualification

D = Graduate

E = Post graduate

When five numbers appear in succession, they refer to all the five categories respectively.

- Whatever be the qualifications of the owner of the units, most units get orders through Government contractors.
- The largest supply of tiles is to Tamilnadu with a majority 77.8 per cent of A, 67.6 per cent of B, 66.7 per cent of C and E, and 65.5 per cent of D.
- 35 units adopt cost-based fixation of price, but cost and demand-based fixation is practised by 66.7 per cent of A, 65.6 per cent of D and 100 per cent of E.
- 44 per cent of A, 67.6 per cent of B, 77.8 per cent of C, 75.9 per cent of D and 66.7 per cent of E sold on cash and credit basis.
- Sale is both directly and through agents in most of the units.
- Period allowed to customers for payment is just one week (Each 55.6 per cent of A and C), 9 units allow one month. But the rest allow between 1 week and 1 month.
- There is keen competition from nearby units and within the district.
- The sale of five units falls below 200 loads a year; but the standard is 200 to 400 loads a year in majority of the units.
- Most of the units don't adopt any promotional techniques to boost their sales.
- Of course, timely supply helps to retain the customers.
- Performance of marketing is good in a maximum 89 per cent of A, 67.6 per cent of B, 66.7 per cent of C and D, and 55.2 per cent of D.

Table 70 gives particulars of marketing on the basis of the production capacity of the units. The following code is used.

A = below 8000 tiles a day

B = 8000 to 16000 tiles a day

C = 16000 to 24000 tiles a day

- Most of the units get orders through Government contractors (74 per cent of A, 57.6 per cent of B and 82.4 per cent of C).
- Irrespective of the capacity, most of the units supply the largest quantity to Tamilnadu (70.6 per cent of A, 69.7 per cent of B and 88.2 per cent of C).
- The most accepted method of fixing the price is the cost and demand-based method (57.6 per cent of B and 70.6 per cent of C).
- Most units sell their goods both on cash and on credit, a majority 64.7 per cent of A, 72.7 per cent of B and 70.6 per cent of C.
- Majority units adopt two methods of selling-direst sale and sale through agents.
- As regards the period allowed to customers for payment, it is one week (11 units of B and 8 units of C) and 2 to 3 weeks (12 units of A).
- It is anybody's guess that the competition is mostly from nearby units (55.9 per cent of A and 72.7 per cent of B) and from units with in the district (70.6 per cent of C). Competition from outside the district is insignificant.
- 12 units of C exceed 400 loads in their sale for a year and 7 units of A fall below 200. But most units sell 200 to 400 loads a year.
- Only very few units (23) adopt some promotional techniques and others don't.
- Timely supply is done to maintain the sales (58.8 per cent of A and 63.6 per cent of B). But quality is also maintained by 58.8 per cent of C.

**Table 67**
**Factors of Marketing Based on Installed Production Capacity Per Day**

| *Factors* | | *Capacity (Tiles per day)* | | |
|---|---|---|---|---|
| | | *Below 8000 (n=34)* | *8000-16000 (n=33)* | *16000-24000 (n=17)* |
| Mode of Getting orders | Regular customers within the state | 1 (2.9) | 4 (12.1) | - |
| | Through agents | 2 (5.9) | 6 (18.2) | 3 (17.6) |
| | Regular customers outside the state | 3 (8.8) | 4 (12.1) | - |
| | Through Govt. Contractors | 25 (73.5) | 19 (57.6) | 14 (82.4) |
| | 1 and 2 | 3 (8.8) | - | - |
| Supply of tiles to other states | Tamilnadu | 24 (70.6) | 23 (69.7) | 15 (88.2) |
| | Pondicherry | 1 (2.9) | 2 (6.1) | 2 (11.8) |
| | Andhra Pradesh | 4 (11.8) | 7 (21.2) | - |
| | Karnataka | 5 (14.7) | 1 (3.0) | - |
| Methods of Price fixation | Cost-based | 17 (50.0) | 13 (39.4) | 5 (29.4) |
| | Demand-based | 1 (2.9) | - | - |
| | Cost and Demand-based | 16 (47.1) | 19 (57.6) | 12 (70.6) |
| | Competition-based | - | 1 (3.0) | - |
| Nature of sales | Cash | 7 (20.6) | 6 (18.2) | 5 (29.4) |
| | Credit | 5 (14.7) | 3 (9.1) | - |
| | Both | 22 (64.7) | 24 (72.7) | 12 (70.6) |
| Mode of sales | Direct sale | 12 (35.3) | 10 (30.3) | 9 (52.9) |
| | Through agents | 2 (5.9) | 6 (18.2) | - |
| | Both | 20 (58.8) | 17 (51.5) | 8 (47.1) |

*Contd...*

| Factors | | Capacity (Tiles per day) | | |
|---|---|---|---|---|
| | | *Below 8000 (n=34)* | *8000-16000 (n=33)* | *16000-24000 (n=17)* |
| Period of credit allowed to customers | Less than 1 week | 11 (32.4) | 11 (33.3) | 8 (47.1) |
| | 1 to 2 weeks | 8 (23.5) | 6 (18.2) | 5 (29.4) |
| | 2 to 3 weeks | 12 (35.3) | 10 (30.3) | 4 (23.5) |
| | Above 1 month | 3 (8.8) | 6 (18.2) | - |
| Location of major competitors [a] | Nearby units | 19 (55.9) | 24 (72.7) | - |
| | Within the district | 15 (44.1) | 9 (27.3) | 12 (70.6) |
| | Outside the district | - | - | 5 (29.4) |
| Average sales in a year (in loads) [a] | Below 200 | 7 (20.6) | - | - |
| | 200-400 | 27 (79.4) | 33 (100.0) | 5 (29.4) |
| | 400 and Above | - | - | 12 (70.6) |
| Promotional techniques adopted [c] | Appointment of agents | 3 (8.8) | 12 (36.4) | 8 (47.1) |
| | None of the Above | 31 (91.2) | 21 (63.6) | 9 (52.9) |
| Strategy adopted to maintain the sales | Timely supply | 20 (58.8) | 21 (63.6) | 7 (41.2) |
| | Giving Quality product | 14 (41.2) | 12 (36.4) | 10 (58.8) |
| Performance of marketing function | Bad | 3 (8.8) | 1 (3.0) | - |
| | Moderate | 9 (26.5) | 6 (18.2) | 3 (17.6) |
| | Good | 21 (61.8) | 23 (69.7) | 11 (64.7) |
| | Excellent | 1 (2.9) | 3 (9.1) | 3 (17.6) |

( ) in Percentage Contingency Coefficient $\geq 0.5$ P-Value $<0.01$[a]
Contingency Coefficient $\geq 0.5$ P-Value $<0.05$[b]
Contingency Coefficient $\leq 0.5$ P-Value $<0.01$[c]
Contingency Coefficient $\leq 0.5$ P-Value $<0.05$[d]

- The overall picture of marketing is good, a maximum of 61.8 per cent of A, 70 per cent of B and 65 per cent of C.

Moreover, the results of the contingency co-efficient suggest that the factors of marketing such as location of major competitors, average sales in a year and promotional techniques adopted for selling the products were associated with the installed production capacity of the units and these were statistically significant at one per cent level.

**Table 68**
**Neural Classification Analysis–The Contribution of Various Marketing Factors to the Performance of Marketing Function in Alagappanagar**

| *Dependent variable: Performance of Marketing function* | | |
|---|---|---|
| *Independent Variables* | *Importance Co-efficient* | *Normalised Weights* |
| Mode of getting work orders | 0.0566 | 5.66 |
| Supply of tiles to other states | 0.0188 | 1.887 |
| Methods adopted for price fixation | 0.1698 | 16.981 |
| Nature of sales | 0.2452 | 24.528 |
| Mode of sales | 0.0754 | 7.547 |
| Credit period allowed to customers | 0.0754 | 7.547 |
| Location of the competitors | 0.0943 | 9.434 |
| Average sales in a year | 0.1320 | 13.208 |
| Promotional techniques followed | 0.0754 | 7.547 |

No. of hidden layers = 32  
Estimation = Sequential Algorithm  
Correct classification rate = 91.30%

Table 68 lists the contribution of various factors to the performance of marketing based on the results of neural classification analysis. The factors of marketing such as nature of sales, methods adopted for price fixation, average sales in a year and location of the competitors attained a greater normalised weights of 24.528 per cent, 16.981 per cent, 13.208 per cent and 9.434 per cent respectively. This shows that the above factors contributed to the performance at a correct classification rate of 91.30 per cent. Moreover the number of hidden layers between the performance of marketing function and various factors was 32 and this confirms that there is a non-linear relationship between these two.

Hence, the level of performance of marketing of the units in Alagappanagar was influenced by the best discriminating factors such as mode of tile sale, methods adopted for price fixation, average number of tiles sold and location of the competitors.

**Table 69**
**Neural Classification Analysis–The Contribution of Various Marketing Factors to the Performance of Marketing Function in Chittissery**

*Dependent variable: Performance of Marketing function*

| *Independent Variables* | *Importance Co-efficient* | *Normalised Weights* |
|---|---|---|
| Mode of getting work orders | 0.0937 | 9.375 |
| Supply of tiles to other states | 0.0625 | 6.25 |
| Methods adopted for price fixation | 0.1562 | 15.625 |
| Nature of sales | 0.1875 | 18.75 |
| Mode of sales | 0.0937 | 9.375 |
| Credit period allowed to customers | 0.25 | 25.0 |
| Location of competitors | 0.1562 | 15.625 |

No. of hidden layers = 34    Estimation = Sequential Algorithm
Correct classification rate = 87.18%

Table 69 shows the contribution of various factors to the performance of marketing based on the results of neural classification analysis. The factors such as credit period allowed to customers, nature of sales, methods adopted for price fixation, location of the competitors, mode of getting work orders and mode of sales were achieved a greater normalised weights of 25.0 per cent, 18.75 per cent, 15.625 per cent and 9.375 per cent respectively. This shows that only the above factors contributed to the performance at a correct classification rate of 87.18 per cent. Moreover the number of hidden layers between the performance of marketing and various factors was 34 and this confirms that there is a non-linear relationship between these two.

Hence, the level of performance of marketing of the units located in Chittissery was influenced by the best discriminating factors such as credit period allowed to customers, nature of sales, methods adopted for price fixation, location of the competitors, mode of getting work orders and mode of sales.

**Table 70**
**Neural Classification Analysis–The Contribution of Various Marketing Factors to the Performance of Marketing Function in Pudukad**

| *Dependent variable: Performance of Marketing function* | | |
|---|---|---|
| *Independent Variables* | *Importance Co-efficient* | *Normalised Weights* |
| Supply of tiles to other states | 0.0588 | 5.882 |
| Methods adopted for price fixation | 0.0588 | 5.882 |
| Nature of sales | 0.7058 | 70.588 |
| Average sales in a year | 0.0588 | 5.882 |
| Promotional techniques followed | 0.0588 | 5.882 |
| Strategy adopted for maintain the sales | 0.0588 | 5.882 |

No. of hidden layers = 0 Estimation = Sequential Algorithm
Correct classification rate = 81.82%

Table 70 depicts the contribution of various factors to the performance of marketing based on the results of neural classification analysis. The marketing factor "Nature of sales" achieved a greater weight of 70.588 per cent followed by the equal contribution of 5.882 per cent made by the remaining factors of marketing. This shows that only the nature of sales emerged and occupied a major portion in classifying the level of performance of marketing to the extent of 81.82 per cent. Moreover the number of hidden layers between the performance of marketing and various factors was 0 and this confirms that there is a high linear relationship between these two. Hence, the level of performance of Marketing was influenced by the best discriminating factor nature of sales in the clay tiles manufacturing units located at Pudukad.

Table 71 shows the contribution of various factors to the performance of marketing based on the results of neural classification analysis. The factors of marketing such as period of credit allowed to customers, mode of sale of tiles and nature of sale of tiles attained a greater normalised weights of 21.782 per cent, 14.851 per cent and 11.881 per cent respectively. This shows that the above factors contributed to the performance at a correct classification rate of 83.33 per cent. Moreover the number of hidden layers between the performance of marketing and various factors was 17 and this confirms that there is a non-linear relationship between these two.

Hence, the level of performance of marketing of the units was influenced by the best discriminating factors such as credit allowed to customers, mode of sale of tiles and nature of sale of tiles in Thrissur District.

**Table 71**
**Neural Classification Analysis–The Contribution of Various Marketing Factors to the Performance of Marketing Function in Thrissur District**

*Dependent variable: Performance of marketing function*

| *Independent Variables* | *Importance Co-efficient* | *Normalised Weights* |
|---|---|---|
| Mode of getting orders | 0.0396 | 3.96 |
| Supply of tiles to other states | 0.0198 | 1.98 |
| Methods of price fixation | 0.10891 | 10.891 |
| Nature of sales | 0.11881 | 11.881 |
| Mode of sales | 0.14851 | 14.851 |
| Period of credit allowed to customers | 0.21782 | 21.782 |
| Major competitors faced | 0.10891 | 10.891 |
| Average sales in a year | 0.10891 | 10.891 |
| Promotional techniques adopted | 0.0198 | 1.98 |
| Strategy adopted to maintain the sales | 0.10891 | 10.891 |

No. of hidden layers = 17 Estimation = Sequential Algorithm
Correct classification rate = 83.33%

Table 72 explains the various problems associated with the marketing function based on the location of the units. The locations of the units were classified into three major areas such as Alagappanagar, Chittissery and Pudukad.

Out of 23 units located in Alagappanagar, 43.5 per cent, 39.1 per cent, 69.6 per cent and 52.2 per cent of the units expressed that they were facing the problems such as high competition, delay in the collection period, high rate of Agents commission and low profit margin respectively. 52.2 per cent, 39.1 per cent and 43.5 per cent of the units did not face the problems of lack of market information, incidents of bad debts and more breakage of tiles respectively. 34.8 per cent of the

**Table 72**
**Problems in Marketing Function Based on the Location of the Units**

| *Problems* | | *Location* | | |
|---|---|---|---|---|
| | | *Alagappanagar (n=23)* | *Chittissery (n=39)* | *Pudukad (n=22)* |
| Lack of market Information | Strongly Disagree | 2 (8.7) | 7 (17.9) | 3 (13.6) |
| | Disagree | 12 (52.2) | 15 (38.5) | 7 (31.8) |
| | Neutral | 3 (13.0) | 5 (12.8) | 2 (9.1) |
| | Agree | 6 (26.1) | 10 (25.6) | 10 (45.5) |
| | Strongly Agree | - | 2 (5.1) | - |
| Stiff competition | Strongly Disagree | 1 (4.3) | 2 (5.1) | 3 (13.6) |
| | Disagree | 9 (39.1) | 10 (25.6) | 6 (27.3) |
| | Neutral | 3 (13.0) | 2 (5.1) | - |
| | Agree | 10 (43.5) | 23 (59.0) | 12 (54.5) |
| | Strongly Agree | - | 2 (5.1) | 1 (4.5) |
| Delay in credit collection process | Strongly Disagree | 2 (8.7) | 2 (5.1) | 2 (9.1) |
| | Disagree | 8 (34.8) | 15 (38.5) | 9 (40.9) |
| | Neutral | 2 (8.7) | 3 (7.7) | - |
| | Agree | 9 (39.1) | 19 (48.7) | 8 (36.4) |
| | Strongly Agree | 2 (8.7) | - | 3 (13.6) |
| Incidence of Bad Debts | Strongly Disagree | 2 (8.7) | 6 (15.4) | 3 (13.6) |
| | Disagree | 9 (39.1) | 19 (48.7) | 12 (54.5) |
| | Neutral | 5 (21.7) | 3 (7.7) | 1 (4.5) |
| | Agree | 6 (26.1) | 11 (28.2) | 4 (18.2) |
| | Strongly Agree | 1 (4.3) | - | 2 (9.1) |

*Contd...*

| *Problems* | | *Location* | | |
|---|---|---|---|---|
| | | *Alagappanagar (n=23)* | *Chittissery (n=39)* | *Pudukad (n=22)* |
| High rate of Agents commission | Strongly Disagree | 2 (8.7) | 4 (10.3) | 2 (9.1) |
| | Disagree | 3 (13.0) | 15 (38.5) | 7 (31.8) |
| | Neutral | 2 (8.7) | 2 (5.1) | 3 (13.6) |
| | Agree | 16 (69.6) | 14 (35.9) | 6 (27.3) |
| | Strongly Agree | - | 4 (10.3) | 4 (18.2) |
| Low profit margin | Strongly Disagree | - | 1 (2.6) | 1 (4.5) |
| | Disagree | 7 (30.4) | 13 (33.3) | 3 (13.6) |
| | Neutral | 3 (13.0) | 3 (7.7) | 6 (27.3) |
| | Agree | 12 (52.2) | 20 (51.3) | 10 (45.5) |
| | Strongly Agree | 1 (4.3) | 2 (5.1) | 2 (9.1) |
| More breakage of tiles | Strongly Disagree | 4 (17.4) | 10 (25.6) | 5 (22.7) |
| | Disagree | 10 (43.5) | 18 (46.2) | 11 (50.0) |
| | Neutral | 3 (13.0) | 1 (2.6) | 2 (9.1) |
| | Agree | 5 (21.7) | 9 (23.1) | 4 (18.2) |
| | Strongly Agree | 1 (4.3) | 1 (2.6) | - |
| High fluctuation in sales | Strongly Disagree | 1 (4.3) | 6 (15.4) | 3 (13.6) |
| | Disagree | 8 (34.8) | 21 (53.8) | 9 (40.9) |
| | Neutral | 5 (21.7) | 3 (7.7) | 2 (9.1) |
| | Agree | 8 (34.8) | 8 (20.5) | 8 (36.4) |
| | Strongly Agree | 1 (4.3) | 1 (2.6) | - |

( ) in Percentage

units revealed that high fluctuation in sales existed whereas same percentage of units disagreed to this.

Among the 39 units located in Chittissery area, 59 per cent, 48.7 per cent and 51.3 per cent of the units agreed that they encountered the problem of high competition, delay in credit collection and low profit margin respectively. The problems of lack of market information, incident of bad debts, high rate of agents commission, more breakage of tiles and high fluctuation in sales were not encountered by 38.5 per cent, 48.7 per cent, 38.5 per cent, 46.2 per cent and 53.8 per cent of the units respectively.

Finally, out of 22 units located in Pudukad area, 45.5 per cent, 44.5 per cent and 45.5 per of the units revealed that they were facing the problems of lack of market information, high competition and low profit margin respectively. The problem of delay in credit collection, incident of bad debts, high rate of Agents commission, more breakage of tiles and high fluctuation in sales were not faced by 40.9 per cent, 54.5 per cent, 31.8 per cent, 50 per cent and 40.9 per cent of the units respectively.

**Table 73**
**Stepwise Multiple Regression Analysis–The Impact of Various Marketing Problems on the Performance of Marketing Function in Alagappanagar**

*Dependent variable: Performance of marketing function (Y)*

| *Independent variable* | *Unstandardised Co-efficient* | *Standard Error* | *Standardised Co-efficient* | *t-value* | *p-value* |
|---|---|---|---|---|---|
| Constant | 4.225 | 0.343 | - | 12.309 | 0.000 |
| More breakage of tiles ($X_1$) | -0.262 | 0.124 | -0.418 | -2.109 | 0.047 |

Multiple R = 0.418 F- value = 4.448 d.f. (1, 21) P-value < 0.05
R square = 0.175

$$\hat{Y} = 4.225 - 0.262X_1$$

Where $\hat{Y}$ is the estimated performance of marketing function.

Table 73 exhibits the impact of various problems on the marketing performance. The equation describes that, on an average if "More breakage of tiles" changes by one unit, there will be a decline of 0.262 units in the performance of marketing.

The result of t-test confirms that, the estimated regression coefficient (-0.262) is significant at five per cent level. The multiple R of 0.418 shows that there exists a relationship of 41.8 per cent between "More breakage of tiles" and performance of marketing. Moreover, the $R^2$ of 0.175 confirms that the problem only explained 17.5 per cent of variation in the performance of marketing function. Finally, the result of f-test signifies that the variation was statistically significant at five per cent level. Hence, the problem of "More breakage of tiles" significantly weakened the performance of marketing function of clay tile manufacturing units located in Alagappanagar.

**Table 74**
**Stepwise Multiple Regression Analysis–The Impact of Various Marketing Problems on the Performance of Marketing Function in Chittissery**

*Dependent variable: Performance of marketing function (Y)*

| *Independent variable* | *Unstandardised Co-efficient* | *Standard Error* | *Standardised Co-efficient* | *t-value* | *p-value* |
|---|---|---|---|---|---|
| Constant | 4.892 | 0.245 | - | 20.002 | 0.000 |
| Low profit margin ($X_1$) | -0.292 | 0.072 | -0.555 | -4.057 | 0.000 |

Multiple R = 0.555    F- value = 16.457    d.f. (1,37)    P-value < 0.01
R square = 0.308

$$\hat{Y} = 4.892 - 0.292X_1$$

Where $\hat{Y}$ is the estimated performance of marketing function.

Table 74 explains the impact of various problems of marketing on its performance. The equation describes that, on an average if "Low profit margin" changes by one unit, there will be a decline of 0.292 units in the performance of marketing.

The result of t-test confirms that, the estimated regression coefficient (-0.292) is highly significant at one per cent level. The multiple R of 0.555 shows that there exists a relationship of 55.5 per cent between "Low profit margin" and performance of marketing function. Moreover, the $R^2$ of 0.308 confirms that the problem only explained 30.8 per cent of variation in the performance of marketing function. Finally, the result of f-test confirms that the variation was statistically significant at one per cent level. Hence, it can be concluded that, among the various problems in marketing, the problem of "Low profit margin" significantly eroded the performance of marketing of clay tile manufacturing units located in Chittissery.

**Table 75**
**Stepwise Multiple Regression Analysis–The Impact of Various Marketing Problems on the Performance of Marketing Function in Pudukad**

| *Dependent variable: Performance of marketing function (Y)* | | | | | |
|---|---|---|---|---|---|
| *Independent variable* | *Unstandardised Co-efficient* | *Standard Error* | *Standardised Co-efficient* | *t-value* | *p-value* |
| Constant | 4.562 | 0.337 | - | 13.517 | 0.000 |
| Delay in credit collection process ($X_1$) | -0.289 | 0.102 | -0.535 | -2.835 | 0.010 |
| Multiple R = 0.535<br>R square = 0.287 | F- value = 8.035 | d.f.. (1, 20) | | P-value < 0.01 | |

$$\hat{Y} = 4.562 - 0.289X_1$$

Where $\hat{Y}$ is the estimated performance of marketing function.

Table 75 shows the impact of various problems of marketing on its performance. The equation describes that, on an average if "Delay in credit collection process" changes by one unit, there will be a decline of 0.289 units in the performance of marketing.

The result of t-test confirms that, the estimated regression coefficient (-0.289) is highly significant at one per cent level. The multiple R of 0.535 shows that there exists a relationship of 53.5 per cent between "Delay in credit collection process" and performance of marketing function. Moreover, the $R^2$ of 0.287 confirms that the problem only explained 28.7 per cent of variation in the performance of marketing. Finally, the result of f-test confirms that the variation was statistically significant at one per cent level. Hence, it can be concluded that, among the various problems in marketing, the problem of "Delay in credit collection process" significantly weakened the performance of marketing of clay tile manufacturing units located in Pudukad.

**Table 76**

**Stepwise Multiple Regression Analysis–The Impact of Various Marketing Problems on the Performance of Marketing Function in Thrissur District**

| *Dependent variable: Performance of marketing function (Y)* | | | | | |
|---|---|---|---|---|---|
| *Independent variable* | *Unstandardised Co-efficient* | *Standard Error* | *Standardised Co-efficient* | *t-value* | *p-value* |
| Constant | 4.352 | 0.172 | - | 25.263 | 0.000 |
| Incidence of bad debts ($X_1$) | -0.224 | 0.061 | -0.374 | -3.649 | 0.000 |

Multiple R = 0.374  F- value = 13.317  d.f. (1,82)  P-value < 0.01
R square = 0.140

$$\hat{Y} = 4.352 - 0.224X_1$$

Where $\hat{Y}$ is the estimated performance of marketing function.

Table 76 exhibits the impact of various problems of marketing on its performance. The equation describes that, on an average if "Incidence of bad debts" changes by one unit, there will be a reduction of 0.224 units in the performance of marketing.

The result of t-test confirms that, the estimated regression coefficient (-0.224) is highly significant at one per cent level. The multiple R of 0.374 shows that there exists a relationship of 37.4 per cent between "Incidence of bad debts" and performance of marketing function. Moreover, the $R^2$ of 0.140 confirms that the problem was only about 14.0 per cent of variation in the performance of marketing function. Finally, the result of f-test confirms that the variation was statistically significant at one per cent level. Hence, it can be concluded that, among the various problems in marketing, the problem of "Incidence of bad debts" significantly decreased the performance of marketing of clay tile manufacturing units located in Thrissur District.

# Chapter 4

# Analysis of Finance and Labour Functions

This chapter is an analysis of the functional areas such as Finance and Labour of clay tiles manufacturing units in Thrissur District. The analysis was done at four different stages for Finance and Labour.

In the first stage, simple frequency tables and cross tabulations were used in order to analyse the organisational background and the various factors of Finance and Labour. Moreover the technique of contingency coefficient was also used to identify the association between organisational background and the various factors of Finance and Labour.

At the second stage, multiple regression analysis was used to scrutinize the contribution of various factors of Finance and Labour to its performance.

At the third stage, various problems in Finance and Labour were cross-classified and stepwise multiple regression analysis was used to identify the impact of various problems on the performance of Finance and Labour.

Table 1 explains the total capital invested by the clay tiles manufacturing units in Thrissur District. From the total of 84 units, 34.5 per cent (29) of the units had invested total capital above Rs. 30 lakhs followed by 32.1 per cent (27) with Rs.10 to 20 lakhs and 29.8 per cent (25) with Rs. 20 to 30 lakhs.

Hence, 34.5 per cent of the units had invested Rs. 30 lakhs and above in their business.

**Table 1**
**Investment of Capital**

| *Amount (Rs. in Lakhs)* | *No. of Units* | *Per cent* |
|---|---|---|
| Less than 10 | 3 | 3.6 |
| 10–20 | 27 | 32.1 |
| 20–30 | 25 | 29.8 |
| More than 30 | 29 | 34.5 |
| Total | 84 | 100.0 |

*Source:* Primary Data.

**Table 2**
**Investment of Owned Fund**

| *Amount (Rs. in Lakhs)* | *No. of Units* | *Per cent* |
|---|---|---|
| Less than 5 | 24 | 28.6 |
| 5–10 | 31 | 36.9 |
| 10–15 | 9 | 10.7 |
| More than 15 | 20 | 23.8 |
| Total | 84 | 100.0 |

*Source:* Primary Data.

Table 2 shows the fund invested by the owners of the units. From the total of 84 units, 36.9 per cent (31) of the units had invested their owned fund of Rs.5 to 10 lakhs followed by 28.6 per cent (24) with below Rs. 5 lakhs and 23.8 per cent (20) with above Rs. 15 lakhs.

Hence, 36.9 per cent of the units had invested Rs. 5 to 10 lakhs.

**Table 3**
**Sources of Borrowed Funds**

| *Sources* | *No. of Units* | *Per cent* |
|---|---|---|
| Kerala Finance Corporation | 69 | 82.1 |
| Friends/Relatives | 3 | 3.6 |
| Other loans from outsiders | 11 | 13.1 |
| None | 1 | 1.2 |
| Total | 84 | 100.0 |

*Source:* Primary Data.

Table 3 discloses the various sources of fund borrowed by the units. 82.1 per cent (69) of the units were raising their funds through Kerala Finance Corporation, 13.1 per cent (11) from the outsiders and 3.6 per cent from their friends and relatives.

Hence, the majority of 82.1 per cent of the units were raising their funds through the Kerala Finance Corporation.

**Table 4**
**Long-term Loans Received**

| *Amount (Rs. in Lakhs)* | *No. of Units* | *Per cent* |
|---|---|---|
| Less than 5 | 5 | 6.0 |
| 5–10 | 26 | 31.0 |
| 10–15 | 31 | 36.8 |
| More than 15 | 22 | 26.2 |
| Total | 84 | 100.0 |

*Source:* Primary Data.

Table 4 presents the amount of long-term loans received by the units. Out of 84 units, 36.8 per cent (31) were raising a long-term loan of Rs. 10 to 15 lakhs, 31 per cent (26) a loan of Rs. 5 to 10 lakhs and 26.2 per cent (22) above 15 lakhs.

Hence, 36.8 per cent of the units were raising long-term loans of Rs.10 to 15 lakhs for their business.

**Table 5**
**Rate of Interest**

| *Rate (in Per cent)* | *No. of Units* | *Per cent* |
|---|---|---|
| Less than 5 | – | – |
| 5–10 | 12 | 14.3 |
| 10–15 | 42 | 50.0 |
| More than 15 | 30 | 35.7 |
| Total | 84 | 100.0 |

*Source:* Primary Data.

Table 5 shows the rate of interest charged by the Banks and Financial Institutions on the loans obtained by the units. Out of 84 units, exactly 50 per cent (42) had stated that the banks and financial institutions charged an interest of 10 to 15 per cent on their loans, 35.7 per cent (30) stated above 15 per cent and 14.3 per cent (12) 5 to 10 per cent.

Hence, the maximum 50 per cent of the units had paid an interest of 10 to 15 per cent per annum.

**Table 6**
**Subsidies Received from the Government**

| *Response* | *No. of Units* | *Per cent* |
|---|---|---|
| Yes | 72 | 85.7 |
| No | 12 | 14.3 |
| Total | 84 | 100.0 |

*Source:* Primary Data.

Table 6 describes the units' responses to the subsidies received from the Government. More than 85 per cent (72) of the units were receiving subsidies from State Government and the remaining 14.3 per cent (12) of the units were not.

Hence, a majority of 85.7 per cent of the units were receiving subsidies from the State Government.

**Table 7**
**Sources of Working Capital**

| *Sources* | *No. of Units* | *Per cent* |
|---|---|---|
| Collection from debtors/cash sales | 28 | 33.3 |
| Short term loans | 2 | 2.4 |
| Friends/Relatives | 4 | 4.8 |
| Advance from customers | 3 | 3.6 |
| Collection from Debtors/cash sales and short term Loans | 1 | 1.2 |
| Collection from debtors/cash sales and Friends/ Relatives | 11 | 13.1 |
| Collection from debtors/cash sales and Advance from customers | 35 | 41.6 |
| Total | 84 | 100.0 |

*Source:* Primary Data.

Table 7 states the various sources of working capital of the units. Out of 84 units the majority of 41.6 per cent (35) of the units were raising their working capital through collection from debtors, cash sales and getting advances from their customers. Similarly, 33.3 per cent (28) of the clay tiles manufacturing units were raising the working capital by the mode collection from debtors and through cash sales. Hence, a majority 41.6 per cent of the units were raising their working capital through collection from debtors, cash sales and getting advances from their customers.

**Table 8**
**Credit Collection Period**

| *Period* | *No. of Units* | *Per cent* |
|---|---|---|
| Less than 10 days | 36 | 42.9 |
| 10–20 days | 35 | 41.6 |
| 1 month | 12 | 14.3 |
| More than 1 month | 1 | 1.2 |
| Total | 84 | 100.0 |

*Source:* Primary Data.

Table 8 presents the average collection period allowed by the units. Out of 84 units, 42.9 per cent (36) allow a collection period of less than 10 days, 41.6 per cent (35) from 10 to 20 days and 14.3 per cent (12) upto 1 month.

Hence, a collection period of ten days is allowed by majority of the 42.9 per cent of units.

**Table 9**
**Selling Price of Tiles Per Unit**

| *Amount (in Rupees)* | *No. of Units* | *Per cent* |
|---|---|---|
| Less than 2 | - | - |
| 2–4 | 64 | 76.2 |
| More than 4 | 20 | 23.8 |
| Total | 84 | 100.0 |

*Source:* Primary Data.

Table 9 shows the range of selling price of flooring/roofing tiles fixed by the units. More than three-fourth of the units were fixing the price between Rs. 2 and 4 and remaining 23.8 per cent (20) Rs. 4 and above.

Hence, a majority of 76.2 per cent of the units were fixing the price for their clay tiles between Rs. 2 and 4.

Table 10 gives the cost of clay make for one load of 6000 tiles. 59.5 per cent of the units were spending Rs.2000 to 4000 to manufacture 6000 clay tiles followed by 16.7 per cent (14) Rs. 4000 to 6000 and 15.5 per cent (13) Rs. 8000 and above.

Hence, the maximum 59.5 per cent of the units were spending Rs. 2000 to 4000 on clay to make a load of 6000 tiles.

**Table 10**
**Cost of Clay Per Load**

| *Amount (in Rupees)* | *No. of Units* | *Per cent* |
|---|---|---|
| 2000–4000 | 50 | 59.5 |
| 4000–6000 | 14 | 16.7 |
| 6000–8000 | 7 | 8.3 |
| More than 8000 | 13 | 15.5 |
| Total | 84 | 100.0 |

*Source:* Primary Data.

**Table 11**
**Cost of Firewood Per Load**

| *Amount (in Rupees)* | *No. of Units* | *Per cent* |
|---|---|---|
| Less than 2500 | 4 | 4.8 |
| 2500–5000 | 59 | 70.2 |
| 5000–7500 | 11 | 13.1 |
| More than 7500 | 10 | 11.9 |
| Total | 84 | 100.0 |

*Source:* Primary Data.

Table 11 provides particulars of the cost of firewood to make one load of 6000 tiles. Out of 84 units, 70.2 per cent (59) of the units were purchasing the firewood for Rs. 2500 to 5000 to manufacture one load of clay tiles, 13.1 per cent (11) from Rs. 5000 to 7500 and 11.9 per cent (10) above Rs. 7500.

Hence, a majority of 70.2 per cent of the units were purchasing firewood for Rs. 2500 to 5000 to manufacture a load of 6000 clay tiles.

**Table 12**
**Cost of Oil Per Load**

| *Amount (in Rupees)* | *No. of Units* | *Per cent* |
|---|---|---|
| Less than 500 | 17 | 20.2 |
| 500–1000 | 47 | 56.0 |
| 1000–1500 | 12 | 14.3 |
| More than 1500 | 8 | 9.5 |
| Total | 84 | 100.0 |

*Source:* Primary Data.

Table 12 shows the cost of oil to produce one load of 6000 tiles. 56 per cent (47) of the units were purchasing oil for Rs. 500 to 1000 to make a load of tiles, 20.2 per cent (17) below Rs. 500 and 14.3 per cent (12) Rs. 1000 to 1500.

Hence, the maximum 56 per cent of the units were purchasing oil for Rs. 500 to 1000 to manufacture the same number of clay tiles.

**Table 13**
**Labour Charges Per Load**

| *Amount (in Rupees)* | *No. of Units* | *Per cent* |
|---|---|---|
| Less than 2500 | 8 | 9.5 |
| 2500–5000 | 45 | 53.6 |
| 5000–7500 | 18 | 21.4 |
| More than 7500 | 13 | 15.5 |
| Total | 84 | 100.0 |

*Source:* Primary Data.

Table 13 provides the labour charges for manufacturing one load of clay tiles. More than 50 per cent (45) of the units incurred an expenditure of Rs. 2500 to 5000 followed by 21.4 per cent (18) Rs. 5000 to 7500 and 15.5 per cent (13) with Rs. 7500 and above.

Hence, the maximum 53.6 per cent of the units were paid labour charges of Rs. 2500 to 5000 for manufacturing a load of clay tiles.

**Table 14**
**Electricity Charges Per Load**

| *Amount (in Rupees)* | *No. of Units* | *Per cent* |
|---|---|---|
| Less than 600 | 6 | 7.1 |
| 600–1200 | 44 | 52.4 |
| 1200–1800 | 29 | 34.5 |
| More than 1800 | 5 | 6.0 |
| Total | 84 | 100.0 |

*Source:* Primary Data.

Table 14 gives a picture of electricity charges incurred by the units. From the total of 84 units, more than 50 per cent (44) of the units incurred the electricity expenditure of Rs. 600 to

1200 to manufacture one load of clay tiles, 34.5 per cent (29) Rs. 1200 to 1800 and 7.1 per cent (6) below Rs. 600.

Hence, a majority of 52.4 per cent of the units paid Rs. 600 to 1200 for electricity to manufacture one load of clay tiles.

**Table 15**
**Investment in Land and Buildings**

| *Amount (Rs. in Lakhs)* | *No. of Units* | *Per cent* |
|---|---|---|
| Less than 5 | 7 | 8.3 |
| 5–10 | 42 | 50.0 |
| 10–15 | 28 | 33.4 |
| More than 15 | 7 | 8.3 |
| Total | 84 | 100.0 |

*Source:* Primary Data.

Table 15 shows the investment made by the units in land and building. Out of 84 units, exactly 50 per cent (42) of the units had invested Rs. 5 to 10 lakhs in land and building followed by 33.4 per cent (28) of them which invested Rs.10 to 15 lakhs.

Hence, a maximum 50 per cent of the units had invested Rs. 5 to 10 lakhs in land and building.

**Table 16**
**Investment in Plant and Machinery**

| *Amount (Rs. in Lakhs)* | *No. of Units* | *Per cent* |
|---|---|---|
| Less than 3 | 6 | 7.1 |
| 3–6 | 22 | 26.2 |
| 6–9 | 21 | 25.0 |
| More than 9 | 35 | 41.7 |
| Total | 84 | 100.0 |

*Source:* Primary Data.

Table 16 gives particulars of the investment made by the units in plant and machinery. From the total of 84 units, 41.7 per cent (35) of the units had invested Rs. 9 lakhs and above in plant and machinery followed by 26.2 per cent (22) with Rs. 3 to 6 lakhs and 25 per cent (21) with Rs. 6 to 9 lakhs.

Hence, a maximum of 41.7 per cent of the units had invested Rs. 9 lakhs and above in plant and machinery.

**Table 17**
**Investment in Electrical Fittings**

| *Amount (in Rupees)* | *No. of Units* | *Per cent* |
|---|---|---|
| Less than 30000 | 11 | 13.1 |
| 30000–60000 | 38 | 45.2 |
| 60000–90000 | 11 | 13.1 |
| More than 90000 | 24 | 28.6 |
| Total | 84 | 100.0 |

*Source:* Primary Data.

Table 17 shows the investment made by the units in electrical fittings. Out of 84 units, 45.2 per cent (38) of the units had invested Rs. 30000 to 60000 in electrical fittings, 28.6 per cent (24) above Rs. 90000 and 13.1 per cent (11) invested below Rs. 30000.

Hence, a majority of 45.2 per cent of the units had invested Rs. 30000 to 60000 in electrical fittings.

**Table 18**
**Investment in Pallets and Frames**

| *Amount (in Rupees)* | *No. of Units* | *Per cent* |
|---|---|---|
| Less than 30000 | 1 | 1.2 |
| 30000–60000 | 15 | 17.8 |
| 60000–90000 | 21 | 25.0 |
| More than 90000 | 47 | 56.0 |
| Total | 84 | 100.0 |

*Source:* Primary Data.

Table 18 shows the investment in pallets and frames. 56 per cent (47) of the units had invested above Rs. 90000 in pallets and frames, 25 per cent (21) had invested Rs. 60000 to 90000 and 17.8 per cent (15) of them Rs. 30000 to 60000.

Hence, a maximum 56 per cent of the units had invested Rs. 30000 to 60000 in pallets and frames.

Table 19 gives the investment in Chimney/Kiln made by the clay tiles manufacturing units. 39.3 per cent (33) of the units had invested Rs.3 to 6 lakhs in kiln followed by 29.8 per cent (25) with Rs. 3 lakhs and 23.8 per cent (20) Rs. 6 to 9 lakhs.

Hence, the maximum 39.3 per cent of the units had invested Rs. 3 to 6 lakhs in chimney/kiln.

**Table 19**
**Investment in Chimney/Kiln**

| *Amount (Rs. in lakhs)* | *No. of Units* | *Per cent* |
|---|---|---|
| Less than 3 | 25 | 29.8 |
| 3–6 | 33 | 39.3 |
| 6–9 | 20 | 23.8 |
| More than 9 | 6 | 7.1 |
| Total | 84 | 100.0 |

*Source:* Primary Data.

**Table 20**
**Investment in Furniture and Fittings**

| *Amount (in Rupees)* | *No. of Units* | *Per cent* |
|---|---|---|
| Less than 7000 | 4 | 4.8 |
| 7000–14000 | 13 | 15.5 |
| 14000–21000 | 35 | 41.6 |
| More than 21000 | 32 | 38.1 |
| Total | 84 | 100.0 |

*Source:* Primary Data.

Table 20 shows the investment in furniture and fittings made by the clay tiles manufacturing units. Out of 84 units, 41.6 per cent (35) had invested Rs. 14000 to 21000 in furniture and followed by 38.1 per cent (32) with Rs. 21000 and above and 15.5 per cent (13) Rs. 7000 to 14000.

Hence, a majority of 41.6 per cent of the units had invested Rs. 14000 to 21000 in furniture and fittings.

**Table 21**
**Expected Rate of Return**

| *Expected Rate of Return (in Per cent)* | *No. of Units* | *Per cent* |
|---|---|---|
| Less than 25 | 5 | 6.0 |
| 25–50 | 77 | 91.6 |
| More than 50 | 2 | 2.4 |
| Total | 84 | 100.0 |

*Source:* Primary Data.

Table 21 describes the rate of return expected by the units. Out of 84 units, more than 90 per cent of the units expected a return of 25 to 50 per cent per annum and the remaining 6 per cent (5) expected below 25 per cent and only two units expected above 50 per cent rate of return.

Hence, the maximum of 91.6 per cent of the units expected a rate of return of 25 to 50 per cent per annum.

**Table 22**
**Average Actual Rate of Return**

| *Average Actual Rate of Return (in Per cent)* | *No. of Units* | *Per cent* |
|---|---|---|
| Less than 15 | 48 | 57.1 |
| 15–30 | 36 | 42.9 |
| More than 30 | - | - |
| Total | 84 | 100.0 |

*Source:* Primary Data.

Table 22 shows the average actual rate of return achieved by the units. Out of 84 units, 57.1 per cent (48) achieved actual return of less than 15 per cent and 42.9 per cent (36) of the units achieved 15 to 30 per cent rate of return per annum.

Hence, the maximum of 57.1 per cent of the units achieved only a rate of return of less than 15 per cent.

**Table 23**
**Performance of Finance Function**

| *Level* | *No. of Units* | *Per cent* |
|---|---|---|
| Bad | 16 | 19.0 |
| Moderate | 23 | 27.4 |
| Good | 43 | 51.2 |
| Excellent | 2 | 2.4 |
| Total | 84 | 100.0 |

*Source:* Primary Data.

Table 23 shows the performance levels of the finance function of the units. Out of 84 units, 51.2 per cent (43) had stated that their performance of finance was good, 27.4 per cent (23) stated that it was moderate and 19 per cent (16) bad.

Hence, a majority of 51.2 per cent of the clay tiles manufacturing units stated that their overall performance of finance was good.

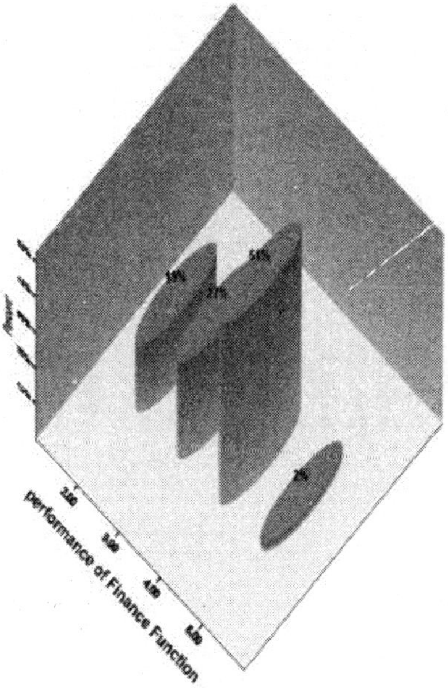


**Diagram 1**

The following key points may be observed from the Table 24.

- In terms of total capital 12 out of 23 units (52.2 per cent) in Alagappanagar have more than Rs.30 lakhs each whereas 19 out of 39 units (48.7 per cent) in Chittissery have Rs.20 to 30 lakhs each and 11 out of 22 units (50 per cent) in Pudukad have Rs.10 to 20 lakhs each. So, units in Alagappanagar lead in terms of total capital.
- In terms of invested own funds, Alagappanagar and Chittissery lead, with 8 out of 23 units (34.8 per cent) and 15 out of 39 units (38.5 per cent) having Rs.5 to 10 lakhs. The other location Pudukad has 40.9 per cent of the units with funds less than Rs.5 lakhs.
- A vast majority of units in all the three location depend on Kerala Finance Corporation for borrowing money.
- 30.4 per cent of Alagappanagar units get a long-term loan of Rs.15 lakhs and above and another 30.4 per cent

**Table 24**
**Factors of Finance Based on the Location of the Units**

| Factors | | Location | | |
|---|---|---|---|---|
| | | *Alagappanagar (n=23)* | *Chittissery (n=39)* | *Pudukad (n=22)* |
| Total investedcapital[c] (Rs. in Lakhs) | Below 10 | 2 (8.7) | - | 1 (4.5) |
| | 10-20 | 6 (26.1) | 10 (25.6) | 11 (50.0) |
| | 20-30 | 3 (13.0) | 19 (48.7) | 3 (13.6) |
| | Above 30 | 12 (52.2) | 10 (25.6) | 7 (31.8) |
| Invested own fund (Rs.in Lakhs) | Below 5 | 6 (26.1) | 9 (23.1) | 9 (40.9) |
| | 5-10 | 8 (34.8) | 15 (38.5) | 8 (36.4) |
| | 10-15 | 2 (8.7) | 7 (17.9) | - |
| | Above 15 | 7 (30.4) | 8 (20.5) | 5 (22.7) |
| Major source of borrowed funds | Kerala Finance Corporation | 20 (87.0) | 30 (76.9) | 19 (86.4) |
| | Friends/Relatives | - | 1 (2.6) | 2 (9.1) |
| | Other loans from outsiders | 3 (13.0) | 7 (17.9) | 1 (4.5) |
| | None | - | 1 (2.6) | - |
| Long term loans received (Rs. in Lakhs) | Below 5 | 2 (8.7) | 1 (2.6) | 2 (9.1) |
| | 5-10 | 7 (30.4) | 9 (23.1) | 10 (45.5) |
| | 10-15 | 7 (30.4) | 18 (46.2) | 6 (27.3) |
| | Above 15 | 7 (30.4) | 11 (28.2) | 4 (18.2) |
| Rate of interest (in Per cent) | 5-10 | 2 (8.7) | 5 (12.8) | 5 (22.7) |
| | 10-15 | 9 (39.1) | 19 (48.7) | 14 (63.6) |
| | Above 15 | 12 (52.2) | 15 (38.5) | 3 (13.6) |
| Subsidies received from Govt. | Yes | 20 (87.0) | 33 (84.6) | 19 (86.4) |
| | No | 3 (13.0) | 6 (15.4) | 3 (13.6) |

*Contd...*

| *Factors* | | *Location* | | |
|---|---|---|---|---|
| | | *Alagappanagar (n=23)* | *Chittissery (n=39)* | *Pudukad (n=22)* |
| Sources of working capital | Collection from debtors/cash sales | 9 (39.1) | 10 (25.6) | 9 (40.9) |
| | Short term loan | 1 (4.3) | - | 1 (4.5) |
| | Friends/Relatives | - | 2 (5.1) | 2 (9.1) |
| | Advance from customers | - | 2 (5.1) | 1 (4.5) |
| | Collection from Debtors/cash sales and short term Loan | 1 (4.3) | - | - |
| | Collection from debtors/cash sales and Friends/Relatives | 3 (13.0) | 5 (12.8) | 3(13.6) |
| | Collection from debtors/cash sales and Advance from customers | 9 (39.1) | 20(51.3) | 6 (27.3) |
| Credit collection period | Less than 10 days | 11(47.8) | 16 (41.0) | 9 (40.9) |
| | 10-20 days | 6(26.1) | 19 (48.7) | 10 (45.5) |
| | 1 month | 6(26.1) | 4 (10.3) | 2 (9.1) |
| | Above 1 month | - | - | 1 (4.5) |
| Selling price of Flooring/Roofing tiles per unit(in Rupees) | 2-4 | 16 (69.6) | 30 (76.9) | 18 (81.8) |
| | Above 4 | 7 (30.4) | 9 (23.1) | 4 (18.2) |
| Cost of clay per load (in Rupees) | 2000-4000 | 13 (56.5) | 23 (59.0) | 14 (63.6) |
| | 4000-6000 | 3 (13.0) | 7 (17.9) | 4 (18.2) |
| | 6000-8000 | 3 (13.0) | 3 (7.7) | 1 (4.5) |
| | Above 8000 | 4 (17.4) | 6 (15.4) | 3 (13.6) |

*Contd...*

| *Factors* | | *Location* | | |
|---|---|---|---|---|
| | | *Alagappanagar (n=23)* | *Chittissery (n=39)* | *Pudukad (n=22)* |
| Cost of Firewood per load (in Rupees) | Below 2500 | 1 (4.3) | 2 (5.1) | 1 (4.5) |
| | 2500-5000 | 14 (60.9) | 28 (71.8) | 17 (77.3) |
| | 5000-7500 | 4 (17.4) | 5 (12.8) | 2 (9.1) |
| | 7500 and Above | 4 (17.4) | 4 (10.3) | 2 (9.1) |
| Cost of Oil per load (in Rupees) | Below 500 | 4 (17.4) | 8 (20.5) | 5 (22.7) |
| | 500-1000 | 12 (52.2) | 22 (56.4) | 13 (59.1) |
| | 1000-1500 | 5 (21.7) | 4 (10.3) | 3 (13.6) |
| | 1500 and Above | 2 (8.7) | 5 (12.8) | 1 (4.5) |
| Labour charges per load (in Rupees) | Below 2500 | 3 (13.0) | 5 (12.8) | - |
| | 2500-5000 | 10 (43.5) | 21 (53.8) | 14 (63.6) |
| | 5000-7500 | 4 (17.4) | 9 (23.1) | 5 (22.7) |
| | 7500 and Above | 6 (26.1) | 4 (10.3) | 3 (13.6) |
| Electricity charges per load (in Rupees) | Below 600 | 2 (8.7) | 3 (7.7) | 1 (4.5) |
| | 600-1200 | 8 (34.8) | 22 (56.4) | 14 (63.6) |
| | 1200-1800 | 10 (43.5) | 13 (33.3) | 6 (27.3) |
| | 1800 and Above | 3 (13.0) | 1 (2.6) | 1 (4.5) |
| Investment in Land and Buildings [d] (Rs.in Lakhs) | Below 5 | 2 (8.7) | 1 (2.6) | 4 (18.2) |
| | 5–10 | 13 (56.5) | 18 (46.2) | 11 (50.0) |
| | 10–15 | 5 (21.7) | 19 (48.7) | 4 (18.2) |
| | Above 15 | 3 (13.0) | 1 (2.6) | 3 (13.6) |
| Investment in Plant and Machinery (Rs.in Lakhs) | Below 3 | 3 (13.0) | - | 3(13.6) |
| | 3–6 | 4 (17.4) | 9 (23.1) | 9 (40.9) |
| | 6–9 | 6 (26.1) | 12 (30.8) | 3 (13.6) |
| | Above 9 | 10 (43.5) | 18 (46.2) | 7 (31.8) |

*Contd...*

| Factors | | Location | | |
|---|---|---|---|---|
| | | *Alagappanagar (n=23)* | *Chittissery (n=39)* | *Pudukad (n=22)* |
| Investment in Plant and Machinery (Rs.in Lakhs) | Below 3 | 3 (13.0) | - | 3(13.6) |
| | 3 – 6 | 4 (17.4) | 9 (23.1) | 9 (40.9) |
| | 6 – 9 | 6 (26.1) | 12 (30.8) | 3 (13.6) |
| | Above 9 | 10 (43.5) | 18 (46.2) | 7 (31.8) |
| Investment in Electrical Fittings (in Rupees) | Below 30000 | 5 (21.7) | 3 (7.7) | 3 (13.6) |
| | 30000-60000 | 7 (30.4) | 20(51.3) | 11 (50.0) |
| | 60000-90000 | 1 (4.3) | 8(20.5) | 2 (9.1) |
| | 90000 and Above | 10 (43.5) | 8(20.5) | 6 (27.3) |
| Investment in Pallets and Frames (in Rupees) | Below 30000 | 1 (4.3) | - | - |
| | 30000-60000 | 5 (21.7) | 4(10.3) | 6 (27.3) |
| | 60000-90000 | 2 (8.7) | 14 (35.9) | 5 (22.7) |
| | 90000 and Above | 15 (65.2) | 21 (53.8) | 11 (50.0) |
| Investment in Chimney (Rs.in Lakhs) | Below 3 | 8 (34.8) | 9 (23.1) | 8 (36.4) |
| | 3 – 6 | 6 (26.1) | 20 (51.3) | 7 (31.8) |
| | 6 – 9 | 6 (26.1) | 10 (25.6) | 4 (18.2) |
| | Above 9 | 3 (13.0) | - | 3 (13.6) |
| Investment in Furniture and Fittings (in Rupees) | Below 7000 | 3 (13.0) | - | 1 (4.5) |
| | 7000-14000 | 1 (4.3) | 10 (25.6) | 2 (9.1) |
| | 14000-21000 | 8 (34.8) | 16 (41.0) | 11 (50.0) |
| | 21000 and Above | 11 (47.8) | 13 (33.3) | 8 (36.4) |

*Contd...*

| *Factors* | | *Location* | | |
|---|---|---|---|---|
| | | *Alagappanagar (n=23)* | *Chittissery (n=39)* | *Pudukad (n=22)* |
| Expected rate of return(in Per cent) | Below 25 | 1 (4.3) | 4 (10.3) | - |
| | 25-50 | 22 (95.7) | 33 (84.6) | 22 (100.0) |
| | 50-75 | - | 2 (5.1) | - |
| Average Actual rate of return (in Per cent) | Below 15 | 14 (60.9) | 23 (59.0) | 11 (50.0) |
| | 15-30 | 9 (39.1) | 16 (41.0) | 11 (50.0) |
| Performance of Finance function [c] | Bad | 3 (13.0) | 3 (7.7) | 10 (45.5) |
| | Moderate | 10 (43.5) | 10 (25.6) | 3 (13.6) |
| | Good | 10 (43.5) | 24 (61.5) | 9 (40.9) |
| | Excellent | - | 2 (5.1) | - |

( ) in Percentage Contingency Coefficient ≥ 0.5 P-Value <0.01[a]
Contingency Coefficient ≥ 0.5 P-Value <0.05[b]
Contingency Coefficient ≤ 0.5 P-Value <0.01[c]
Contingency Coefficient ≤ 0.5 P-Value <0.05[d]

Rs. 10-15 lakhs and a third 30.4 per cent Rs. 5 to 10 lakhs. 46.2 per cent units in Chittissery get Rs. 10 to 15 lakhs and 45.5 per cent units of Pudukad get Rs. 5 lakhs. So, Alagappanagar units lead in getting long-term loans.

- 52.5 per cent of the Alagappanagar units are prepared to pay an interest of 15 per cent and above whereas 48.7 per cent of Chittissery units and 63.3 per cent of Pudukad units pay 10 to 15 per cent interest.
- A vast majority of the units of all the three location get subsidies from the Government.
- Major sources of working capital are collection from debtors, cash sales and advances from customers -39.1 per cent of Alagappanagar units, 51.3 per cent of Chittissery units and 40.9 per cent of Pudukad units.
- Most of the units are unwilling to allow the customers a long period for payment. 47.8 per cent of Alagappanagar units insist on 10 days or earlier. 48.7 per cent and 45.5 per cent of the units in Chittissery and Pudukad allow 10 to 20 days and very few units a month or more for payment.
- The selling price of a tile is just Rs. 2 to 4 in 69.6 per cent, 76.9 per cent and 81.8 per cent of the units of the three localities.
- A majority of units in Alagappanagar 56.5 per cent, Chittissery 59 per cent and Pudukad 63.6 per cent keep the cost of clay lowest i.e. Rs.2000 to 4000 per load of 6000 tiles.
- The cost of firewood is maintained considerably low Rs. 2500 to 5000 per load–by a majority of units in Alagappanagar 60.9 per cent, Chittissery 71.8 per cent and Pudukad 77.3 per cent.
- Most of the units of all three locations (52.2 per cent, 56.4 per cent and 59.1 per cent) manage to keep the cost of oil at Rs. 500 to 1000 per load. This is moderate.
- Again, most of the units of all three locations viz., 43.5 per cent, 53.8 per cent and 63.6 per cent manage to keep

the cost of labour between Rs. 2500 and 5000 which is neither too low, nor too high.

- The units of Chittissery (56.4 per cent) and Pudukad (63.6 per cent) manage to keep electricity charges comparatively low i.e. between Rs. 600 and 1200, while 43.5 per cent of Alagappanagar spend Rs. 1200 to 1800 on every load of 6000 tiles. The highest consumption of electricity Rs. 1800 and above is by 13 per cent of Alagappanagar, 2.6 per cent of Chittissery and 4.5 per cent of Pudukad units.
- While 56.5 per cent of Alagappanagar units and 50 per cent of Pudukad units have invested Rs. 5 to 10 lakhs, 48.7 per cent of Chittissery units have invested Rs.10 to 15 lakhs in land and buildings. Only very few units invest more than Rs. 15 lakhs (altogether only 7 out of 84 units).
- Investment in plant and machinery is indispensable. 43.5 per cent of Alagappanagar units and 46.2 per cent of Chittissery units make the highest investment of more than Rs.9 lakhs, as compared with 31.8 per cent of Pudukad units.
- While 43.5 per cent of Alagappanagar units spend Rs. 90000 and above on electrical fittings, 51.3 per cent of Chittissery and 50 per cent of Pudukad units spend only Rs. 30000 to 60000.
- No unit can escape spending on pallets and frames. Naturally, 65.2 per cent of units in Alagappanagar, 53.8 per cent of units in Chittissery and 50 per cent of units in Pudukad spend the maximum of almost Rs. 1 lakh on acquiring pallets and frames.
- Expenses on chimney are kept at a minimum (below Rs.3 lakhs) by 34.8 per cent in Alagappanagar units and 36.4 per cent in Pudukad units, while 51.3 per cent in Chittissery units spend between Rs.3 and 6 lakhs.
- While 47.8 per cent of Alagappanagar units spend the maximum amount of Rs. 21000 and above on furniture

and fittings, a majority of the units in the other two locations (41 per cent and 50 per cent) keep the expenses between Rs. 14000 and 21000.

- Most of the units in three locations viz., 95.7 per cent, 84.6 per cent and 100 per cent expected a return of 25 to 50 per cent.
- Expectation is one thing; achievement is another! Most of the units (60.9 per cent, 59 per cent and 50 per cent) realized return of 15 per cent or below.
- Financial performance is fairly good in the case of 43.5 per cent of the units in Alagappanagar and 61.5 per cent in the case of Chittissery. But 40.5 per cent of Pudukad units have registered bad performance.

Moreover, the results of the contingency co-efficient suggest that the factors of finance such as total capital invested, investment in land and buildings and performance of finance function were associated with the location of the units and these were statistically significant at one per cent and five per cent level.

The salient features of Table 25 are:

- 80 per cent of the units established upto 1981, 57.1 per cent set up between 1981 and 1985 and 40 per cent of the units established between 1985 and 1990 have invested above Rs. 30 lakhs each but only 18 out of 42 units established after 1990 have invested Rs. 10 to 20 lakhs.
- Invested owner fund exceeds Rs.15 lakhs in the case of 60 per cent of units established prior to 1980 and 28 per cent in the case of units established in 1981 to 1985. It is less than Rs. 5 lakhs in the case of 40.5 per cent of the units established after 1990 and between Rs.5 and 10 lakhs in the case of 46.7 per cent of units established in 1985 to 1990. The invested owner fund shows a decreasing trend.
- Kerala Finance Corporation remains the major source of borrowing over the whole period.

**Table 25**
**Factors of Finance Based on the Year of Establishment**

| *Factors* | | *Year* | | | |
|---|---|---|---|---|---|
| | | *Before 1981 (n=5)* | *1981-1985 (n=7)* | *1985-1990 (n=30)* | *1990 and After (n=42)* |
| Total invested capital (Rs. in lakhs) | Below 10 | - | - | 1 (3.3) | 2 (4.8) |
| | 10-20 | - | 2 (28.6) | 7 (23.3) | 18 (42.9) |
| | 20-30 | 1 (20.0) | 1 (14.3) | 10 (33.3) | 13 (31.0) |
| | Above 30 | 4 (80.0) | 4 (57.1) | 12 (40.0) | 9 (21.4) |
| Invested own fund (Rs. in lakhs) | Below 5 | - | 2 (28.6) | 5 (16.7) | 17 (40.5) |
| | 5-10 | - | 2 (28.6) | 14 (46.7) | 15 (35.7) |
| | 10-15 | 2 (40.0) | 1 (14.3) | 3 (10.0) | 3 (7.1) |
| | Above 15 | 3 (60.0) | 2 (28.6) | 8 (26.7) | 7 (16.7) |
| Major source of borrowed funds [c] | Kerala Finance Corporation | 3 (60.0) | 4 (57.1) | 25 (83.3) | 37 (88.1) |
| | Friends / Relatives | - | - | 1 (3.3) | 2 (4.8) |
| | Other loans from outsiders | 1 (20.0) | 3 (42.9) | 4 (13.3) | 3 (7.1) |
| | None | 1 (20.0) | - | - | - |
| Long term loans received (Rs. in lakhs) | Below 5 | - | - | 1 (3.3) | 4 (9.5) |
| | 5-10 | 1 (20.0) | 2 (28.6) | 8 (26.7) | 15 (35.7) |
| | 10-15 | 2 (40.0) | 2 (28.6) | 13 (43.3) | 14 (33.3) |
| | Above 15 | 2 (40.0) | 3 (42.9) | 8 (26.7) | 9 (21.4) |
| Rate of interest (in Per cent) | 5-10 | 2 (40.0) | 1 (14.3) | 4 (13.3) | 5 (11.9) |
| | 10-15 | 1 (20.0) | 2 (28.6) | 14 (46.7) | 25 (59.5) |
| | Above 15 | 2 (40.0) | 4 (57.1) | 12 (40.0) | 12 (28.6) |

*Contd...*

| Factors | | Year | | | |
|---|---|---|---|---|---|
| | | *Before 1981 (n=5)* | *1981-1985 (n=7)* | *1985-1990 (n=30)* | *1990 and After (n=42)* |
| Rate of interest (in Per cent) | 5-10 | 2 (40.0) | 1 (14.3) | 4 (13.3) | 5 (11.9) |
| | 10-15 | 1 (20.0) | 2 (28.6) | 14 (46.7) | 25 (59.5) |
| | Above 15 | 2 (40.0) | 4 (57.1) | 12 (40.0) | 12 (28.6) |
| Subsidies received from Govt. | Yes | 3 (60.0) | 5 (71.4) | 25 (83.3) | 39 (92.9) |
| | No | 2 (40.0) | 2 (28.6) | 5 (16.7) | 3 (7.1) |
| Sources of working capital | Collection from debtors/ cash sales | 1 (20.0) | 2 (28.6) | 12 (40.0) | 13 (31.0) |
| | Short term loan | - | - | 2 (6.7) | - |
| | Friends/Relatives | - | - | 1 (3.3) | 3 (7.1) |
| | Advance from customers | - | - | 2 (6.7) | 1 (2.4) |
| | Collection from Debtors/ cash sales and short term Loan | - | - | - | 1 (2.4) |
| | Collection from debtors/cash sales and Friends/Relatives | 1 (20.0) | 1 (14.3) | 3 (10.0) | 6 (14.3) |
| | Collection from debtors / cash sales and Advance from customers | 3 (60.0) | 4 (57.1) | 10 (33.3) | 18 (42.9) |
| Credit collection period | Less than 10 days | 3 (60.0) | 3 (42.9) | 15 (50.0) | 15 (35.7) |
| | 10-20 days | 2 (40.0) | 1 (14.3) | 11 (36.7) | 21 (50.0) |
| | 1 month | - | 3 (42.9) | 4 (13.3) | 5 (11.9) |
| | Above 1 month | - | - | - | 1 (2.4) |

*Contd...*

| Factors | | Year | | | |
|---|---|---|---|---|---|
| | | *Before 1981 (n=5)* | *1981-1985 (n=7)* | *1985-1990 (n=30)* | *1990 and After (n=42)* |
| Selling price of Flooring/Roofing tiles per unit[c] (in Rupees) | 2-4 | 3 (60.0) | - | 26 (86.7) | 35 (83.3) |
| | Above 4 | 2 (40.0) | 7 (100.0) | 4 (13.3) | 7 (16.7) |
| Cost of clay per load[c] (in Rupees) | 2000-4000 | 2 (40.0) | - | 20 (66.7) | 28 (66.7) |
| | 4000-6000 | 1 (20.0) | - | 6 (20.0) | 7 (16.7) |
| | 6000-8000 | - | 2 (28.6) | 1 (3.3) | 4 (9.5) |
| | Above 8000 | 2 (40.0) | 5 (71.4) | 3 (10.0) | 3 (7.1) |
| Cost of Firewood per load[a] (in Rupees) | Below 2500 | - | - | 1 (3.3) | 3 (7.1) |
| | 2500-5000 | 3 (60.0) | - | 24 (80.0) | 32 (76.2) |
| | 5000-7500 | 2 (40.0) | 5 (71.4) | 2 (6.7) | 2 (4.8) |
| | 7500 and Above | - | 2 (28.6) | 3 (10.0) | 5 (11.9) |
| Cost of Oil per load[a] (in Rupees) | Below 500 | - | - | 7 (23.3) | 10 (23.8) |
| | 500-1000 | 3 (60.0) | - | 19 (63.3) | 25 (59.5) |
| | 1000-1500 | 2 (40.0) | 5 (71.4) | 2 (6.7) | 3 (7.1) |
| | 1500 and Above | - | 2 (28.6) | 2 (6.7) | 4 (9.5) |
| Labour charges per load[c] (in Rupees) | Below 2500 | 1 (20.0) | - | 4 (13.3) | 3 (7.1) |
| | 2500-5000 | 1 (20.0) | - | 21 (70.0) | 23 (54.8) |
| | 5000-7500 | 3 (60.0) | 3 (42.9) | 1 (3.3) | 11 (26.2) |
| | 7500 and Above | - | 4 (57.1) | 4 (13.3) | 5 (11.9) |
| Electricity charges per load[a] (in Rupees) | Below 600 | - | - | 4 (13.3) | 2 (4.8) |
| | 600-1200 | 2 (40.0) | - | 15 (50.0) | 27 (64.3) |
| | 1200-1800 | 2 (40.0) | 4 (57.1) | 10 (33.3) | 13 (31.0) |
| | 1800 and Above | 1 (20.0) | 3 (42.9) | 1 (3.3) | - |

*Contd...*

| Factors | | Year: Before 1981 (n=5) | 1981-1985 (n=7) | 1985-1990 (n=30) | 1990 and After (n=42) |
|---|---|---|---|---|---|
| Investment in Land and Buildings (Rs.in lakhs) | Below 5 | - | 1 (14.3) | 2 (6.7) | 4 (9.5) |
| | 5–10 | 2 (40.0) | 4 (57.1) | 12 (40.0) | 24 (57.1) |
| | 10–15 | 2 (40.0) | 2 (28.6) | 13 (43.3) | 11 (26.2) |
| | Above 15 | 1 (20.0) | - | 3 (10.0) | 3 (7.1) |
| Investment in Plant and Machinery (Rs.in lakhs) | Below 3 | - | - | 2 (6.7) | 4 (9.5) |
| | 3–6 | - | 2 (28.6) | 8 (26.7) | 12 (28.6) |
| | 6–9 | 1 (20.0) | 1 (14.3) | 5 (16.7) | 14 (33.3) |
| | Above 9 | 4 (80.0) | 4 (57.1) | 15 (50.0) | 12 (28.6) |
| Investment in Electrical Fittings (in Rupees) | Below 30000 | - | 1 (14.3) | 5 (16.7) | 5 (11.9) |
| | 30000-60000 | 2 (40.0) | 1 (14.3) | 12 (40.0) | 23 (54.8) |
| | 60000-90000 | 1 (20.0) | 2 (28.6) | 2 (6.7) | 6 (14.3) |
| | 90000 and Above | 2 (40.0) | 3 (42.9) | 11 (36.7) | 8 (19.0) |
| Investment in Pallets and Frames (in Rupees) | Below 30000 | - | - | - | 1 (2.4) |
| | 30000-60000 | - | - | 6 (20.0) | 9 (21.4) |
| | 60000-90000 | - | 3 (42.9) | 7 (23.3) | 11 (26.2) |
| | 90000 and Above | 5 (100.0) | 4 (57.1) | 17 (56.7) | 21 (50.0) |
| Investment in Chimney (Rs.in lakhs) | Below 3 | - | 1 (14.3) | 10 (33.3) | 14 (33.3) |
| | 3 – 6 | 2 (40.0) | 2 (28.6) | 9 (30.0) | 20 (47.6) |
| | 6 – 9 | 3 (60.0) | 3 (42.9) | 8 (26.7) | 6 (14.3) |
| | Above 9 | - | 1 (14.3) | 3 (10.0) | 2 (4.8) |

*Contd...*

| *Factors* | | *Year* Before 1981 (n=5) | 1981-1985 (n=7) | 1985-1990 (n=30) | 1990 and After (n=42) |
|---|---|---|---|---|---|
| Investment in Furniture and Fittings (in Rupees) | Below 7000 | - | - | 2 (6.7) | 2 (4.8) |
| | 7000-14000 | - | 1 (14.3) | 6 (20.0) | 6 (14.3) |
| | 14000-21000 | 2 (40.0) | 3 (42.9) | 11 (36.7) | 19 (45.2) |
| | 21000 and Above | 3 (60.0) | 3 (42.9) | 11 (36.7) | 15 (35.7) |
| Expected rate of return (in Per cent) | Below 25 | - | 1 (14.3) | 2 (6.7) | 2 (4.8) |
| | 25-50 | 5 (100.0) | 6 (85.7) | 28 (93.3) | 38 (90.5) |
| | 50-75 | - | - | - | 2 (4.8) |
| Average Actual rate of return (in Per cent) | Below 15 | 2 (40.0) | 4 (57.1) | 16 (53.3) | 26 (61.9) |
| | 15-30 | 3 (60.0) | 3 (42.9) | 14 (46.7) | 16 (38.1) |
| Performance of Finance function | Bad | 1 (20.0) | 1 (14.3) | 5 (16.7) | 9 (21.4) |
| | Moderate | 1 (20.0) | 3 (42.9) | 9 (30.0) | 10 (23.8) |
| | Good | 2 (40.0) | 3 (42.9) | 16 (53.3) | 22 (52.4) |
| | Excellent | 1 (20.0) | - | - | 1 (2.4) |

( ) in Percentage Contingency Coefficient ≥ 0.5 P-Value <0.01[a]
Contingency Coefficient ≥ 0.5 P-Value <0.05[b]
Contingency Coefficient ≤ 0.5 P-Value <0.01[c]
Contingency Coefficient ≤ 0.5 P-Value <0.05[d]

- 5 out of 12 units (41.6per cent) got long-term loans of Rs. 15 lakhs or above each before 1985, but the trend changed; and only 17 out of 72 units (23.6 per cent) established since 1985 have got such heavy loans.
- 50 per cent of the units established prior to 1985 paid an interest of 15 per cent on the loans, but only 33.3 per cent of the units established since 1985 pay such an interest.
- Subsidies received from the Government have been uniformly substantial. Only 12 out of 84 units have not received subsidies.
- Collection from debtors, cash sales and advances from customers remain the most important sources of working capital since the inception of the units' upto the 1990's.
- 50 per cent of the units established prior to 1985 prefer to allow a period of 10 days only for credit collection, but 50 per cent of those established since 1990 allow a period of 20 days for collection.
- Selling price of a tile has been fixed between Rs. 2 and 4 by 60 per cent of units established prior to 1980, 86.7 per cent of units 1985 to 90 and 83.3 per cent of units since 1990 but all the units established between 1981 and 85, fix the price above Rs. 4.
- A majority of the units maintain the cost of clay at Rs. 2000 to 4000 a load, except those units started in 1981 to 1985, 71 per cent of units spend Rs.8000 or above on a load. This explains why these units fix the selling price at Rs. 4 and above.
- Most of the units have succeeded in keeping the cost of firewood between Rs.2500 and 5000, but units established between 1981 and 1985 spend more than Rs. 5000.
- The cost of oil is maintained at Rs. 500 to 1000 per load by most of the units, whereas the 71 per cent of the units of 1981 to 1985 spend Rs. 1000 to 1500 on every load.

- Labour charges are kept at Rs. 5000 to 7500 per load by 60 per cent of the units established prior to 1981 and at Rs. 7500 and above by units of 1981 and 1985. But 70 per cent of the units established from 1985 to 1990 and 54.8 per cent of the units established since 1990 spend only less than Rs.5000 per load.
- Most of the units pay Rs. 600 to 1200 as electricity charges per load, except 57.1 per cent of units from 1981 to 1985 which pay upto Rs. 1800.
- Investment in land and buildings is Rs. 5 to 10 lakhs by 40 per cent of units established prior to 1981, 57.1 per cent of units from 1981 to 1985 and 57.1 of units since 1990, whereas units established 1985 to 1990 have invested Rs.10 to 15 lakhs.
- Investment in plant and machinery is more than Rs. 9 lakhs by a majority of the units established prior to 1990, but only 33.3 per cent of the units established in 1990 spend Rs. 6 to 9 lakhs.
- 40 per cent of the units established prior to 1981 and 42.9 per cent of units from 1981 to 1985 have spent about 90000 each on Investment in Electrical fittings; whereas only 36.7 per cent of units from 1980 to 1990 and 19 per cent of units established since 1990 spend so much; most of these units have kept it between Rs. 30000 and 60000.
- It is an obvious fact that spending on pallets and frames cannot be avoided. A remarkable majority of all the units irrespective of the year of establishment spend more than Rs.90000 each on pallets and frames.
- Expenses on chimney/kiln is neither too high nor too low. 60 per cent of the units established prior to 1981 and 42.9 per cent established between 1981 and 1985 spend about Rs. 6 to 9 lakhs. 33 per cent of the units from 1985 to 1990 spend below Rs. 3 lakhs and 47.6 per cent of units established since 1990 spend between Rs. 3 and 6 lakhs.

- With regard to furniture and fittings, the two slabs– Rs. 14000 to 21000 and above 21000 are prominent. Very few units, about 17 established prior to 1990 spent Rs. 21000 and above. Remaining units established after 1990 spend Rs. 14000 to 21000.
- Most of the units expected a return of 25 to 50 per cent but the actual return was below 15 per cent, except 60 per cent of units prior to 1981, 42 per cent of 1981 to 1985, 46.7 per cent of 1985 to 1990 and 38 per cent since 1990 - all of which have got a return of 15 to 30 per cent.
- Most of the units ranging from 40 per cent to 52 per cent have had good financial performance.

Moreover, the results of the contingency co-efficient suggest that the factors of finance such as major source of borrowed funds, selling price of the tiles, cost of clay, cost of firewood, cost of oil, labour charges and electricity charges per load were associated with the year of establishment of the units and these were statistically significant at one per cent level.

Table 26 shows that there are 74 units in Panchayat limits, 9 units under Municipality and 1 unit in the Corporation area. For the sake of convenience;

Panchayat = A

Municipality = B

Corporation = C

- Regarding total capital invested, 35.1 per cent of A and 33 per cent of B have invested above Rs. 30 lakhs each, 28.4 per cent of A and 44.4 per cent of B have Rs. 20 to 30 lakhs whereas the only unit of C has Rs. 10 to 20 lakhs.
- Only 23 per cent of A and 33.3 per cent of B have invested own fund of Rs.15 lakhs and above and Rs.5 to 10 lakhs dominates the scenario with 36.5 per cent of A and 33.3 per cent of B and the only unit of C.
- Undoubtedly the major source of borrowing is Kerala Finance Corporation, with the result that other

**Table 26**
**Factors of Finance Based on the Jurisdiction of the Units**

| Factors | | Jurisdiction | | |
|---|---|---|---|---|
| | | Panchayat (n=74) | Municipality (n=9) | Corporation (n=1) |
| Total invested capital (Rs.in lakhs) | Below 10 | 3 (4.1) | - | - |
| | 10-20 | 24 (32.4) | 2 (22.2) | 1 (100.0) |
| | 20-30 | 21 (28.4) | 4 (44.4) | - |
| | Above 30 | 26 (35.1) | 3 (33.3) | - |
| Invested own fund(Rs.in lakhs) | Below 5 | 22 (29.7) | 2 (22.2) | - |
| | 5-10 | 27 (36.5) | 3 (33.3) | 1 (100.0) |
| | 10-15 | 8 (10.8) | 1 (11.1) | - |
| | Above 15 | 17 (23.0) | 3 (33.3) | - |
| Major source of borrowed funds | Kerala Finance Corporation | 60 (81.1) | 8 (88.9) | 1 (100.0) |
| | Friends/Relatives | 3 (4.1) | - | - |
| | Other loans from outsiders | 10 (13.5) | 1 (11.1) | - |
| | None | 1 (1.4) | - | - |
| Long term loans received (Rs.in lakhs) | Below 5 | 5 (6.8) | - | - |
| | 5-10 | 22 (29.7) | 3 (33.3) | 1 (100.0) |
| | 10-15 | 27 (36.5) | 4 (44.4) | - |
| | Above 15 | 20 (27.0) | 2 (22.2) | - |
| Rate of interest (in Per cent) | 5-10 | 11 (14.9) | 1 (11.1) | - |
| | 10-15 | 36 (48.6) | 6 (66.7) | - |
| | Above 15 | 27 (36.5) | 2 (22.2) | 1 (100.0) |
| Subsidies received from Govt. | Yes | 63 (85.1) | 8 (88.9) | 1 (100.0) |
| | No | 11 (14.9) | 1 (11.1) | - |

*Contd...*

| Factors | | Jurisdiction | | |
|---|---|---|---|---|
| | | *Panchayat* (*n*=74) | *Municipality* (*n*=9) | *Corporation* (*n*=1) |
| Sources of working capital [a] | Collection from debtors/cash sales | 24 (32.4) | 4 (44.4) | - |
| | Short term loan | 1 (1.4) | 1 (11.1) | - |
| | Friends / Relatives | 4 (5.4) | - | - |
| | Advance from customers | 2 (2.7) | - | 1 (100.0) |
| | Collection from Debtors/cash sales and short term Loan | 1 (1.4) | - | - |
| | Collection from debtors/cash sales and Friends/Relatives | 10 (13.5) | 1 (11.1) | - |
| | Collection from debtors/cash sales and Advance from customers | 32 (43.2) | 3 (33.3) | - |
| Credit collection period | Less than 10 days | 32 (43.2) | 4 (44.4) | - |
| | 10-20 days | 29 (39.2) | 5 (55.6) | 1 (100.0) |
| | 1 month | 12 (16.2) | - | - |
| | Above 1 month | 1 (1.4) | - | - |
| Selling price of Flooring/Roofing tiles per unit (in Rupees) | 2-4 | 54 (73.0) | 9 (100.0) | 1 (100.0) |
| | Above 4 | 20 (27.0) | - | - |
| Cost of clay per load (in Rupees) | 2000-4000 | 40 (54.1) | 9 (100.0) | 1 (100.0) |
| | 4000-6000 | 14 (18.9) | - | - |
| | 6000-8000 | 7 (9.5) | - | - |
| | Above 8000 | 13 (17.6) | - | - |
| Cost of Firewood per load (in Rupees) | Below 2500 | 3 (4.1) | 1 (11.1) | - |
| | 2500-5000 | 50 (67.6) | 8 (88.9) | 1 (100.0) |
| | 5000-7500 | 11 (14.9) | - | - |
| | 7500 and Above | 10 (13.5) | - | - |

*Contd...*

| Factors | | Jurisdiction | | |
|---|---|---|---|---|
| | | *Panchayat (n=74)* | *Municipality (n=9)* | *Corporation (n=1)* |
| Cost of Oil per load (in Rupees) | Below 500 | 13 (17.6) | 3 (33.3) | 1 (100.0) |
| | 500-1000 | 41 (55.4) | 6 (66.7) | - |
| | 1000-1500 | 12 (16.2) | - | - |
| | 1500 and Above | 8 (10.8) | - | - |
| Labour charges per load (in Rupees) | Below 2500 | 6 (8.1) | 2 (22.2) | - |
| | 2500-5000 | 37 (50.0) | 7 (77.8) | 1 (100.0) |
| | 5000-7500 | 18 (24.3) | - | - |
| | 7500 and Above | 13 (17.6) | - | - |
| Electricity charges per load [d] (in Rupees) | Below 600 | 5 (6.8) | - | 1 (100.0) |
| | 600-1200 | 37 (50.0) | 7 (77.8) | - |
| | 1200-1800 | 27 (36.5) | 2 (22.2) | - |
| | 1800 and Above | 5 (6.8) | - | - |
| Investment in Land and Buildings (Rs.in lakhs) | Below 5 | 5 (6.8) | 2 (22.2) | - |
| | 5–10 | 40 (54.1) | 1 (11.1) | 1 (100.0) |
| | 10–15 | 22 (29.7) | 6 (66.7) | - |
| | Above 15 | 7 (9.5) | - | - |
| Investment in Plant and Machinery (Rs.in lakhs) | Below 3 | 6 (8.1) | - | - |
| | 3–6 | 19 (25.7) | 2 (22.2) | 1 (100.0) |
| | 6–9 | 19 (25.7) | 2 (22.2) | - |
| | Above 9 | 30 (40.5) | 5 (55.6) | - |

*Contd...*

| *Factors* | | *Jurisdiction* | | |
|---|---|---|---|---|
| | | *Panchayat (n=74)* | *Municipality (n=9)* | *Corporation (n=1)* |
| Investment in Electrical Fittings (in Rupees) | Below 30000 | 9 (12.2) | 2 (22.2) | - |
| | 30000-60000 | 35 (47.3) | 2 (22.2) | 1 (100.0) |
| | 60000-90000 | 9 (12.2) | 2 (22.2) | - |
| | 90000 and Above | 21 (28.4) | 3 (33.3) | - |
| Investment in Pallets and Frames (in Rupees) | Below 30000 | 1 (1.4) | - | - |
| | 30000-60000 | 13 (17.6) | 1 (11.1) | 1 (100.0) |
| | 60000-90000 | 19 (25.7) | 2 (22.2) | - |
| | 90000 and Above | 41 (55.4) | 6 (66.7) | - |
| Investment in Chimney (Rs. in lakhs) | Below 3 | 23 (31.1) | 1 (11.1) | 1 (100.0) |
| | 3–6 | 29 (39.2) | 4 (44.4) | - |
| | 6-9 | 16 (21.6) | 4 (44.4) | - |
| | Above 9 | 6 (8.1) | - | - |
| Investment in Furniture and Fittings (in Rupees) | Below 7000 | 3 (4.1) | - | 1 (100.0) |
| | 7000-14000 | 12 (16.2) | 1 (11.1) | - |
| | 14000-21000 | 31 (41.9) | 4 (44.4) | - |
| | 21000 and Above | 28 (37.8) | 4 (44.4) | - |

*Contd...*

| Factors | | Jurisdiction | | |
|---|---|---|---|---|
| | | *Panchayat* (*n*=74) | *Municipality* (*n*=9) | *Corporation* (*n*=1) |
| Expected rate of return (in Per cent) | Below 25 | 5 (6.8) | - | - |
| | 25-50 | 68 (91.9) | 8 (88.9) | 1 (100.0) |
| | 50-75 | 1 (1.4) | 1 (11.1) | - |
| Average Actual rate of return (in Per cent) | Below 15 | 43 (58.1) | 4 (44.4) | 1 (100.0) |
| | 15-30 | 31 (41.9) | 5 (55.6) | - |
| Performance of Finance function | Bad | 13 (17.6) | 2 (22.2) | 1 (100.0) |
| | Moderate | 20 (27.0) | 3 (33.3) | - |
| | Good | 39 (52.7) | 4 (44.4) | - |
| | Excellent | 2 (2.7) | - | - |

( ) i n Percentage Contingency Coefficient ≥ 0.5 P-Value <0.01[a]
Contingency Coefficient ≥ 0.5 P-Value <0.05[b]
Contingency Coefficient ≤ 0.5 P-Value <0.01[c]
Contingency Coefficient ≤ 0.5 P-Value <0.05[d]

sources like friends, relatives and outsiders fade into insignificance.

- Rs. 10 to 15 lakhs of long-term loans were obtained by 36.5 per cent of A, and 44.4 of B. The only unit of C has availed itself of a loan less than Rs. 10 lakhs.
- Regarding the rate of interest, 48.6 per cent of A and 66.7 per cent of B pay between 10 to 15 per cent per annum, whereas the only unit of C pay 15 per cent or above.
- Except 14.9 per cent of A and 11.1 per cent of B, all the units are getting subsidies from the Government.
- The only unit of C gets all its working capital from advances paid by the customers. 43.2 per cent of A and 44.4 per cent of B get their working capital from debtors, cash sales and advances from customers.
- The period of collection is less than 10 days with 43.2 per cent of A and 44.4 per cent of B. It is 10 to 20 days with 39.2 per cent of A and 55.6 per cent of B and the unit of C. Only one unit of A allows a month as period of collection.
- Except 20 units of A, all the units fix the selling price of a tile at Rs. 2 to 4.
- The cost of clay per load is Rs. 2000 to 4000 by 54.1 per cent of A, and all the units of B and C.
- The cost of firewood is maintained at Rs. 2500 to 5000 by 67.6 per cent of A, 88.9 per cent of B and the sole unit of C. Only 21 units of A spend more than Rs. 5000.
- The cost of oil is kept at Rs.500 to 1000 per load by 55.4 per cent of A and 66.7 per cent of B. The unit in C keeps it at the lowest i.e. below Rs.500.
- Labour charges are Rs. 2500 to 5000 per load in 50 per cent of A, 77.8 per cent of B and C. 31 units of A spend more than Rs.5000.
- Electricity charges are Rs. 600 to 1200 per load in 50 per cent of A and 77.8 per cent of B. The C unit keeps it at minimum–below Rs. 600.

- 39.2 per cent of A and 66.7 per cent of B have spent more than Rs.10 lakhs on land and buildings whereas 54.1 per cent of A and C units have spent Rs.5 to 10 lakhs.
- C unit has invested Rs. 3 to 6 lakhs in plant and machinery. 40.5 per cent of A has 9 lakhs and above. 55.6 per cent of B has invested more than Rs.9 lakhs.
- 28.4 per cent of A and 33.3 per cent of B have spent more than Rs. 90000 each on electrical fittings whereas 47.3 per cent of A and C unit have kept it between Rs. 30000 and 6000.
- 55.4 per cent of A and 66.7 per cent of B have spent the maximum of Rs.90000 or more, and unit C below Rs. 60000 on pallets and frames.
- Expenses on chimney are Rs. 3 to 6 lakhs in 39.2 per cent of A and 44.4 per cent of B, Rs.6 to 9 lakhs in 21.6 per cent of A and 44.4 per cent of B. The sole unit of C has kept it below Rs. 3 lakhs.
- As regards furniture and fittings 37.8 per cent of A and 44.4 per cent of B have spent the maximum of Rs. 21000 or above whereas unit C keeps it at the lowest below Rs. 7000.
- 91.9 per cent of A and 88.9 per cent of B and the unit C expected a return of 25 to 50 per cent per annum but the actual was below 15 per cent for 58.1 per cent of A, 44.4 per cent of B and C, but return of 15 per cent or more was realized by 41.9 per cent of A and 55.6 per cent of B.
- 52.7 per cent of A and 44.4 of B have recorded good financial performance, while C has fared badly.

Moreover, the results of the contingency co-efficient suggest that the factors of finance such as major source of working capital, electricity charges per load and furniture and fittings were associated with the jurisdiction of the units and these were statistically significant at one per cent and five per cent level.

Table 27 examines the financial performance of the units on the types of tiles they make. For the sake of convenience the following codes may be adopted.

A = 4 units manufacturing roofing tiles.

B = 42 units manufacturing flooring tiles.

C = 9 units manufacturing other clay tiles.

D = 8 units manufacturing both flooring and roofing tiles.

E = 20 units manufacturing flooring and decorative tiles.

F = 1 unit manufacturing decorative and other tiles.

- Total capital invested is Rs. 10 to 20 lakhs in almost all cases. 23.8 per cent of B, 33.3 per cent of C, 62.5 per cent of D, 40 per cent of E and the sole unit F. 75 per cent of A, 40.5 per cent of B have between Rs. 20 and 30 lakhs.
- As regards invested own fund, 31 out of 84 units have Rs. 5 to 10 lakhs.
- Kerala Finance Corporation is the single major source of borrowing for 69 units.
- As regards long-term loans, 31 units obtain Rs.10 to 15 lakhs and 26 units get Rs. 5 to 10 lakhs and 22 obtain more than Rs. 15 lakhs.
- 42 units (i.e. 50 per cent) pay an interest of 10 to 15 per cent on their loans and 30 units above 15 per cent.
- 72 out of 84 units avail themselves of the subsidies from the Government.
- Sources of working capital are collection from debtors, cash sales and advances from customers for 63 out of 84 units (i.e. 75 per cent)
- 35 units allow a period of 10 to 20 days for collection, whereas 36 less than 10 days. Only one unit of C allows a month.
- Regarding the selling price, 64 units have it from Rs.2 to 4 but all the units of C, D and 75 per cent of A fix it above Rs. 4

**Table 27**
**Factors of Finance Based on Type of Clay Tiles Manufactured By The Units**

| *Factors* | | *Types of Clay Tiles* | | | | | |
|---|---|---|---|---|---|---|---|
| | | *Roofing (n=4)* | *Flooring (n=42)* | *Other tiles (n=9)* | *Roofing & Flooring (n=8)* | *Flooring & Decorative (n=20)* | *Decorative & other tiles (n=1)* |
| Total invested capital [a] | Below 10 | - | - | - | 2 (25.0) | 1 (5.0) | - |
| (Rs.in lakhs) | 10-20 | - | 10 (23.8) | 3 (33.3) | 5 (62.5) | 8 (40.0) | 1 (100.0) |
| | 20-30 | 3 (75.0) | 17 (40.5) | - | - | 5 (25.0) | - |
| | Above 30 | 1 (25.0) | 15 (35.7) | 6 (66.7) | 1 (12.5) | 6 (30.0) | - |
| Invested own fund | Below 5 | - | 8 (19.0) | 2 (22.2) | 4 (50.0) | 9 (45.0) | 1 (100.0) |
| (Rs.in lakhs) | 5-10 | 3 (75.0) | 17 (40.5) | 3 (33.3) | 2 (25.0) | 6 (30.0) | - |
| | 10-15 | 1 (25.0) | 4 (9.5) | 1 (11.1) | 2 (25.0) | 1 (5.0) | - |
| | Above 15 | - | 13 (31.0) | 3 (33.3) | - | 4 (20.0) | - |
| Major source of borrowed funds | Kerala Finance Corporation | 3 (75.0) | 36 (85.7) | 7 (77.8) | 6 (75.0) | 16 (80.0) | 1 (100.0) |
| | Friends/Relatives | - | 1 (2.4) | - | 1 (12.5) | 1 (5.0) | - |
| | Other loans from outsiders | 1 (25.0) | 4 (9.5) | 2 (22.2) | 1 (12.5) | 3 (15.0) | - |
| | None | - | 1 (2.4) | - | - | - | - |
| Long term loans received [d] | Below 5 | - | 1 (2.4) | - | 3 (37.5) | 1 (5.0) | - |
| (Rs.in lakhs) | 5-10 | - | 10 (23.8) | 5 (55.6) | 2 (25.0) | 8 (40.0) | 1 (100.0) |
| | 10-15 | 2 (50.0) | 17 (40.5) | 2 (22.2) | 2 (25.0) | 8 (40.0) | - |
| | Above 15 | 2 (50.0) | 14 (3.3) | 2 (22.2) | 1 (12.5) | 3 (15.0) | - |
| Rate of interest (in Per cent) | 5-10 | - | 5 (11.9) | 1 (11.1) | 3 (37.5) | 3 (15.0) | - |
| | 10-15 | 1 (25.0) | 24 (57.1) | 2 (22.2) | 4 (50.0) | 10 (50.0) | 1 (100.0) |
| | Above 15 | 3 (75.0) | 13 (31.0) | 6 (66.7) | 1 (12.5) | 7 (35.0) | - |

*Contd...*

| Factors | | Types of Clay Tiles | | | | | |
|---|---|---|---|---|---|---|---|
| | | Roofing (n=4) | Flooring (n=42) | Other tiles (n=9) | Roofing & Flooring (n=8) | Flooring & Decorative (n=20) | Decorative & other tiles (n=1) |
| Subsidies received from Govt. | Yes | 4 (100.0) | 37 (88.1) | 7 (77.8) | 7 (87.5) | 16 (80.0) | 1 (100.0) |
| | No | - | 5 (11.9) | 2 (22.2) | 1 (12.5) | 4 (20.0) | - |
| Sources of working capital | Collection from debtors/ cash sales | - | 13 (31.0) | 4 (44.4) | 2 (25.0) | 8 (40.0) | 1 (100.0) |
| | Short term loan | - | 1 (2.4) | - | - | 1 (5.0) | - |
| | Friends / Relatives | - | 3 (7.1) | - | 1 (12.5) | - | - |
| | Advance from customers | - | 3 (7.1) | - | - | - | - |
| | Collection from Debtors/ cash sales and short term Loan | - | - | - | 1 (12.5) | - | - |
| | Collection from debtors/ cash sales and Friends/ Relatives | - | 8 (19.0) | 1 (11.1) | - | 2 (10.0) | - |
| | Collection from debtors/ cash sales and Advance from customers | 4 (100.0) | 14 (33.3) | 4 (44.4) | 4 (50.0) | 9 (45.0) | - |
| Credit collection period (in days) | Less than 10 | 2 (50.0) | 18 (42.9) | 4 (44.4) | 4 (50.0) | 8 (40.0) | - |
| | 10-20 | 2 (50.0) | 21 (50.0) | 2 (22.2) | 1 (12.5) | 8 (40.0) | 1 (100.0) |
| | 1 month | - | 3 (7.1) | 2 (22.2) | 3 (37.5) | 4 (20.0) | - |
| | Above 1 month | - | - | 1 (11.1) | - | - | - |
| Selling price of Flooring / Roofing tiles per unit[a] (in Rupees) | 2-4 | 1 (25.0) | 42 (100.0) | - | - | 20 (100.0) | 1 (100.0) |
| | Above 4 | 3 (75.0) | - | 9 (100.0) | 8 (100.0) | - | - |

*Contd...*

| Factors | | Types of Clay Tiles | | | | | |
|---|---|---|---|---|---|---|---|
| | | *Roofing (n=4)* | *Flooring (n=42)* | *Other tiles (n=9)* | *Roofing & Flooring (n=8)* | *Flooring & Decorative (n=20)* | *Decorative & other tiles (n=1)* |
| Cost of clay per load [a] (in Rupees) | 2000-4000 | - | 33 (78.6) | - | - | 16 (80.0) | 1 (100.0) |
| | 4000-6000 | 1 (25.0) | 9 (21.4) | - | - | 4 (20.0) | - |
| | 6000-8000 | 2 (50.0) | - | 3 (33.3) | 2 (25.0) | - | - |
| | Above 8000 | 1 (25.0) | - | 6 (66.7) | 6 (75.0) | - | - |
| Cost of Firewood per load [a] (in Rupees) | Below 2500 | - | 3 (7.1) | - | - | 1 (5.0) | |
| | 2500-5000 | 1 (25.0) | 39 (92.9) | - | - | 18 (90.0) | 1 (100.0) |
| | 5000-7500 | 1 (25.0) | - | 6 (66.7) | 4 (50.0) | - | - |
| | 7500 and Above | 2 (50.0) | - | 3 (33.3) | 4 (50.0) | 1 (5.0) | - |
| Cost of Oil per load [a] (in Rupees) | Below 500 | - | 14 (33.3) | - | - | 3 (15.0) | - |
| | 500-1000 | 1 (25.0) | 28 (66.7) | - | - | 17 (85.0) | 1 (100.0) |
| | 1000-1500 | 1 (25.0) | - | 6 (66.7) | 5 (62.5) | - | - |
| | 1500 and Above | 2 (50.0) | - | 3 (33.3) | 3 (37.5) | - | - |
| Labour charges per load [a] (in Rupees) | Below 2500 | - | 6 (14.3) | - | - | 2 (10.0) | - |
| | 2500-5000 | - | 29 (69.0) | - | - | 15 (75.0) | 1 (100.0) |
| | 5000-7500 | 2 (50.0) | 6 (14.3) | 4 (44.4) | 3 (37.5) | 3 (15.0) | - |
| | 7500 and Above | 2 (50.0) | 1 (2.4) | 5 (55.6) | 5 (62.5) | - | - |
| Electricity charges per load [a] (in Rupees) | Below 600 | - | 5 (11.9) | - | - | 1 (5.0) | - |
| | 600-1200 | 1 (25.0) | 27 (64.3) | - | 1 (12.5) | 14 (70.0) | 1 (100.0) |
| | 1200-1800 | 3 (75.0) | 9 (21.4) | 5 (55.6) | 7 (87.5) | 5 (25.0) | - |
| | 1800 and Above | - | 1 (2.4) | 4 (44.4) | - | - | - |

*Contd...*

| Factors | | Types of Clay Tiles | | | | | |
|---|---|---|---|---|---|---|---|
| | | *Roofing (n=4)* | *Flooring (n=42)* | *Other tiles (n=9)* | *Roofing & Flooring (n=8)* | *Flooring & Decorative (n=20)* | *Decorative & other tiles (n=1)* |
| Investment in Land and Buildings[a] (Rs.in lakhs) | Below 5 | - | - | 1 (11.1) | 3 (37.5) | 2 (10.0) | 1 (100.0) |
| | 5–10 | 1 (25.0) | 20 (47.6) | 6 (66.7) | 5 (62.5) | 10 (50.0) | - |
| | 10–15 | 3 (75.0) | 17 (40.5) | 2 (22.2) | - | 6 (30.0) | - |
| | Above 15 | - | 5 (11.9) | - | - | 2 (10.0) | - |
| Investment in Plant and Machinery (Rs. in lakhs) | Below 3 | - | 1 (2.4) | 1 (11.1) | 3 (37.5) | 1 (5.0) | - |
| | 3–6 | - | 9 (21.4) | 2 (22.2) | 3 (37.5) | 7 (35.0) | 1 (100.0) |
| | 6–9 | 1 (25.0) | 12 (28.6) | 2 (22.2) | 2 (25.0) | 4 (20.0) | - |
| | Above 9 | 3 (75.0) | 20 (47.6) | 4 (44.4) | - | 8 (40.0) | - |
| Investment in Electrical Fittings[a] (in Rupees) | Below 30000 | - | 2 (4.8) | 2 (22.2) | 5 (62.5) | 1 (5.0) | 1 (100.0) |
| | 30000-60000 | 3 (75.0) | 20 (47.6) | 2 (22.2) | 2 (25.0) | 11 (55.0) | - |
| | 60000-90000 | - | 5 (11.9) | 2 (22.2) | 1 (12.5) | 3 (15.0) | - |
| | 90000 and Above | 1 (25.0) | 15 (35.7) | 3 (33.3) | - | 5 (25.0) | - |
| Investment in Pallets and Frames[d] (in Rupees) | Below 30000 | - | - | - | 1 (12.5) | - | - |
| | 30000-60000 | - | 6 (14.3) | 1 (11.1) | 3 (37.5) | 5 (25.0) | - |
| | 60000-90000 | 3 (75.0) | 8 (19.0) | 2 (22.2) | 3 (37.5) | 4 (20.0) | 1 (100.0) |
| | 90000 and Above | 1 (25.0) | 28 (66.7) | 6 (66.7) | 1 (12.5) | 11 (55.0) | - |
| Investment in Chimney (Rs.in lakhs) | Below 3 | 1 (25.0) | 9 (21.4) | 3 (33.3) | 4 (50.0) | 8 (40.0) | - |
| | 3–6 | 3 (75.0) | 18 (42.9) | - | 3 (37.5) | 8 (40.0) | 1 (100.0) |
| | 6–9 | - | 12 (28.6) | 5 (55.6) | 1 (12.5) | 2 (10.0) | - |
| | Above 9 | - | 3 (7.1) | 1 (11.1) | - | 2 (10.0) | - |

| Factors | | Types of Clay Tiles | | | | | |
|---|---|---|---|---|---|---|---|
| | | *Roofing (n=4)* | *Flooring (n=42)* | *Other tiles (n=9)* | *Roofing & Flooring (n=8)* | *Flooring & Decorative (n=20)* | *Decorative & other tiles (n=1)* |
| Investment in Furniture and Fittings [a] (in Rupees) | Below 7000 | - | 1 (2.4) | - | 3 (37.5) | - | - |
| | 7000-14000 | - | 6 (14.3) | 2 (22.2) | - | 5 (25.0) | - |
| | 14000-21000 | 2 (50.0) | 15 (35.7) | 3 (33.3) | 5 (62.5) | 9 (45.0) | 1 (100.C) |
| | 21000 and Above | 2 (50.0) | 20 (47.6) | 4 (44.4) | - | 6 (30.0) | - |
| Expected rate of return (in Per cent) | Below 25 | - | 3 (7.1) | 1 (11.1) | 1 (12.5) | - | - |
| | 25-50 | 4 (100.0) | 38 (90.5) | 8 (88.9) | 7 (87.5) | 19 (95.0) | 1 (100.0) |
| | 50-75 | - | 1 (2.4) | - | - | 1 (5.0) | - |
| Average Actual rate of return[d] (in Per cent) | Below 15 | 3 (75.0) | 19 (45.2) | 5 (55.6) | 8 (100.0) | 13 (65.0) | - |
| | 15-30 | 1(25.0) | 23 (54.8) | 4 (44.4) | - | 7 (35.0) | 1 (100.0) |
| Performance of Finance function | Bad | 2 (50.0) | 6 (14.3) | 1 (11.1) | 2 (25.0) | 5 (25.0) | - |
| | Moderate | 1 (25.0) | 9 (21.4) | 4 (44.4) | 2 (25.0) | 6 (30.0) | 1 (100.0) |
| | Good | 1 (25.0) | 26 (61.9) | 3 (33.3) | 4 (50.0) | 9 (45.0) | - |
| | Excellent | - | 1 (2.4) | 1 (11.1) | - | - | - |

( ) in Percentage
Contingency Coefficient ≥ 0.5 P-Value <0.01[a]
Contingency Coefficient ≥ 0.5 P-Value <0.05[b]
Contingency Coefficient ≤ 0.5 P-Value <0.01[c]
Contingency Coefficient ≤ 0.5 P-Value <0.05[d]

- 50 units maintain the cost of clay between Rs. 2000 and 4000 per load; only 13 units spend more than Rs. 8000
- The cost of firewood is between Rs. 2500 and 5000 per load for 59 units. Only 10 units spend more than Rs. 7500.
- 47 units maintain the cost of oil between Rs. 500 and 1000 per load. Only 8 units spend more than Rs. 1500.
- 45 units keep labour cost low at Rs. 2500 to 5000 per load. Only 2 units of A, 1 unit of B, 5 each of C and D spend more than Rs. 7500.
- Regarding Electricity charges 44 units pay Rs. 600 to 1200 per load. Only one unit of B and four of C pay Rs. 1800 or above.
- 42 out of 84 units (51 per cent) have invested Rs. 5 to 10 lakhs in land and buildings. The highest investment of Rs. 15 lakhs or above by 5 units of B and 2 units of E.
- 35 units have made the highest investment of Rs.9 lakhs in plant and machinery.
- 38 units have spent Rs. 30000 to 60000 on electrical fittings. One unit of A, 15 units of B, 3 of C and 5 of E have spent the highest amount of around Rs. 1 lakh.
- Pallets and frames are indispensable for any unit. Therefore 47 out of 84 units have spent Rs. 90000 or more on this equipment.
- While 33 units spend Rs. 3 to 6 lakhs each on chimney, the highest spending of about Rs. 9 lakhs is by 3 units of B, 1 unit of C and 2 units of E.
- 35 out of 84 units spend Rs.14000 to 21000 on furniture and fittings and 32 units have spent more than Rs. 21000.
- Against the expected return of 25 to 50 per cent (expected by 77 units) the annual return was below 15 per cent in 48 units and between 15 and 30 per cent in 36 units.
- As regards financial performance, 50 per cent of A have fared badly, but 61 per cent of B, 50 per cent of D and

45 per cent of E have done well. The overall picture is satisfactory.

Moreover, the results of the contingency co-efficient suggest that the factors of finance namely total capital invested, long-term loan received, selling price of the clay tiles, cost of clay, cost of firewood, cost of oil, labour charges, electricity charges per load, electrical fittings, pallets and frames, furniture and fittings and average actual rate of return were associated with the type of clay tiles manufactured by the units and these were statistically significant at one per cent and five per cent level.

Table 28 shows the financial performance of the units based on their ownership. For the sake of convenience, the following code is used:

A = Sole Proprietorship (48 units)

B = Partnership (29 units)

C = Co-operative Society (4 units)

D = Private Company (3 units)

- Units of c don't touch the highest capital of Rs. 30 lakhs and above; whereas all the three private companies have invested Rs.30 lakhs and above. Rs. 10 to 20 lakhs of total capital have been invested in 27 units each of A, B and C.
- Rs. 5 to 10 lakhs of invested own fund with 35.4 per cent of A, 44.8 per cent of B and 25 per cent of C. All the three private units have the highest invested own fund above Rs.15 lakhs.
- Kerala Finance Corporation is the major source of borrowing for 69 units. But the units of C and D depend equally on friends, relatives and other sources. One co-operative unit does not borrow any amount.
- Long-term borrowing is Rs. 10 to 15 lakhs with 31 units and above Rs. 15 lakhs with 22 units.
- The rate of interest is 10 to 15 per cent with 42 units and 30 units pay the highest rate above 15 per cent.

**Table 28**

**Factors of Finance Based on Ownership of the Units**

| *Factors* | | *Ownership* | | | |
|---|---|---|---|---|---|
| | | *Sole Proprietor (n=48)* | *Partnership (n=29)* | *Co-op. Society (n=4)* | *Private company (n=3)* |
| Total invested capital (Rs. in lakhs) | Below 10 | 3 (6.3) | - | - | - |
| | 10-20 | 18 (37.5) | 7 (24.1) | 2 (50.0) | - |
| | 20-30 | 11 (22.9) | 12 (41.4) | 2 (50.0) | - |
| | Above 30 | 16 (33.3) | 10 (34.5) | - | 3 (100.0) |
| Invested own fund (Rs. in lakhs) | Below 5 | 16 (33.3) | 7 (24.1) | 1 (25.0) | - |
| | 5-10 | 17 (35.4) | 13 (44.8) | 1 (25.0) | - |
| | 10-15 | 4 (8.3) | 4 (13.8) | 1 (25.0) | - |
| | Above 15 | 11 (22.9) | 5 (17.2) | 1 (25.0) | 3 (100.0) |
| Major source of borrowed funds [a] | Kerala Finance Corporation | 44 (91.7) | 23 (79.3) | 1 (25.0) | 1 (33.3) |
| | Friends/Relatives | 1 (2.1) | - | 1 (25.0) | 1 (33.3) |
| | Other loans from outsiders | 3 (6.3) | 6 (20.7) | 1 (25.0) | 1 (33.3) |
| | None | - | - | 1 (25.0) | - |
| Long term loans received (Rs. in lakhs) | Below 5 | 5 (10.4) | - | - | - |
| | 5-10 | 15 (31.3) | 8 (27.6) | 3 (75.0) | - |
| | 10-15 | 18 (37.5) | 12 (41.4) | - | 1 (33.3) |
| | Above 15 | 10 (20.8) | 9 (31.0) | 1 (25.0) | 2 (66.7) |
| Rate of interest (in Per cent) | 5-10 | 7 (14.6) | 3 (10.3) | 2 (50.0) | - |
| | 10-15 | 24 (50.0) | 14 (48.3) | 1 (25.0) | 3 (100.0) |
| | Above 15 | 17 (35.4) | 12 (41.4) | 1 (25.0) | - |
| Subsidies received from Govt. [c] | Yes | 45 (93.8) | 25 (86.2) | 1 (25.0) | 1 (33.3) |
| | No | 3 (6.3) | 4 (13.8) | 3 (75.0) | 2 (66.7) |

*Contd...*

| *Factors* | | *Ownership* | | | |
|---|---|---|---|---|---|
| | | *Sole Proprietor (n=48)* | *Partnership (n=29)* | *Co-op. Society (n=4)* | *Private company (n=3)* |
| Sources of working capital | Collection from debtors/cash sales | 13 (27.1) | 12 (41.4) | 1 (25.0) | 2 (66.7) |
| | Short term Loan | 1 (2.1) | - | 1 (25.0) | - |
| | Friends/Relatives | 2 (4.2) | 2 (6.9) | - | - |
| | Advance from customers | 1 (2.1) | 1 (3.4) | 1 (25.0) | |
| | Collection from Debtors/cash salesand short term Loan | 1 (2.1) | - | - | - |
| | Collection from debtors/cash salesand Friends/Relatives | 9 (18.8) | 1 (3.4) | - | 1 (33.3) |
| | Collection from debtors /cash salesand Advance from customers | 21 (43.8) | 13 (44.8) | 1 (25.0) | - |
| Credit collection period (in days) | Less than 10 | 20 (41.7) | 13 (44.8) | 1 (25.0) | 2 (66.7) |
| | 10-20 | 21 (43.8) | 10 (34.5) | 3 (75.0) | 1 (33.3) |
| | 1 month | 7 (14.6) | 5 (17.2) | - | - |
| | Above 1 month | - | 1 (3.4) | - | - |
| Selling price of Flooring/ Roofing tiles per unit (in Rupees) | 2-4 | 37 (77.1) | 20 (69.0) | 4 (100.0) | 3 (100.0) |
| | Above 4 | 11 (22.9) | 9 (31.0) | - | - |
| Cost of clay per load (in Rupees) | 2000-4000 | 31 (64.6) | 13 (44.8) | 3 (75.0) | 3 (100.0) |
| | 4000-6000 | 6 (12.5) | 7 (24.1) | 1 (25.0) | - |
| | 6000-8000 | 6 (12.5) | 1 (3.4) | - | - |
| | Above 8000 | 5 (10.4) | 8 (27.6) | - | - |

*Contd...*

| *Factors* | | *Ownership* | | | |
|---|---|---|---|---|---|
| | | *Sole Proprietor (n=48)* | *Partnership (n=29)* | *Co-op. Society (n=4)* | *Private company (n=3)* |
| Cost of Firewood per load (in Rupees) | Below 2500 | 2 (4.2) | 1 (3.4) | - | 1 (33.3) |
| | 2500-5000 | 34 (70.8) | 19 (65.5) | 4 (100.0) | 2 (66.7) |
| | 5000-7500 | 5 (10.4) | 6 (20.7) | - | - |
| | 7500 and Above | 7 (14.6) | 3 (10.3) | - | - |
| Cost of Oil per load (in Rupees) | Below 500 | 9 (18.8) | 4 (13.8) | 2 (50.0) | 2 (66.7) |
| | 500-1000 | 28 (58.3) | 16 (55.2) | 2 (50.0) | 1 (33.3) |
| | 1000-1500 | 5 (10.4) | 7 (24.1) | - | - |
| | 1500 and Above | 6 (12.5) | 2 (6.9) | - | - |
| Labour charges per load (in Rupees) | Below 2500 | 5 (10.4) | 2 (6.9) | - | 1 (33.3) |
| | 2500-5000 | 28 (58.3) | 12 (41.4) | 4 (100.0) | 1 (33.3) |
| | 5000-7500 | 7 (14.6) | 11 (37.9) | - | - |
| | 7500 and Above | 8 (16.7) | 4 (13.8) | - | 1 (33.3) |
| Electricity charges per load (in Rupees) | Below 600 | 4 (8.3) | 1 (3.4) | 1 (25.0) | - |
| | 600-1200 | 24 (50.0) | 16 (55.2) | 3 (75.0) | 1 (33.3) |
| | 1200-1800 | 17 (35.4) | 10 (34.5) | - | 2 (66.7) |
| | 1800 and Above | 3 (6.3) | 2 (6.9) | - | - |
| Investment in Land and Buildings (Rs. in lakhs) | Below 5 | 6 (12.5) | 1 (3.4) | - | - |
| | 5–10 | 22 (45.8) | 16 (55.2) | 3 (75.0) | 1 (33.3) |
| | 10–15 | 16 (33.3) | 9 (31.0) | 1 (25.0) | 2 (66.7) |
| | Above 15 | 4 (8.3) | 3 (10.3) | - | - |

*Contd...*

| Factors | | Ownership | | | |
|---|---|---|---|---|---|
| | | Sole Proprietor (n=48) | Partnership (n=29) | Co-op. Society (n=4) | Private company (n=3) |
| Investment in Plant and Machinery | Below 3 | 5 (10.4) | 1 (3.4) | - | - |
| (Rs. in lakhs) | 3–6 | 14 (29.2) | 5 (17.2) | 3 (75.0) | - |
| | 6–9 | 12 (25.0) | 8 (27.6) | - | 1 (33.3) |
| | Above 9 | 17 (35.4) | 15 (51.7) | 1 (25.0) | 2 (66.7) |
| Investment in Electrical Fittings | Below 30000 | 7 (14.6) | 3 (10.3) | 1 (25.0) | - |
| (in Rupees) | 30000-60000 | 20 (41.7) | 16 (55.2) | 2 (50.0) | - |
| | 60000-90000 | 8 (16.7) | 2 (6.9) | 1 (25.0) | - |
| | 90000 and Above | 13 (27.1) | 8 (27.6) | - | 3 (100.0) |
| Investment in Pallets and Frames | Below 30000 | 1 (2.1) | - | - | - |
| (in Rupees) | 30000-60000 | 10 (20.8) | 4 (13.8) | 1 (25.0) | - |
| | 60000-90000 | 13 (27.1) | 7 (24.1) | 1 (25.0) | - |
| | 90000 and Above | 24 (50.0) | 18 (62.1) | 2 (50.0) | 3 (100.0) |
| Investment in Chimney (Rs. in lakhs) | Below 3 | 19 (39.6) | 4 (13.8) | 2 (50.0) | - |
| | 3–6 | 15 (31.3) | 15 (51.7) | 2 (50.0) | 1 (33.3) |
| | 6–9 | 11 (22.9) | 8 (27.6) | - | 1 (33.3) |
| | Above 9 | 3 (6.3) | 2 (6.9) | - | 1 (33.3) |

Contd...

| *Factors* | | *Ownership* | | | |
|---|---|---|---|---|---|
| | | *Sole Proprietor (n=48)* | *Partnership (n=29)* | *Co-op. Society (n=4)* | *Private company (n=3)* |
| Investment in Furniture and Fittings [d] (in Rupees) | Below 7000 | 3 (6.3) | - | 1 (25.0) | - |
| | 7000-14000 | 12 (25.0) | 1 (3.4) | - | - |
| | 14000-21000 | 16 (33.3) | 17 (58.6) | 2 (50.0) | - |
| | 21000 and Above | 17 (35.4) | 11 (37.9) | 1 (25.0) | 3 (100.0) |
| Expected rate of return (in Per cent) | Below 25 | 2 (4.2) | 3 (10.3) | - | - |
| | 25-50 | 45 (93.8) | 25 (86.2) | 4 (100.0) | 3 (100.0) |
| | 50-75 | 1 (2.1) | 1 (3.4) | - | - |
| Average Actual rate of return (in Per cent) | Below 15 | 30 (62.5) | 15 (51.7) | 3 (75.0) | - |
| | 15-30 | 18 (37.5) | 14 (48.3) | 1 (25.0) | 3 (100.0) |
| Performance of Finance function | Bad | 8 (16.7) | 6 (20.7) | 2 (50.0) | - |
| | Moderate | 15 (31.3) | 6 (20.7) | 1 (25.0) | 1 (33.3) |
| | Good | 25 (52.1) | 15 (51.7) | 1 (25.0) | 2 (66.7) |
| | Excellent | - | 2 (6.9) | - | - |

( ) in Percentage

Contingency Coefficient ≥ 0.5 P-Value <0.01[a]
Contingency Coefficient ≥ 0.5 P-Value <0.05[b]
Contingency Coefficient ≤ 0.5 P-Value <0.01[c]
Contingency Coefficient ≤ 0.5 P-Value <0.05[d]

- While 72 units avail themselves of the subsidies from the Government, 3 units of A, 4 units of B, 3 units of C and 2 units of D do not get any subsidies.
- As sources of income, collection from debtors, cash sales and advance received from customers are dominant.
- Only one unit of B allows a period of 1 month, while 36 units have fixed 10 days and 35 units have 10 to 15 days as period of collection.
- As regards selling prices, 11 units of A and 9 units of B fix it at Rs. 4 and above a tile whereas all the other 64 units fix it between Rs. 2 and 4.
- The cost of clay per load has been kept at the minimum of Rs. 2000 to 4000 by 50 units, but 10.4 per cent of A and 27.6 per cent of B spend Rs. 8000 or above.
- The cost of firewood is between 2500 and 5000 per load in 59 units, but 7 units of A and 3 units of B spend the maximum of Rs. 7500 or above.
- The cost of oil is between Rs.500 and 1000 per load for 47 units, but exceeds Rs. 1500 with 12.5 per cent of A and 6.9 per cent of B.
- Labour charges are maintained at Rs.2500 to 5000 per load by 45 units, but 8 units of A, 4 units of B and 1 unit of D spend Rs. 7500 or above.
- The electricity charges are normal in 44 units (52.4 per cent) Rs. 600 to 1200 per load. But 3 units of A and 2 units of B pay more than Rs. 1800.
- Investment in land and buildings by 42 units (50 per cent) is between Rs. 5 and 10 lakhs. Four units of A and three units of B have invested Rs. 15 lakhs or more.
- Investment in plant and machinery exceed Rs.9 lakhs in 35.4 per cent units of A, 51.7 per cent of B, 25 per cent of C and 67 per cent of D.
- 38 units have electrical fittings of Rs. 60000 whereas 13 units of A, 8 units of B and all the three units of D have exceeds Rs. 90000 or above.

- As regards pallets and frames 37 units have spent Rs. 90000 or more.
- Chimney cost is between Rs. 3 and 6 lakhs in 15 units of A, 15 units of B, 2 units of C and 1 unit of D (total = 33), but the maximum of Rs.9 lakhs has been spent by 3 units of A, 2 units of B and 1 unit of D.
- As regards furniture and fittings 35 units have spent Rs. 14000 to 21000 but 32 units have spent more than Rs. 21000.
- 77 units expected return ranging 25 to 50 per cent but 48 units actually realized a return of 15 per cent or below and 36 units have recorded 15 to 30 per cent per annum.
- As regards financial performance, more than 52 per cent of A, 51 per cent of B, one unit of C and 2 units of D have done well. The overall picture is satisfactory.

Moreover, the results of the contingency co-efficient suggest that the factors of finance such as major source of borrowed funds, subsidies received from the Government and investment in furniture and fittings were associated with the ownership of the units and these were statistically significant at one per cent and five per cent level.

The tiles manufacturing units may be studied on the basis of the educational qualifications of the owners. The following code is use:

A = below S.S.L.C
B = Pre-degree
C = Technical qualification
D = Graduates
E = Post-graduate

- 66.7 per cent of E have ventured to invest more than Rs. 30 lakhs. 1 unit of A, 10 of B, 3 of C and 13 of D all have invested above Rs. 30 lakhs.
- 31 units have Rs. 5 to 10 lakhs as invested own fund. 20 units have above Rs. 15 lakhs.
- Kerala Finance Corporation is the major source of borrowing for the majority of the units.

**Table 29**
**Factors of Finance Based on the Educational Qualifications of the Unit Owner**

| Factors | | Qualification | | | | |
|---|---|---|---|---|---|---|
| | | *Below S.S.L.C (n=9)* | *Pre-Degree (n=34)* | *Technical (n=9)* | *Graduate (n=29)* | *Post-graduate (n=3)* |
| Total invested capital (Rs. in lakhs) | Below 10 | - | 2 (5.9) | - | 1 (3.4) | - |
| | 10-20 | 4 (44.4) | 11 (32.4) | 4 (44.4) | 7 (24.1) | 1 (33.3) |
| | 20-30 | 4 (44.4) | 11 (32.4) | 2 (22.2) | 8 (27.6) | - |
| | Above 30 | 1 (11.1) | 10 (29.4) | 3 (33.3) | 13 (44.8) | 2 (66.7) |
| Invested own fund (Rs. in lakhs) | Below 5 | 3 (33.3) | 10 (29.4) | 3 (33.3) | 7 (24.1) | 1 (33.3) |
| | 5-10 | 2 (22.2) | 15 (44.1) | 4 (44.4) | 10 (34.5) | - |
| | 10-15 | 3 (33.3) | 2 (5.9) | - | 3 (10.3) | 1 (33.3) |
| | Above 15 | 1 (11.1) | 7 (20.6) | 2 (22.2) | 9 (31.0) | 1 (33.3) |
| Major source of borrowed funds | Kerala Finance Corporation | 6 (66.7) | 29 (85.3) | 7 (77.8) | 24 (82.8) | 3 (100.0) |
| | Friends / Relatives | 1 (11.1) | 1 (2.9) | - | 1 (3.4) | - |
| | Other loansfrom outsiders | 2 (22.2) | 4 (11.8) | 1 (11.1) | 4 (13.8) | - |
| | None | - | - | 1 (11.1) | - | - |
| Long term loan received (Rs. in lakhs) | Below 5 | 1 (11.1) | 2 (5.9) | - | 2 (6.9) | - |
| | 5-10 | 4 (44.4) | 10 (29.4) | 3 (33.3) | 7 (24.1) | 2 (66.7) |
| | 10-15 | 2 (22.2) | 16 (47.1) | 4 (44.4) | 9 (31.0) | - |
| | Above 15 | 2 (22.2) | 6 (17.6) | 2 (22.2) | 11 (37.9) | 1 (33.3) |
| Rate of interest (in Per cent) | 5-10 | 2 (22.2) | 6 (17.6) | 1 (11.1) | 3 (10.3) | - |
| | 10-15 | 3 (33.3) | 13 (38.2) | 6 (66.7) | 17 (58.6) | 3 (100.0) |
| | Above 15 | 4 (44.4) | 15 (44.1) | 2 (22.2) | 9 (31.0) | - |

*Contd...*

| Factors | | Qualification | | | | |
|---|---|---|---|---|---|---|
| | | *Below S.S.L.C (n=9)* | *Pre-Degree (n=34)* | *Technical (n=9)* | *Graduate (n=29)* | *Post-graduate (n=3)* |
| Subsidies received from Govt. | Yes | 7 (77.8) | 30 (88.2) | 7 (77.8) | 25 (86.2) | 3 (100.0) |
| | No | 2 (22.2) | 4 (11.8) | 2 (22.2) | 4 (13.8) | - |
| Sources of working capital[b] | Collection from debtors/ cash sales | - | 14 (41.2) | 3 (33.3) | 10 (34.5) | 1 (33.3) |
| | Short term loan | 1 (11.1) | - | - | 1 (3.4) | - |
| | Friends/Relatives | 1 (11.1) | | 3 (33.3) | - | - |
| | Advance from customers | 1 (11.1) | 2 (5.9) | - | - | - |
| | Collection from Debtors/ cash sales and short term Loan | - | - | - | 1 (3.4) | - |
| | Collection from debtors/ cash sales and Friends/ Relatives | - | 2 (5.9) | 2 (22.2) | 6 (20.7) | 1 (33.3) |
| | Collection from debtors/ cash sales and Advance from customers | 6 (66.7) | 16 (47.1) | 1 (11.1) | 11 (37.9) | 1 (33.3) |
| Period of credit collection[a] (in days) | Less than 10 | 5 (55.6) | 12 (35.3) | 4 (44.4) | 13 (44.8) | 2 (66.7) |
| | 10-20 | 4 (44.4) | 15 (44.1) | 3 (33.3) | 13 (44.8) | - |
| | 1 month | - | 7 (20.6) | 2 (22.2) | 3 (10.3) | - |
| | Above 1 month | - | - | - | - | 1 (33.3) |

*Contd...*

| Factors | | Qualification | | | | |
|---|---|---|---|---|---|---|
| | | *Below S.S.L.C (n=9)* | *Pre-Degree (n=34)* | *Technical (n=9)* | *Graduate (n=29)* | *Post-graduate (n=3)* |
| Selling price of Flooring/ | 2-4 | 6 (66.7) | 25 (73.5) | 8 (88.9) | 23 (79.3) | 2 (66.7) |
| Roofing tiles per unit (in Rupees) | Above 4 | 3 (33.3) | 9 (26.5) | 1 (11.1) | 6 (20.7) | 1 (33.3) |
| Cost of clay per load (in Rupees) | 2000-4000 | 5 (55.6) | 18 (52.9) | 7 (77.8) | 19 (65.5) | 1 (33.3) |
| | 4000-6000 | 1 (11.1) | 7 (20.6) | 1 (11.1) | 4 (13.8) | 1 (33.3) |
| | 6000-8000 | 3 (33.3) | 3 (8.8) | - | 1 (3.4) | - |
| | Above 8000 | - | 6 (17.6) | 1 (11.1) | 5 (17.2) | 1(33.3) |
| Cost of Firewood per load (in Rupees) | Below 2500 | 1 (11.1) | - | - | 3 (10.3) | - |
| | 2500-5000 | 5 (55.6) | 24 (70.6) | 8 (88.9) | 20 (69.0) | 2 (66.7) |
| | 5000-7500 | 2 (22.2) | 5 (14.7) | - | 4 (13.8) | - |
| | 7500 and Above | 1 (11.1) | 5 (14.7) | 1 (11.1) | 2 (6.9) | 1 (33.3) |
| Cost of Oil per load (in Rupees) | Below 500 | 3 (33.3) | 2 (5.9) | 3 (33.3) | 8 (27.6) | 1 (33.3) |
| | 500-1000 | 3 (33.3) | 23 (67.6) | 5 (55.6) | 15 (51.7) | 1 (33.3) |
| | 1000-1500 | 1 (11.1) | 7 (20.6) | - | 4 (13.8) | - |
| | 1500 and Above | 2 (22.2) | 2 (5.9) | 1 (11.1) | 2 (6.9) | 1 (33.3) |
| Labour charges per load (in Rupees) | Below 2500 | - | 3 (8.8) | - | 5 (17.2) | - |
| | 2500-5000 | 5 (55.6) | 18 (52.9) | 6 (66.7) | 15 (51.7) | 1 (33.3) |
| | 5000-7500 | 4 (44.4) | 6 (17.6) | 3 (33.3) | 4 (13.8) | 1 (33.3) |
| | 7500 and Above | - | 7 (20.6) | - | 5 (17.2) | 1 (33.3) |
| Electricity charges per load (in Rupees) | Below 600 | 3 (33.3) | 2 (5.9) | - | 1 (3.4) | - |
| | 600-1200 | 3 (33.3) | 19 (55.9) | 6 (66.7) | 15 (51.7) | 1 (33.3) |
| | 1200-1800 | 2 (22.2) | 10 (29.4) | 3 (33.3) | 12 (41.4) | 2 (66.7) |
| | 1800 and Above | 1 (11.1) | 3 (8.8) | - | 1 (3.4) | - |

*Contd...*

| Factors | | Qualification | | | | |
|---|---|---|---|---|---|---|
| | | *Below S.S.L.C (n=9)* | *Pre-Degree (n=34)* | *Technical (n=9)* | *Graduate (n=29)* | *Post-graduate (n=3)* |
| Investment in Land and Buildings | Below 5 | - | 4 (11.8) | - | 3 (10.3) | - |
| (Rs. in lakhs) | 5–10 | 7 (77.8) | 17 (50.0) | 6 (66.7) | 11 (37.9) | 1 (33.3) |
| | 10–15 | 2 (22.2) | 11 (32.4) | 1 (11.1) | 13 (44.8) | 1 (33.3) |
| | Above 15 | - | 2 (5.9) | 2 (22.2) | 2 (6.9) | 1 (33.3) |
| Investment in Plant and Machinery | Below 3 | 1 (11.1) | 4 (11.8) | - | 1 (3.4) | - |
| (Rs. in lakhs) | 3–6 | 3 (33.3) | 8 (23.5) | 3 (33.3) | 7 (24.1) | 1 (33.3) |
| | 6–9 | 3 (33.3) | 8 (23.5) | 1 (11.1) | 9 (31.0) | - |
| | Above 9 | 2 (22.2) | 14 (41.2) | 5 (55.6) | 12 (41.4) | 2 (66.7) |
| Investment in Electrical fittings(in Rupees) | Below 30000 | 2 (22.2) | 6 (17.6) | - | 3 (10.3) | - |
| | 30000-60000 | 5 (55.6) | 16 (47.1) | 5 (55.6) | 10 (34.5) | 2 (66.7) |
| | 60000-90000 | 1 (11.1) | 4 (11.8) | 2 (22.2) | 4 (13.8) | - |
| | 90000 and Above | 1 (11.1) | 8 (23.5) | 2 (22.2) | 12 (41.4) | 1 (33.3) |
| Investment in Pallets and Frames | Below 30000 | - | - | - | 1 (3.4) | - |
| (in Rupees) | 30000-60000 | 2 (22.2) | 6 (17.6) | 1 (11.1) | 6 (20.7) | - |
| | 60000-90000 | 5 (55.6) | 7 (20.6) | 2 (22.2) | 6 (20.7) | 1 (33.3) |
| | 90000 and Above | 2 (22.2) | 21 (61.8) | 6 (66.7) | 16 (55.2) | 2 (66.7) |
| Investment in Chimney(Rs.in lakhs) | Below 3 | 3 (33.3) | 12 (35.3) | 3 (33.3) | 6 (20.7) | 1 (33.3) |
| | 3 – 6 | 5 (55.6) | 13 (38.2) | 3 (33.3) | 11 (37.9) | 1 (33.3) |
| | 6 – 9 | - | 9 (26.5) | 2 (22.2) | 9 (31.0) | - |
| | Above 9 | 1 (11.1) | - | 1 (11.1) | 3 (10.3) | 1 (33.3) |

*Contd...*

| Factors | | Qualification | | | | |
|---|---|---|---|---|---|---|
| | | *Below S.S.L.C (n=9)* | *Pre-Degree (n=34)* | *Technical (n=9)* | *Graduate (n=29)* | *Post-graduate (n=3)* |
| Investment in Furniture and Fittings (in Rupees) | Below 7000 | 1 (11.1) | 2 (5.9) | - | 1 (3.4) | - |
| | 7000-14000 | 2 (22.2) | 4 (11.8) | 3 (33.3) | 4 (13.8) | - |
| | 14000-21000 | 4 (44.4) | 16 (47.1) | 3 (33.3) | 10 (34.5) | 2 (66.7) |
| | 21000 and Above | 2 (22.2) | 12 (35.3) | 3 (33.3) | 14 (48.3) | 1 (33.3) |
| Expected rate of return(in Per cent) | Below 25 | 1 (11.1) | 2 (5.9) | 2 (22.2) | - | - |
| | 25-50 | 8 (88.9) | 32 (94.1) | 7 (77.8) | 27 (93.1) | 3 (100.0) |
| | 50-75 | - | - | - | 2 (6.9) | - |
| Average Actual rate of return(in Per cent) | Below 15 | 7 (77.8) | 22 (64.7) | 6 (66.7) | 12 (41.4) | 1 (33.3) |
| | 15-30 | 2 (22.2) | 12 (35.3) | 3 (33.3) | 17 (58.6) | 2 (66.7) |
| Performance of Finance function | Bad | 1 (11.1) | 7 (20.6) | 1 (11.1) | 5 (17.2) | 2 (66.7) |
| | Moderate | 2 (22.2) | 10 (29.4) | 2 (22.2) | 9 (31.0) | - |
| | Good | 6 (66.7) | 16 (47.1) | 6 (66.7) | 14 (48.3) | 1 (33.3) |
| | Excellent | - | 1 (2.9) | - | 1 (3.4) | - |

( ) in Percentage Contingency Coefficient ≥ 0.5 P-Value <0.01[a]
Contingency Coefficient ≥ 0.5 P-Value <0.05[b]
Contingency Coefficient ≤ 0.5 P-Value <0.01[c]
Contingency Coefficient ≤ 0.5 P-Value <0.05[d]

- Regarding long-term loans, 37.9 per cent of D have received Rs. 15 lakhs and above. 31 units have received Rs. 10 to 15 lakhs whereas 26 units Rs. 5 to 10 lakhs.
- 44.4 per cent of A and 44.1 per cent of B venture to pay an interest of 15 per cent and 66.7 per cent of C, 58.6 per cent of D and 100 per cent of E pay 10 to 15 per cent per annum.
- As for subsidies from the Government except 12 units, all the other 74 units receive subsidies.
- It is obvious that the sources of working capital are mainly collections from debtors, cash sales and advance from customers.
- Except 44 per cent of B and 44 per cent of D, all the other units allow a period of less than 10 days for collection.
- As regards selling price, a good majority of the units fix it in the range of Rs. 2 and 4.
- Cost of clay is kept at the minimum of Rs. 2000 to 4000 for a load by a vast majority of the units. Only 17.6 per cent of B, 11.1 per cent of C, 17.2 per cent of D and 33.3 per cent of E spend Rs. 8000 or above.
- Cost of firewood is between Rs. 2500 and 5000 for a vast majority of units. Only 10 units spend Rs. 7500 or above.
- The cost of oil per load is kept between Rs. 500 and 1000 per load which is neither too low nor too high. Only 8 units spend Rs. 1500 or above.
- Labour charges are also moderate, between Rs. 2500 and 5000 per load for more than 50 per cent of the units.
- Electricity charges are between Rs. 600 and 1200 for a majority of the units; only 5 units Rs. 1800 per load.
- Investment in land and buildings is normal for all the units. It is Rs. 5 to 10 lakhs. Only seven units have invested more than Rs. 15 lakhs.

- Investment in plant and machinery is high with a majority of the units. They have invested more than Rs. 9 lakhs.
- Expenses on electrical fittings in Rs. 30000 to 60000 with all the units except 24 units which spend the maximum of Rs. 90000 or above.
- 47 units spend Rs.90000 or above on pallets and frames. This is natural.
- The expenses on chimney are between Rs.3 and 6 lakhs with a vast majority of the units.
- Furniture and fittings take Rs. 14000 to 21000 for 35 units of 84, whereas 32 units spend Rs. 21000 or more.
- Almost all the units had expected a return of 25 to 50 per cent but the actual return was below 15 per cent for 48 units and between 15 and 30 per cent for 36 units.
- Performance is adjudged good for all the units.

Moreover, the results of the contingency co-efficient suggest that the factors of finance namely source of working capital and period of credit collection were associated with the qualification of the units owner of the clay tiles manufacturing units and these were statistically significant at one per cent and five per cent level.

Table 30 examines the units on the basis of their production capacity. The following code is used:

A = units producing 8000 tiles per day

B = units producing 8000 to 16000 tiles per day

C = units producing above 16000 tiles per day

- 94.1 per cent of units of C have invested more than Rs. 30 lakhs. Only 3 units of A have invested less than Rs. 10 lakhs.
- Invested own capital is highest with Rs. 15 lakhs in the case of 88 per cent of C but 58.8 per cent of A have only less than 5 lakhs.
- Only one unit of B does not borrow. Otherwise Kerala Finance Corporation is the major source of borrowing for the units – 88.2 per cent, 75.8 per cent and 82.4 per cent.

**Table 30**

**Factors of Finance Based in Installed Production Capacity Per Day**

| *Factors* | | *Capacity* | | |
|---|---|---|---|---|
| | | *Below8000 tiles (n=34)* | *8000-16000 tiles(n=33)* | *16000-24000 tiles (n=17)* |
| Total invested capital[a] (Rs.in lakhs) | Below 10 | 3 (8.8) | - | - |
| | 10-20 | 25 (73.5) | 2 (6.1) | - |
| | 20-30 | 6 (17.6) | 18 (54.5) | 1 (5.9) |
| | Above 30 | - | 13 (39.4) | 16 (94.1) |
| Invested own fund[a] (Rs.in lakhs) | Below 5 | 20 (58.8) | 4 (12.1) | - |
| | 5-10 | 11 (32.4) | 19 (57.6) | 1 (5.9) |
| | 10-15 | 3 (8.8) | 5 (15.2) | 1 (5.9) |
| | Above 15 | - | 5 (15.2) | 15 (88.2) |
| Major source of borrowed funds | Kerala Finance Corporation | 30 (88.2) | 25 (75.8) | 14 (82.4) |
| | Friends / Relatives | 2 (5.9) | 1 (3.0) | - |
| | Other loans from outsiders | 2 (5.9) | 6 (18.2) | 3 (17.6) |
| | None | - | 1 (3.0) | - |
| Long term loans received[a] (Rs. in lakhs) | Below 5 | 5 (14.7) | - | - |
| | 5-10 | 18 (52.9) | 3 (9.1) | 5 (29.4) |
| | 10-15 | 9 (26.5) | 18 (54.5) | 4 (23.5) |
| | Above 15 | 2 (5.9) | 12 (36.4) | 8 (47.1) |
| Rate of interest (in Per cent) | 5-10 | 6 (17.6) | 2 (6.1) | 4 (23.5) |
| | 10-15 | 19 (55.9) | 18 (54.5) | 5 (29.4) |
| | Above 15 | 9 (26.5) | 13 (39.4) | 8 (47.1) |
| Subsidies received from the Govt. | Yes | 31 (91.2) | 27 (81.8) | 14 (82.4) |
| | No | 3 (8.8) | 6 (18.2) | 3 (17.6) |

*Contd...*

| Factors | | Capacity | | |
|---|---|---|---|---|
| | | *Below8000 tiles (n=34)* | *8000-16000 tiles(n=33)* | *16000-24000 tiles (n=17)* |
| Sources of working capital | Collection from debtors/cash sales | 12 (35.3) | 13 (39.4) | 3 (17.6) |
| | Short term loan | 2 (5.9) | - | - |
| | Friends/Relatives | 3 (8.8) | - | 1 (5.9) |
| | Advance from customers | 2 (5.9) | 1 (3.0) | - |
| | Collection from Debtors/cash sales and short term Loan | 1 (2.9) | - | - |
| | Collection from debtors/cash sales and Friends/Relatives | 1 (2.9) | 4 (12.1) | 6 (35.3) |
| | Collection from debtors/cash sales and Advance from customers | 13 (38.2) | 15 (45.5) | 7 (41.2) |
| Credit collection period | Less than 10 days | 14 (41.2) | 12 (36.4) | 10 (58.8) |
| | 10-20 days | 13 (38.2) | 17 (51.5) | 5 (29.4) |
| | 1 month | 6 (17.6) | 4 (12.1) | 2 (11.8) |
| | Above 1 month | 1 (2.9) | - | - |
| Selling price of Flooring/Roofing tiles per unit (in Rupees) | 2-4 | 25 (73.5) | 25 (75.8) | 14(82.4) |
| | Above 4 | 9 (26.5) | 8 (24.2) | 3 (17.6) |
| Cost of clay per load (in Rupees) | 2000-4000 | 21 (61.8) | 16 (48.5) | 13 (76.5) |
| | 4000-6000 | 4 (11.8) | 9 (27.3) | 1 (5.9) |
| | 6000-8000 | 3 (8.8) | 2 (6.1) | 2 (11.8) |
| | Above 8000 | 6 (17.6) | 6 (18.2) | 1 (5.9) |
| Cost of Firewood per load (in Rupees) | Below 2500 | 1 (2.9) | - | 3 (17.6) |
| | 2500-5000 | 23 (67.6) | 25 (75.8) | 11 (64.7) |
| | 5000-7500 | 5 (14.7) | 3 (9.1) | 3 (17.6) |
| | 7500 and Above | 5 (14.7) | 5 (15.2) | - |

*Contd...*

| Factors | | Capacity | | |
|---|---|---|---|---|
| | | *Below8000 tiles (n=34)* | *8000-16000 tiles(n=33)* | *16000-24000 tiles (n=17)* |
| Cost of oil per load [c] (in Rupees) | Below 500 | 3(8.8) | 5(15.2) | 9(52.9) |
| | 500-1000 | 22(64.7) | 20(60.6) | 5(29.4) |
| | 1000-1500 | 6(17.6) | 3(9.1) | 3(17.6) |
| | 1500 and Above | 3(8.8) | 5(15.2) | - |
| Labour charges per load (in Rupees) | Below 2500 | - | - | 8(47.1) |
| | 2500-5000 | 20(58.8) | 19(57.6) | 6(35.3) |
| | 5000-7500 | 7(20.6) | 9(27.3) | 2(11.8) |
| | 7500 and Above | 7(20.6) | 5(15.2) | 1(5.9) |
| Electricity charges per load [a] (in Rupees) | Below 600 | 5(14.7) | 1(3.0) | - |
| | 600-1200 | 21(61.8) | 22(66.7) | 1(5.9) |
| | 1200-1800 | 7(20.6) | 9(27.3) | 13(76.5) |
| | 1800 and Above | 1(2.9) | 1(3.0) | 3(17.6) |
| Investment in Land and Buildings [a] (Rs. in lakhs) | Below 5 | 7(20.6) | - | - |
| | 5 –10 | 25(73.5) | 12(36.4) | 5(29.4) |
| | 10 – 15 | 2(5.9) | 20(60.6) | 6(35.3) |
| | Above 15 | - | 1(3.0) | 6(35.3) |
| Investment in Plant and Machinery [a] (Rs. in lakhs) | Below 3 | 6(17.6) | - | - |
| | 3 – 6 | 20(58.8) | 2(6.1) | - |
| | 6 – 9 | 7(20.6) | 14(42.4) | - |
| | Above 9 | 1(2.9) | 17(51.5) | 17(100.0) |
| Investment in Electrical fittings [a] (in Rupees) | Below 30000 | 10(29.4) | 1(3.0) | - |
| | 30000-60000 | 21(61.8) | 17(51.5) | - |
| | 60000-90000 | 2(5.9) | 9(27.3) | - |
| | 90000 and Above | 1(2.9) | 6(18.2) | 17(100.0) |

*Contd...*

| Factors | | Capacity | | |
|---|---|---|---|---|
| | | *Below8000 tiles (n=34)* | *8000-16000 tiles(n=33)* | *16000-24000 tiles (n=17)* |
| Investment in Pallets and Frames [a] (in Rupees) | Below 30000 | 1(2.9) | - | - |
| | 30000-60000 | 13(38.2) | 2(6.1) | - |
| | 60000-90000 | 14(41.2) | 7(21.2) | - |
| | 90000 and Above | 6(17.6) | 24(72.7) | 17(100.0) |
| Investment in Chimney [a] (Rs. in lakhs) | Below 3 | 23(67.6) | 2(6.1) | - |
| | 3 – 6 | 11(32.4) | 22(66.7) | - |
| | 6 – 9 | - | 9(27.3) | 11(64.7) |
| | Above 9 | - | - | 6(35.3) |
| Investment in Furniture and Fittings [a] (in Rupees) | Below 7000 | 4(11.8) | - | - |
| | 7000-14000 | 9(26.5) | 4(12.1) | - |
| | 14000-21000 | 18(52.9) | 16(48.5) | 1(5.9) |
| | 21000 and Above | 3(8.8) | 13(39.4) | 16(94.1) |
| Expected rate of return [d] (in Per cent) | Below 25 | 3(8.8) | 2(6.1) | - |
| | 25-50 | 31(91.2) | 31(93.9) | 15(88.2) |
| | 50-75 | - | - | 2(11.8) |
| Average Actual rate of return [c] (in Per cent) | Below 15 | 28(82.4) | 18(54.5) | 2(11.8) |
| | 15-30 | 6(17.6) | 15(45.5) | 15(88.2) |
| Performance of Financefunction [d] | Bad | 10(29.4) | 6(18.2) | - |
| | Moderate | 12(35.3) | 4(12.1) | 7(41.2) |
| | Good | 12(35.3) | 21(63.6) | 10(58.8) |
| | Excellent | - | 2(6.1) | - |

( ) in Percentage

Contingency Coefficient ≥ 0.5 P-Value < 0.01[a]
Contingency Coefficient ≥ 0.5 P-Value < 0.05[b]
Contingency Coefficient ≤ 0.5 P-Value < 0.01[c]
Contingency Coefficient ≤ 0.5 P-Value < 0.05[d]

- The heaviest borrowing of Rs. 15 lakhs is by 12 units of B and 8 units of C. Otherwise the long-term loans are mainly Rs. 5 to 10 lakhs and 10 to 15 lakhs.
- 55.9 per cent of A and 54.5 per cent of B pay an interest of 10 to 15 per cent on their loans, whereas 47.1 per cent of C pays a heavier interest of 15 per cent.
- Except 12 units, all the other units receive subsidies from the Government.
- 38.2 per cent of A, 45.5 per cent of B and 41.2 per cent of C depend on collection from debtors, cash sales and advances from customers for their working capital. The rest depend upon other sources like friends and relatives and short-term loans.
- 41.2 per cent of A and 58.8 per cent of C for collection grants a period of less than 10 days. 51.5 per cent of B gives 10 to 20 days. Only one unit of A allows more than a month.
- Selling price – 73.5 per cent of A, 75.8 per cent of B and 82.4 per cent of C fix it between Rs. 2 and 4 and the rest above Rs. 4.
- Cost of clay is kept at the minimum of Rs.2000 to 4000 by 61.8 per cent, 48.5 per cent and 76.5 per cent. Only 13 units spend more than Rs.8000.
- Cost of firewood per load is moderate (Rs.2500 to 5000) with 67.6 per cent, 75.8 per cent and 64.7 per cent. Only 5 units of each A and B spend more than Rs. 7500.
- Cost of oil for a load is Rs. 500 to 1000 in 64.7 per cent of A and 60.6 per cent of B. But a good proportion of C (52 per cent) manage to keep it below Rs. 500.
- Labour charges per load is below Rs. 2500 in 47 per cent of C, while it is Rs. 2500 to 5000 in 58.8 per cent of A and 57.6 per cent of B. 13 units spend more than Rs. 7500.
- Electricity charges are between Rs. 600 and 1200 per load in 61.5 per cent of A and 66.7 per cent of B. It is a little higher (1200 to 1800) in 76 per cent of C, probably because of the higher production capacity.

- Investment in land and buildings shows considerable variation. 73.5 per cent of A invested Rs. 5 to 10 lakhs, 60.6 per cent of B Rs. 10 to 15 lakhs and 35.3 per cent of C above Rs. 15 lakhs. It increases with the production capacity.
- Investment in plant and machinery also shows considerable variation. 58.8 per cent of A invested Rs. 3 to 6 lakhs, 51.5 per cent of B and 100 per cent of C above Rs.9 lakhs.
- Electrical fittings also vary according to the production capacity. All the units of C have spent more than Rs. 90000.
- All the units of C and 72.7 per cent of B have spent more than Rs. 90000 on pallets and frames.
- Chimney charges are also proportionate to the production capacity. 67.6 per cent of A have spent less than Rs. 3 lakhs, 66.7 per cent of B between Rs. 3 and 6 lakhs and 64 per cent of C Rs. 6 to 9 lakhs.
- 94.1 per cent of C have incurred an expense of more than Rs. 21000, whereas a good proportion of A and B have spent anywhere between Rs. 14000 and 21000.
- When compared with the expected return of 25 to 50 per cent, the actual return was below 15 per cent in 82.4 per cent of A, 54.5 per cent of B and between 15 and 30 per cent in 88.2 per cent of C.
- 2 units of B record excellent performance, otherwise the overall performance is good.

Moreover, the results of the contingency co-efficient suggest that the factors of finance such as total capital invested, invested own fund, long-term loan received, cost of oil, electricity charges, investment in land and building, investment in plant and machinery, electrical fittings, pallets and frames, chimney, furniture and fittings, expected rate of return, average rate of return and performance of finance function were associated with the installed production capacity of the units and these were statistically significant at one per cent and five per cent level.

Table 31

**Neural Classification Analysis–The Contribution of Various Finance Factors to the Performance of Finance Function in Alagappanagar**

*Dependent variable: Performance of Finance function*

| *Independent Variables* | *Importance Co-efficient* | *Normalised Weights* |
|---|---|---|
| Investment of capital | 0.03165 | 3.165 |
| Investment of owned fund | 0.05063 | 5.063 |
| Source of borrowed fund | 0.01899 | 1.899 |
| Long-term loans received | 0.05063 | 5.063 |
| Rate of Interest | 0.05063 | 5.063 |
| Subsidies received from Government | 0.01899 | 1.899 |
| Sources of working capital | 0.06329 | 6.329 |
| Credit collection period | 0.05063 | 5.063 |
| Selling price of tiles | 0.03797 | 3.797 |
| Cost of clay per load | 0.06962 | 6.962 |
| Cost of firewood per load | 0.03165 | 3.165 |
| Cost of oil per load | 0.09494 | 9.494 |
| Labour charges per load | 0.05696 | 5.696 |
| Electricity charges per load | 0.02532 | 2.532 |
| Investment in Land and buildings | 0.05696 | 5.696 |
| Investment in plant and machinery | 0.0443 | 4.43 |
| Investment in electrical fittings | 0.05063 | 5.063 |
| Investment in pallets and frames | 0.03797 | 3.797 |
| Investment in chimney / kiln | 0.05696 | 5.696 |
| Investment in furniture and fittings | 0.03797 | 3.797 |
| Expected rate of return | 0.0443 | 4.43 |
| Average actual rate of return | 0.01899 | 1.899 |

No. of hidden layers = 6 Estimation = Sequential Algorithm
Correct classification rate = 82.61%

Table 31 lists the contribution of various factors to the performance of finance based on the results of neural classification analysis. It is inferred from the table, the factors of finance such as cost of oil per load, cost of clay per load, sources of working capital, labour expenses per load, investment in land and building and investment in kiln attained a greater normalised weights of 9.494 per cent, 6.962 per cent, 6.329 per cent and 5.696 per cent respectively. This shows, that the above factors contributed to the performance of finance at a correct classification rate of 82.61 per cent. Moreover the number of hidden layers between the performance of finance and various factors was 6 and this confirms that there is a non-linear relationship between these two.

Hence, the level of performance of finance of the units in Alagappanagar was classified by the best discriminating factors such as cost of oil per load, cost of clay per load, sources of working capital, labour expenses per load, investment in land and building and investment in kiln.

**Table 32**

**Neural Classification Analysis–The Contribution of Various Finance Factors to the Performance of Finance Function in Chittissery**

*Dependent variable: Performance of Finance function*

| *Independent Variables* | *Importance Co-efficient* | *Normalised Weights* |
|---|---|---|
| Investment of capital | 0.03571 | 3.571 |
| Investment of owned fund | 0.03571 | 3.571 |
| Sources of working capital | 0.32143 | 32.143 |
| Cost of clay per load | 0.07143 | 7.143 |
| Cost of firewood per load | 0.07143 | 7.143 |
| Cost of oil per load | 0.03571 | 3.571 |
| Labour charges per load | 0.17857 | 17.857 |
| Investment in land and buildings | 0.03571 | 3.571 |
| Investment in plant and machinery | 0.03571 | 3.571 |
| Investment in electrical fittings | 0.03571 | 3.571 |
| Investment in chimney/kiln | 0.07143 | 7.143 |
| Investment in furniture and fittings | 0.07143 | 7.143 |

No. of hidden layers = 1    Estimation = Sequential Algorithm
Correct classification rate = 82.05%

Table 32 shows the contribution of various factors to the performance of finance based on the results of neural classification analysis. The factors such as sources of working capital and labour charges per load attained a greater normalised weights of 32.143 per cent and 17.857 per cent respectively. The other factors such as cost of clay per load, cost of firewood per load, investment in kiln and investment in furniture and fittings have made equal contribution of 7.143 per cent to the finance function. This shows that only the above factors contributed to the performance of finance at a correct classification rate of 82.05 per cent. Moreover the number of hidden layers between the performance of finance and various factors was 1 and this confirms that there is a non-linear relationship between these two.

Hence, the level of performance of finance of the units in Chittissery was predicted by the best discriminating factors such as Sources of working capital, labour charges per load, cost of clay per load and cost of firewood per load.

**Table 33**

**Neural Classification Analysis–The Contribution of Various Finance Factors to the Performance of Finance Function in Pudukad**

*Dependent variable: Performance of Finance function*

| *Independent Variables* | *Importance Co-efficient* | *Normalised Weights* |
|---|---|---|
| Investment of capital | 0.09091 | 9.091 |
| Sources of working capital | 0.09091 | 9.091 |
| Credit collection period | 0.09091 | 9.091 |
| Cost of firewood per load | 0.09091 | 9.091 |
| Cost of oil per load | 0.09091 | 9.091 |
| Cost of electricity charges per load | 0.09091 | 9.091 |
| Investment in plant and machinery | 0.09091 | 9.091 |
| Investment in electrical fittings | 0.18182 | 18.182 |
| Investment in chimney / kiln | 0.09091 | 9.091 |
| Investment in furniture and fittings | 0.09091 | 9.091 |

No. of hidden layers = 0 Estimation = Sequential Algorithm
Correct classification rate = 95.45%

Table 33 portrays the contribution of various factors to the finance based on the results of neural classification analysis. The factors of finance namely investment in electrical fittings alone contributed a major portion of 18.182 per cent; the remaining factors made an equal contribution of 9.091 per cent to the performance of finance. This shows that only the above factors contributed to the level of performance of finance at a correct classification rate of 95.45 per cent. Moreover the number of hidden layers between the performance of finance and various factors was 0 and this confirms that there is a linear relationship between these two.

Hence, the level of performance of finance of the units in Pudukad was predicted by the best discriminating factors namely investment in electrical fittings, investment of capital, sources of working capital, credit collection period, cost of firewood per load, cost of oil per load, cost of electricity charges per load, investment in plant and machinery, investment in kiln and investment in furniture and fittings.

**Table 34**

**Neural Classification Analysis–The Contribution of Various Finance Factors to the Performance of Finance Function in Thrissur District**

*Dependent variable: Performance of Finance function*

| *Independent Variables* | *Importance Co-efficient* | *Normalised Weights* |
|---|---|---|
| Investment of capital | 0.01471 | 1.471 |
| Investment of owned fund | 0.04412 | 4.412 |
| Long-term loans received | 0.10294 | 10.294 |
| Rate of Interest | 0.02941 | 2.941 |
| Sources of working capital | 0.02941 | 2.941 |
| Credit collection period | 0.01471 | 1.471 |
| Cost of clay per 6000 tiles | 0.01471 | 1.471 |
| Cost of oil per load | 0.10294 | 10.294 |
| Labour charges per load | 0.17647 | 17.647 |
| Investment in land and buildings | 0.01471 | 1.471 |
| Investment in plant and machinery | 0.08824 | 8.824 |
| Investment in electrical fittings | 0.22059 | 22.059 |
| Investment in pallets and frames | 0.01471 | 1.471 |
| Investment in furniture and fittings | 0.07353 | 7.353 |
| Expected rate of return | 0.01471 | 1.471 |
| Average actual rate of return | 0.04412 | 4.412 |

No. of hidden layers = 0

Estimation = Sequential Algorithm
Correct classification rate = 85.71%

Table 34 presents the contribution of various factors to the performance of finance based on the results of neural classification analysis. The factors of finance such as investment in electrical fittings, labour charges per load, long-term loans received, cost of oil per load and investment in plant and machinery attained a greater normalised weights of 22.059 per cent, 17.647 per cent, 10.294 per cent and 8.824 per cent respectively. This shows that only the above factors contributed to the performance of finance at a correct classification rate of 85.71 per cent. Moreover the number of hidden layers between the performance of finance and various factors was 0 and this confirms that there is a linear relationship between these two.

Hence, the level of performance of finance of the units in Thrissur District was classified by the best discriminating factors such as investment in electrical fittings, labour charges per load, long term loans received, cost of oil per load and investment in plant and machinery.

Table 35 visualises the various problems related to finance function based on the location of the units. The locations of the units were classified into three major areas such as Alagappanagar, Chittissery and Pudukad.

Out of 23 units located in Alagappanagar area, 43.5 per cent, 73.9 per cent, 78.3 per cent, 52.2 per cent, 39.1 per cent and 52.2 per cent of the units expressed that they encountered with the problems of insufficient subsidy, high rate of bank interest, shortage of working capital, irregular cash inflow, delay in debt collection and low sales respectively. 39.1 per cent of the units were not happy with the financial assistance provided by banks and other institutions.

Among the 39 units located in Chittissery area, two-third and 53.8 per cent of the units agreed that they were facing the problems of insufficient subsidy and irregular cash inflow respectively. Out of the two groups, each comprises of 51.3 per cent. The units stated that one was suffering with high rate of bank interest whereas the other one with shortage of working capital.

Finally, among the 22 units located in Pudukad area, 31.8 per cent, 72.7 per cent, 50 per cent, 40.9 per cent and 36.4 per cent of the units encountered with the problems of poor financial assistance by banks and other institutions, high rate of bank interest, shortage of working capital, irregular cash inflow and delay in debt collection respectively. Out of two groups each consists of 31.8 per cent of the units, one agreed that it suffered by insufficient subsidy whereas the other group disagreed to this. Similarly, another two groups each comprises

**Table 35**
**Problems in Finance Function Based on the Location of the Units**

| Problems | | Location | | |
|---|---|---|---|---|
| | | *Alagappanagar (n=23)* | *Chittissery (n=39)* | *Pudukad (n=22)* |
| Poor financial assistance received | Strongly Disagree | 2 (8.7) | 6 (15.4) | 3 (13.6) |
| | Disagree | 9 (39.1) | 20 (51.3) | 6 (27.3) |
| | Neutral | 2 (8.7) | 2 (5.1) | 2 (9.1) |
| | Agree | 6 (26.1) | 7 (17.9) | 7 (31.8) |
| | Strongly Agree | 4 (17.4) | 4 (10.3) | 4 (18.2) |
| Insufficient subsidy | Strongly Disagree | 2 (8.7) | 2 (5.1) | 1 (4.5) |
| | Disagree | 4 (17.4) | 5 (12.8) | 7 (31.8) |
| | Neutral | 3 (13.0) | 3 (7.7) | 2 (9.1) |
| | Agree | 10 (43.5) | 26 (66.7) | 7 (31.8) |
| | Strongly Agree | 4 (17.4) | 3 (7.7) | 5 (22.7) |
| High rate of Bank interest [d] | Strongly Disagree | - | - | - |
| | Disagree | - | 7 (17.9) | - |
| | Neutral | - | 1 (2.6) | 2 (9.1) |
| | Agree | 17 (73.9) | 20 (51.3) | 16 (72.7) |
| | Strongly Agree | 6 (26.1) | 11 (28.2) | 4 (18.2) |
| Shortage of working capital | Strongly Disagree | 1 (4.3) | 2 (5.1) | 2 (9.1) |
| | Disagree | 4 (17.4) | 9 (23.1) | 4 (18.2) |
| | Neutral | - | 3 (7.7) | 1 (4.5) |
| | Agree | 18 (78.3) | 20 (51.3) | 11 (50.0) |
| | Strongly Agree | - | 5 (12.8) | 4 (18.2) |
| Irregular cash Inflow | Strongly Disagree | 1 (4.3) | 2 (5.1) | 3 (13.6) |
| | Disagree | 6 (26.1) | 11 (28.2) | 5 (22.7) |
| | Neutral | 1 (4.3) | 2 (5.1) | 1 (4.5) |
| | Agree | 12 (52.2) | 21 (53.8) | 9 (40.9) |
| | Strongly Agree | 3 (13.0) | 3 (7.7) | 4 (18.2) |
| Delay in debt collection [d] | Strongly Disagree | - | 2 (5.1) | 4 (18.2) |
| | Disagree | 9 (39.1) | 23 (59.0) | 7 (31.8) |
| | Neutral | 3 (13.0) | 7 (17.9) | 2 (9.1) |
| | Agree | 9 (39.1) | 7 (17.9) | 8 (36.4) |
| | Strongly Agree | 2 (8.7) | - | 1 (4.5) |
| Slow sales | Strongly Disagree | - | 1 (2.6) | 2 (9.1) |
| | Disagree | 6 (26.1) | 21 (53.8) | 8 (36.4) |
| | Neutral | 4 (17.4) | 3 (7.7) | 2 (9.1) |
| | Agree | 12 (52.2) | 13 (33.3) | 8 (36.4) |
| | Strongly Agree | 1 (4.3) | 1 (2.6) | 2 (9.1) |

( ) in Percentage
Contingency Coefficient ≥ 0.5 P-Value < 0.01[a]
Contingency Coefficient ≥ 0.5 P-Value < 0.05[b]
Contingency Coefficient ≤ 0.5 P-Value < 0.01[c]
Contingency Coefficient ≤ 0.5 P-Value < 0.05[d]

of 36.4 per cent of the units, one agreed that it suffered with the problem of low sales whereas the other group disagreed to this.

Thus, the results of contingency co-efficient suggest that there is some relationship between the problems of finance function namely high rate of bank interest & delay in debt collection and the location of the units and these were statistically significant at 5 per cent level.

**Table 36**
**Stepwise Multiple Regression Analysis–The Impact of Various Finance Problems on the Performance of Finance Function in Chittissery**

*Dependent variable. Performance of Finance function (Y)*

| *Independent variable* | *Unstandardised Co-efficient* | *Standard Error* | *Standardised Co-efficient* | *t-value* | *p-value* |
|---|---|---|---|---|---|
| Constant | 4.743 | 0.314 | - | 15.080 | 0.000 |
| Shortage of working capital ($X_1$) | -0.321 | 0.087 | -0.518 | -3.686 | 0.001 |

Multiple R = 0.518 F- value = 13.587 D.F. (1,37) P-value < 0.01
R square = 0.269

$$\hat{Y} = 4.743 - 0.321X_1$$

Where $\hat{Y}$ is the estimated performance of finance.

Table 36 explains the impact of various problems on financial performance. The equation describes that, on an average if "Shortage of working capital" changes by one unit, there will be a decrease of 0.321 units in the performance of finance function.

The result of the t-test confirms that, the estimated regression coefficient (-0.321) is highly significant at one per cent level. The multiple R of 0.518 shows that there exists a relationship of 51.8 per cent between "Shortage of working capital" and performance of finance. Moreover, the $R^2$ of 0.269 confirms that the problem only explained 26.9 per cent of variation in the performance of finance function. Finally, the result of the f-test signifies that the variation was statistically significant at one per cent level. Hence, it can be concluded that the problem of "Shortage of working capital" significantly weakened the performance of finance function of clay tile manufacturing units located in Chittissery.

**Table 37**
**Stepwise Multiple Regression Analysis–The Impact of Various Finance Problems on the Performance of Finance Function in Pudukad**

*Dependent variable. Performance of Finance function (Y)*

| *Independent variable* | *Unstandardised Co-efficient* | *Standard Error* | *Standardised Co-efficient* | *t-value* | *p-value* |
|---|---|---|---|---|---|
| Constant | 4.783 | 0.449 | - | 10.649 | 0.000 |
| Shortage of working capital ($X_1$) | -0.522 | 0.121 | -0.694 | -4.317 | 0.000 |

Multiple R = 0.694  F- value = 18.632  D.F. (1,20)  P-value < 0.01
R square = 0.482

$$\hat{Y} = 4.783 - 0.522X_1$$

Where $\hat{Y}$ is the estimated performance of finance.

Table 37 explains the impact of various problems of finance on its performance. The equation describes that, on an average if "Shortage of working capital" changes by one unit, there will be a decrease of 0.522 units in the performance of finance function.

The result of the t-test confirms that, the estimated regression coefficient (-0.522) is highly significant at one per cent level. The multiple R of 0.694 shows that there exists a relationship of 69.4 per cent between "Shortage of working capital" and performance of finance function. Moreover, the $R^2$ of 0.482 confirms that the problem only explained 48.2 per cent of variation in the performance of finance function. Finally, the result of the f-test signifies that the variation was statistically significant at one per cent level. Hence, it can be concluded that the problem of "Shortage of working capital" significantly weakened the performance of finance function of clay tile manufacturing units located in Pudukad.

Table 38 shows the impact of various problems of finance on its performance. The equation describes that, on an average if "Shortage of working capital" changes by one unit, there will be a decrease of 0.213 units in the performance of finance when other problems such as "Delay in debt collection" and "Insufficient subsidy" are kept constant and vise versa.

**Table 38**
**Stepwise Multiple Regression Analysis–The Impact of Various Finance Problems on the Performance of Finance Function in Thrissur District**

*Dependent variable. Performance of Finance function (Y)*

| *Independent variables* | *Unstandardised Co-efficient* | *Standard Error* | *Standardised Co-efficient* | *t-value* | *p-value* |
|---|---|---|---|---|---|
| Constant | 5.226 | 0.305 | - | 17.127 | 0.000 |
| Shortage of working capital ($X_1$) | -0.213 | 0.080 | -0.290 | -2.669 | 0.009 |
| Delay in debt collection ($X_2$) | -0.229 | 0.081 | -0.298 | -2.840 | 0.006 |
| Insufficient subsidy ($X_3$) | -0.140 | 0.068 | -0.194 | -2.049 | 0.044 |

Multiple R = 0.591 F- value = 14.299 D.F. (3,80) P-value < 0.01
R square = 0.349

$$\hat{Y} = 5.226 - 0.213X_1 - 0.229X_2 - 0.140X_3$$

Where $\hat{Y}$ is the estimated performance of finance.

The results of the t-test confirm that, the estimated regression coefficients (-0.213), (-0.229) and (-0.140) are highly significant at one per cent level and five per cent respectively. The multiple R of 0.591 shows that there exists a relationship of 59.1 per cent between the above problems and finance. Moreover, the $R^2$ of 0.349 confirms that the problems only explain 34.9 per cent of variation in the performance of finance. Finally, the result of f-test signifies that the variation was statistically significant at one per cent level.

Hence, it can be concluded that the problems of "Delay in debt collection" significantly decreased the performance of finance followed by "Shortage of working capital" and "Insufficient subsidy" in Thrissur District.

Table 39 amplifies the number of workers employed in the clay tiles manufacturing units in Thrissur District. The numbers of workers were classified as below 20, 20 to 40 and 40 to 60. More than 55 per cent of the units were employing 20 to 40 workers and remaining 42.8 per cent (36) and 1.2 per cent (1) of them employed 40 to 60 and below 20 workers respectively.

**Table 39**
**Number of Workers in the Units**

| *Workers (in Numbers)* | *No. of Units* | *Per cent* |
|---|---|---|
| Less than 20 | 1 | 1.2 |
| 20–40 | 47 | 56.0 |
| 40–60 | 36 | 42.8 |
| More than 60 | - | - |
| Total | 84 | 100.0 |

*Source:* Primary Data.

Hence, the maximum 56 per cent of the clay tiles manufacturing units were employing 20 to 40 workers in their units.

**Table 40**
**Demand for Labour**

| *Nature* | *No. of Units* | *Per cent* |
|---|---|---|
| Adequate | 20 | 23.8 |
| Normal Demand | 48 | 57.2 |
| High demand | 16 | 19.0 |
| Excess | - | - |
| Total | 84 | 100.0 |

*Source:* Primary Data.

Table 40 shows the employment market of the clay tiles manufacturing units in Thrissur District. The nature of employment market was categorized as adequate, normal demand, high demand and excess. The employment market of 48 units had a normal demand, whereas that of 20 had an adequate demand and that of 16 a high demand.

Hence, the majority of 57.2 per cent of the clay tiles manufacturing units stated that there existed a normal demand for labour in their units.

**Table 41**
**Mode of Recruitment**

| *Mode* | *No. of Units* | *Per cent* |
|---|---|---|
| Interview | 9 | 10.7 |
| Contractors | 13 | 15.5 |
| Factory gate | 25 | 29.8 |
| Recommendation by existing labour | 37 | 44.0 |
| Total | 84 | 100.0 |

*Source:* Primary Data.

Table 41 gives the mode of recruitment of clay tiles manufacturing units. 44 per cent (37) of the units recruited the workers through the recommendation of labourers working in the same units; 29.8 per cent (25) recruited their workers from the factory gate and 15.5 per cent (13) through contractors.

Hence, the maximum 44 per cent of the clay tiles manufacturing units in Thrissur District were recruiting their workers based on the recommendations by existing labourers.

**Table 42**
**Basis of Selection of Workers**

| *Basis* | *No. of Units* | *Per cent* |
|---|---|---|
| Apprenticeship | 46 | 54.8 |
| Technical qualification | 9 | 10.7 |
| Previous experience | 29 | 34.5 |
| Total | 84 | 100.0 |

*Source:* Primary Data.

Table 42 clearly gives the basis of selection of workers in the units in Thrissur District. More than half of the units selected the workers by giving apprenticeship training; 34.5 per cent (29) selected the workers based on previous experience and 10.7 per cent (9) on the basis of technical qualifications acquired by them.

Hence, the majority 54.8 per cent of the clay tiles manufacturing units selected the workers on the basis of apprenticeship training.

**Table 43**
**Types of Labour**

| *Nature* | *No. of Units* | *Per cent* |
|---|---|---|
| Skilled labour | 50 | 59.5 |
| Semi-skilled labour | 18 | 21.5 |
| Unskilled labour | 16 | 19.0 |
| Total | 84 | 100.0 |

*Source:* Primary Data.

Table 43 provides the types of labour in the units located in Thrissur District. Out of 84 units, 59.5 per cent of the units were employing skilled workers; 21.5 per cent (18) employed the workers as semi-skilled and 19 per cent (16) unskilled.

Hence, the maximum 59.5 per cent of the clay tiles manufacturing units employed skilled workers.

**Table 44**
**Number of Shifts in a Day**

| *Shifts* | *No. of Units* | *Per cent* |
|---|---|---|
| Three | - | - |
| Two | 10 | 11.9 |
| One | 74 | 88.1 |
| Total | 84 | 100.0 |

*Source:* Primary Data.

Table 44 shows the number of shifts in a day. More than 85 per cent of the units were operating only one shift a day and remaining 11.9 per cent (10) of them operated two shifts.

Hence, the majority 88.1 per cent of the units were operating only one shift.

**Table 45**
**Basis of Payment of Remuneration**

| *Basis* | *No. of units* | *Per cent* |
|---|---|---|
| Time rate | 24 | 28.6 |
| Piece rate | - | - |
| Both | 60 | 71.4 |
| Total | 84 | 71.4.0 |

*Source:* Primary Data.

Table 45 gives the mode of payment of wages. From the total of 84 units, 71.4 per cent (60) of the units were using both time and piece rate for paying their workers and the remaining 28.6 per cent (24) followed the time rate method.

Hence, the maximum 71.4 per cent of the clay tiles manufacturing units in Thrissur District were following both time rate and piece rate for paying their workers.

**Table 46**
**Overtime Remuneration to Workers**

| *Basis* | *No. of units* | *Per cent* |
|---|---|---|
| Normal rate | - | - |
| 1.5 times of normal rate | 48 | 57.1 |
| 2 times or normal rate | - | - |
| None | 36 | 42.9 |
| Total | 84 | 42.9.0 |

*Source:* Primary Data.

Table 46 shows the overtime wages given to the by the units in Thrissur District. More than half of the units were paying overtime wages to their workers at the rate of 150 per cent of normal rate and remaining 42.9 per cent (36) of the units did not allow overtime facilities to their workers.

Hence, the majority 57.1 per cent of the clay tiles manufacturing units were paying overtime wages at the rate of 1.5 times normal rate.

**Table 47**
**Weekend Leave with Wages**

| *Response* | *No. of Units* | *Per cent* |
|---|---|---|
| Yes | 1 | 1.2 |
| No | 83 | 98.8 |
| Total | 84 | 100.0 |

*Source:* Primary Data.

Table 47 clearly gives the responses of the units to the weekend leave with wages. More than 95 per cent of the units did not allow their workers weekend off with pay. Only one unit allowed it.

Hence, the maximum 98.8 per cent of the units did not allow their workers weekend off with pay.

Table 4.48 clearly shows medical expenditure incurred on any accident at work site. From the total of 84 units, 66.7 per cent of the units did not provide the workers with medical allowances in case of any accident at work site but 33.3 per cent (28) of the units partly bore the medical expenses. However, the medical expenses may also be met from group insurance contributed by the employees and employer.

**Table 48**
**Medical Expenditure Incurred on Accident**

| *Response* | *No. of Units* | *Per cent* |
|---|---|---|
| Partly borne by unit | 28 | 33.3 |
| Borne by the unit itself | - | - |
| Fully borne by the worker | 56 | 66.7 |
| Total | 84 | 100.0 |

*Source:* Primary Data.

Hence, the majority 66.7 per cent of the units did not meet the medical expenses of the employees incase of any accident.

**Table 49**
**Reasons for Leave Allowed to Workers**
**(Other Than Week End and Govt. Holidays)**

| *Reasons* | *No. of Units* | *Per cent* |
|---|---|---|
| Shortage of Raw materials | 5 | 6.0 |
| Inadequate demand for product | 2 | 2.3 |
| Stoppage of production | 4 | 4.8 |
| Shortage of working capital | 6 | 7.1 |
| Not applicable | 67 | 79.8 |
| Total | 84 | 100.0 |

*Source:* Primary Data.

Table 49 lists the reasons for leave allowed to workers other than weekend leave and Government holidays. More than 75 per cent of the units were not giving any voluntary holidays to the workers. 7.1 per cent gave voluntary holidays to the workers due to shortage of working capital and 6 per cent of the units for shortage of raw materials.

Hence, the majority 79.8 per cent of the units did not give any voluntary holidays to the workers.

Table 50 shows the workers' membership in the unions. Out of 84 units, more than half of the unit workers did not join any unions; but 28.6 per cent (24) joined Indian National Trade Union Congress (INTUC) and 16.6 per cent (14) Centre of Indian Trade Union (CITU).

Hence, the maximum 54.8 per cent of the workers of the units in Thrissur District were not members of any of the unions.

**Table 50**
**Workers Membership in Union**

| *Union* | *No. of Units* | *Per cent* |
|---|---|---|
| CITU | 14 | 16.6 |
| INTUC | 24 | 28.6 |
| None | 46 | 54.8 |
| Total | 84 | 1000 |

*Source:* Primary Data.

**Table 51**
**Performance of Labour Function**

| *Level* | *No. of Units* | *Per cent* |
|---|---|---|
| Bad | 8 | 9.5 |
| Moderate | 16 | 19.0 |
| Good | 57 | 67.9 |
| Excellent | 3 | 3.6 |
| Total | 84 | 100.0 |

*Source:* Primary Data.

Table 51 gives the performance levels of the labour. 67.9 per cent (57) of the units agreed that the performance of labour

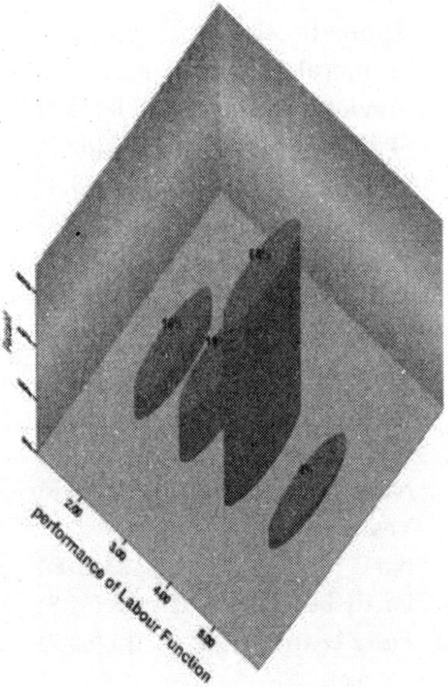


**Diagram 2**

was good; 19 per cent (16) stated that their labour performance was moderate and 9.5 per cent (8) bad.

Hence, majority 67.9 per cent of the units stated that their overall performance of labour was good.

**Table 52**
**Factors of Labour Based on the Location of the Units**

| *Factors* | | *Location* | | |
|---|---|---|---|---|
| | | *Alagappanagar (n=23)* | *Chittissery (n=39)* | *Pudukad (n=22)* |
| Number of workers | Below 20 | - | 1 (2.6) | - |
| | 20-40 | 13 (56.5) | 25 (64.1) | 9 (40.9) |
| | 40-60 | 10 (43.5) | 13 (33.3) | 13 (59.1) |
| Demand for Labour | Adequate | 6 (26.1) | 7 (17.9) | 7 (31.8) |
| | Normal Demand | 13 (56.5) | 23 (59) | 12 (54.5) |
| | High demand | 4 (17.4) | 9 (23.1) | 3 (13.6) |
| Mode of recruitment | Interview | 1 (4.3) | 5 (12.8) | 3 (13.6) |
| | Contractor | 6 (26.1) | 6 (15.4) | 1 (4.5) |
| | Factory gate | 5 (21.7) | 15 (38.5) | 5 (22.7) |
| | Recommendation by existing labour | 11 (47.8) | 13 (33.3) | 13 (59.1) |
| Basis of selection of workers | Apprenticeship | 13 (56.5) | 22 (56.4) | 11 (50) |
| | Technical qualification | 2 (8.7) | 3 (7.7) | 4 (18.2) |
| | Previous experience | 8 (34.8) | 14 (35.9) | 7 (31.8) |
| Type of Labour | Skilled labour | 15 (65.2) | 23 (59) | 12 (54.5) |
| | Semi-skilled labour | 4 (17.4) | 12 (30.8) | 2 (9.1) |
| | Unskilled labour | 4 (17.4) | 4 (10.3) | 8 (36.4) |
| Number of shifts in a day | Two | 4 (17.4) | 5 (12.8) | 1 (4.5) |
| | One | 19 (82.6) | 34 (87.2) | 21 (95.5) |
| Method of payment of remuneration | Time rate | 7 (30.4) | 10 (25.6) | 7 (31.8) |
| | Time and Piece rate | 16 (69.6) | 29 (74.4) | 15 (68.2) |
| Overtime remuneration to workers | 1.5 times of normal rate | 13 (56.5) | 22 (56.4) | 13 (59.1) |
| | None | 10 (43.5) | 17 (43.6) | 9 (40.9) |
| Providing weekend leave with wages | Yes | - | 1 (2.6) | - |
| | No | 23 (100) | 38 (97.4) | 2 2 (100) |
| Medical expenditure incurred for accident | Partly beard by unit | 8 (34.8) | 12 (30.8) | 8 (36.4) |
| | Fully beard by the worker | 15 (65.2) | 27 (69.2) | 14 (63.6) |

*Contd...*

| Factors | | Location | | |
|---|---|---|---|---|
| | | *Alagappanagar (n=23)* | *Chittissery (n=39)* | *Pudukad (n=22)* |
| Reasons for leave allowed to workers | Shortage of Raw materials | 1 (4.3) | 3 (7.7) | 1 (4.5) |
| | Inadequate demand for product | - | 2 (5.1) | - |
| | Stoppage of production | - | 3 (7.7) | 1 (4.5) |
| | Shortage of working capital | 5 (21.7) | - | 1 (4.5) |
| | Not applicable | 17 (73.9) | 31 (79.5) | 19 (86.4) |
| Workers membership in union | CITU | 6 (26.1) | 6 (15.4) | 2 (9.1) |
| | INTUC | 7 (30.4) | 13 (33.3) | 4 (18.2) |
| | None | 10 (43.5) | 20 (51.3) | 16 (72.7) |
| Performance of labour function | Bad | 2 (8.7) | 2 (5.1) | 4 (18.2) |
| | Moderate | 6 (26.1) | 6 (15.4) | 4 (18.2) |
| | Good | 15 (65.2) | 28 (71.8) | 14 (63.6) |
| | Excellent | - | 3 (7.7) | - |

( ) in Percentage

Table 52 examines labour on the basis of the location of the units. The following code is used.

A = Alagappanagar

B = Chittissery

C = Pudukad

- 13 units of C employ 40 to 60 workers whereas 56.3 per cent of A and 64.1 per cent of B employ 20 to 40 workers.
- Demand for labour is normal in all three locations (56.5 per cent of A, 59 per cent of B and 54.5 per cent of C).
- Mode of recruitment is mainly the recommendation of the present workers – 47.8 per cent of A, 59 per cent of C.
- Apprenticeship forms the basis for selection of workers- a majority 56.5 per cent of A, 56.4 per cent of B and half of the units of C.
- Skilled labour is the largest in most of the units. It holds good in 65.2 per cent of A, 59 per cent of B and 54.5 per cent of C.

- A large majority of units run only one shift a day (82.6 per cent of A, 87.2 per cent of B and 95.5 per cent of C)
- Most of the units pay their workers both by time rate and piece rate.
- Most of the units pay 1.5 times the regular wages as overtime allowance, a majority of above each 56 per cent of A and B, and 59 per cent of C.
- Except one unit of B, no unit grants weekend leave with wages.
- Regarding medical expenses on account of any accident at work spot, a maximum of 65.2 per cent of A, 69.2 per cent of B and 63.6 per cent of C do not meet the expenses; they are borne by the workers. The employer provides only group insurance claim.
- Most of the units function normally and there is no reason for leave. Shortage of working capital or raw materials and stoppage of production affect only very few units and 67 units did not have any reason to give leave to the workers on account of stoppage of work.
- Centre of Indian Trade Union (CITU) has poor membership and Indian National Trade Union Congress (INTUC) fares no better. A majority of workers are non-members of the trade unions.
- Performance of labour has been good, a maximum of 65.2 per cent of A, 71.8 per cent of B and 63.6 per cent of C.

Table 53 shows particulars of labour with reference to the establishment of the units. The following code is used.

A = establishment before 1981
B = establishment between 1981 and 1985
C = establishment between 1985 and 1990
D = establishment 1990 and after

- The number of workers in most of the units is between 20 and 40, irrespective of the year of establishment. But 43.3 per cent of C and 47.6 per cent of D employ more than 40 workers.

**Table 53**
**Factors of Labour Based on the Year of Establishment**

| *Factors* | | *Year* | | | |
|---|---|---|---|---|---|
| | | *Before) 1981 (n=5)* | *1981-1985 (n=7)* | *1985-1990 (n=30)* | *1990 and After (n=42)* |
| Number of workers | Below 20 | 1 (20.0) | - | - | - |
| | 20-40 | 3 (60.0) | 5 (71.4) | 17 (56.7) | 22 (52.4) |
| | 40-60 | 1 (20.0) | 2 (28.6) | 13 (43.3) | 20 (47.6) |
| Demand for Labour | Adequate | - | - | 10 (33.3) | 10 (23.8) |
| | Normal Demand | 4 (80.0) | 6 (85.7) | 11 (36.7) | 27 (64.3) |
| | High demand | 1 (20.0) | 1 (14.3) | 9 (30) | 5 (11.9) |
| Mode of recruitment | Interview | 2 (40.0) | - | 2 (6.7) | 5 (11.9) |
| | Contractor | 1 (20.0) | - | 6 (20) | 6 (14.3) |
| | Factory gate | 2 (40.0) | 1 (14.3) | 9 (30) | 13 (31) |
| | Recommendation by existing labour | - | 6 (85.7) | 13 (43.3) | 18 (42.9) |
| Basis of selection of workers | Apprenticeship | 1 (20.0) | 3 (42.9) | 19 (63.3) | 23 (54.8) |
| | Technical qualification | 1 (20.0) | 1 (14.3) | 2 (6.7) | 5 (11.9) |
| | Previous experience | 3 (60.0) | 3 (42.9) | 9 (30) | 14 (33.3) |
| Types of Labour | Skilled labour | 4 (80.0) | 4 (57.1) | 19 (63.3) | 23 (54.8) |
| | Semi-skilled labour | 1 (20.0) | 1 (14.3) | 9 (30) | 7 (16.7) |
| | Unskilled labour | - | 2 (28.6) | 2 (6.7) | 12 (28.6) |
| Number of shifts in a day | Two | 1 (20.0) | 2 (28.6) | 5 (16.7) | 2 (4.8) |
| | One | 4 (80.0) | 5 (71.4) | 25 (83.3) | 40 (95.2) |
| Method of payment of remuneration | Time rate | 2 (40.0) | - | 9 (30) | 13 (31) |
| | Time and Piece rate | 3 (60.0) | 7 (100) | 21 (70) | 29 (69) |

*Contd...*

| *Factors* | | *Year* | | | |
|---|---|---|---|---|---|
| | | *Before) 1981 (n=5)* | *1981- 1985 (n=7)* | *1985- 1990 (n=30)* | *1990 and After (n=42)* |
| Overtime remuneration to workers | 1.5 times of normal rate | 2 (40.0) | 4 (57.1) | 17 (56.7) | 25 (59.5) |
| | None | 3 (60.0) | 3 (42.9) | 13 (43.3) | 17 (40.5) |
| Providing weekend leave with wages | Yes | - | - | - | 1 (2.4) |
| | No | 5 (100.0) | 7 (100) | 30 (100) | 41 (97.6) |
| Medical expenditure incurred for accident | Partly beard by unit | 1 (20.0) | 3 (42.9) | 12 (40) | 12 (28.6) |
| | Fully beard by the worker | 4 (80.0) | 4 (57.1) | 18 (60) | 30 (71.4) |
| Reasons for leave allowed to workers | Shortage of Raw materials | - | - | 1 (3.3) | 4 (9.5) |
| | Inadequate demand for product | - | - | 1 (3.3) | 1 (2.4) |
| | Stoppage of production | 1 (20.0) | 1 (14.3) | - | 2 (4.8) |
| | Shortage of working capital | - | - | 5 (16.7) | 1 (2.4) |
| | Not applicable | 4 (80.0) | 6 (85.7) | 23 (76.7) | 34 (81) |
| Workers membership in union [a] | CITU | 2 (40.0) | 1 (14.3) | 9 (30) | 2 (4.8) |
| | INTUC | 3 (60.0) | 5 (71.4) | 14 (46.7) | 2 (4.8) |
| | NONE | - | 1 (14.3) | 7 (23.3) | 38 (90.5) |
| Performance of labour function | Bad | 1 (20.0) | 1 (14.3) | 1 (3.3) | 5 (11.9) |
| | Moderate | - | 2 (28.6) | 5 (16.7) | 9 (21.4) |
| | Good | 3 (60.0) | 3 (42.9) | 24 (80) | 27 (64.3) |
| | Excellent | 1 (20.0) | 1 (14.3) | - | 1 (2.4) |

( )in Percentage Contingency Coefficient $\geq 0.5$ P-Value $<0.01$ [a]
Contingency Coefficient $\geq 0.5$ P-Value $<0.05$ [b]
Contingency Coefficient $\geq 0.5$ P-Value $<0.01$ [c]
Contingency Coefficient $\geq 0.5$ P-Value $<0.05$ [d]

- Normal demand for labour prevails with a majority of 80 per cent of A, 85.7 per cent of B, 36.7 per cent of C and 64 3 per cent of D.
- None of A care for recruitment on the recommendations but 85.7 per cent of B, 43.3 per cent of C and 42.9 per cent of D make their recruitment on the recommendations of present employees.
- 46 units select workers after apprenticeship whereas 29 units give preference to previous experience.
- The proportion of skilled labour to other types of labour is preponderant with a majority of 80 per cent of A, 57.1 per cent of B, 63.3 per cent of C and 54.8 per cent of D.
- Most units work one shift a day, irrespective of the year of establishment.
- Regarding the basis of payment 100 per cent of B, 70 per cent of C, 69 per cent of D and 60 per cent of A adopt both time and piece-rate.
- 60 per cent of A don't allow any overtime allowance but 57.1 per cent of B, 56.7 per cent of C and 59.5 per cent of D make overtime payment of 150 per cent of normal rate.
- Except one unit of D, no unit accepts weekend leave with pay.
- Medical expenses on account of accident have to be borne by the workers in most of the units. The employer provides only groups insurance claim.
- Shortage of working capital or raw materials and stoppage of production affect only very few units and 67 units did not have any reason to give leave to the workers on account of stoppage of work.
- Indian National Trade Union Congress was more popular than Centre of Indian Trade Union with A, B and C, but 90 per cent of D have no membership of any trade union.

**Table 54**

**Factors of Labour Based on the Jurisdiction of the Units**

| Factors | | *Jurisdiction* Panchayat (n=74) | Municipality (n=9) | Corporation (n=1) |
|---|---|---|---|---|
| Number of workers | Below 20 | 1 (1.4) | - | - |
| | 20-40 | 40 (54.1) | 7 (77.8) | - |
| | 40-60 | 33 (44.6) | 2 (22.2) | 1 (100) |
| Demand for Labour | Adequate | 18 (24.3) | 2 (22.2) | - |
| | Normal Demand | 43 (58.1) | 4 (44.4) | 1 (100) |
| | High demand | 13 (17.6) | 3 (33.3) | - |
| Mode of recruitment | Interview | 7 (9.5) | 2 (22.2) | - |
| | Contractor | 9 (12.2) | 4 (44.4) | - |
| | Factory gate | 23 (31.1) | 1 (11.1) | 1 (100) |
| | Recommendation by existing labour | 35 (47.3) | 2 (22.2) | - |
| Basis of selection of workers | Apprenticeship | 41 (55.4) | 5 (55.6) | - |
| | Technical qualification | 7 (9.5) | 2 (22.2) | - |
| | Previous experience | 26 (35.1) | 2 (22.2) | 1 (100) |
| Types of Labour | Skilled labour | 42 (56.8) | 7 (77.8) | 1 (100) |
| | Semi-skilled labour | 16 (21.6) | 2 (22.2) | - |
| | Unskilled labour | 16 (21.6) | - | - |
| Number of shifts in a day | Two | 7 (9.5) | 3 (33.3) | - |
| | One | 67 (90.5) | 6 (66.7) | 1 (100) |

*Contd...*

| Factors | | Jurisdiction<br>Panchayat (n=74) | <br>Municipality (n=9) | <br>Corporation (n=1) |
|---|---|---|---|---|
| Method of payment of remuneration | Time rate | 19 (25.7) | 5 (55.6) | - |
| Overtime remuneration to workers | Time and Piece rate | 55 (74.3) | 4 (44.4) | 1 (100) |
| | 1.5 times of normal rate | 41 (55.4) | 6 (66.7) | 1 (100) |
| | None | 33 (44.6) | 3 (33.3) | - |
| Weekend leave with wages | Yes | 1 (1.4) | - | - |
| | No | 73 (98.6) | 9 (100) | 1 (100) |
| Medical expenditure | Partly beard by unit | 26 (35.1) | 2 (22.2) | - |
| incurred for accident | Fully beard by the worker | 48 (64.9) | 7 (77.8) | 1 (100) |
| Reasons for leave allowed to workers | Shortage of Raw materials | 5 (6.8) | - | - |
| | Inadequate demand for product | 2 (2.7) | - | - |
| | Stoppage of production | 3 (4.1) | 1 (11.1) | - |
| | Shortage of working capital | 6 (8.1) | - | - |
| | Not applicable | 58 (78.4) | 8 (88.9) | 1 (100) |
| Workers membership in union | CITU | 13 (17.6) | 1 (11.1) | - |
| | INTUC | 20 (27) | 3 (33.3) | 1 (100) |
| | None | 41 (55.4) | 5 (55.6) | - |
| Performance of labour function | Bad | 8 (10.8) | - | - |
| | Moderate | 15 (20.3) | 1 (11.1) | - |
| | Good | 48 (64.9) | 8 (88.9) | 1 (100) |
| | Excellent | 3 (4.1) | - | - |

( )in Percentage

- The performance of C (80 per cent) exceeds that of other groups, and the performance of the most of the units has been uniformly good.

Moreover, the results of the contingency co-efficient suggest that the factors of labour such as number of workers, membership of workers and performance of labour function were associated with the year of establishment of the units and these were statistically significant at one per cent level.

Table 54 gives particulars of labour with reference to the Jurisdiction of the units. The following code is used.

A = Panchayat

B = Municipality

C = Corporation

- 44.6 per cent of A and 22 per cent of B and the one unit of C employ more than 40 workers. Only one unit of A employs less than 20. Otherwise, 47 units employ 20 to 40 workers.
- Demand for labour is normal in 58.1 per cent in A, 44.4 per cent in B and 100 per cent in C.
- Regarding the mode of recruitment the only unit of C recruits at factory gate (open selection), while 44.4 per cent of B contacts the contractors, and 47.3 per cent of A goes by the recommendations of present workers.
- The only unit of C made the selection on the basis of previous experience, while 55.4 per cent of A and 55.6 per cent of B made the selection by apprenticeship.
- Regarding the type of labour, the skilled labour is predominant - 56.8 per cent of A, 77.8 per cent of B and 100 per cent of C of the units appointed skilled labourers.
- Except 7 units of A and 3 units of B, all the units work one shift a day.
- The only unit of C adopts both time rate and piece rate methods of payment and also 74.3 per cent of A and 44.4 per cent of B.

- 55.4 per cent of A, 66.7 per cent of B and the only unit of C gives overtime allowance of 1.5 times the normal wages.
- Except one unit of A, no unit grants weekend leave with wages.
- The workers (64.9 per cent of A and 77.8 per cent of B and one unit of C) had to bear all the medical expenses. The employer provides only group insurance.
- Except 17 units of A and one unit of B, there was no reason for stoppage of work and leave with pay.
- Indian National Trade Union Congress was more popular than Centre of Indian Trade Union with A, B and C. Sizable majority of A, B and the only unit of C have no union membership.
- 64.9 per cent of A, 88.9 per cent of B and one unit of C have recorded good performance, while 3 units of A have done excellently well.

Table 55 explains the particulars of labour on the basis of the type of tiles manufactured by the units. The following codes are used.

A = Roofing tiles
B = Flooring tiles
C = Other tiles
D = Roofing and flooring tiles
E = Flooring and decorative tiles
F = Decorative and other tiles

- Only one unit of B employs fewer than 20 workers. All the four units of A and 64.3 per cent of B, 55.6 per cent of C, 12.5 per cent of D, 50 per cent of E employed 20 to 40 labourers.
- Normal demand for labour prevailed in a vast majority of 3 units of A, 57.1 per cent of B, 44.4 per cent of C, 75 per cent of D and 55 per cent of E.
- Recommendations by the present workers weighed with the recruitment.

**Table 55**

**Factors of Labour Based on the Type of Clay Tiles Manufactured by the Units**

| Factors | | Types of Clay Tiles | | | | | |
|---|---|---|---|---|---|---|---|
| | | *Roofing (n=4)* | *Flooring (n=42)* | *Other tiles (n=9)* | *Roofing & Flooring (n=8)* | *Flooring & Decorative & (n=20)* | *Decorative & other tiles (n=1)* |
| Number of workers | Below 20 | - | 1(2.4) | - | - | - | - |
| | 20-40 | 4(100.0) | 27(64.3) | 5(55.6) | 1(12.5) | 10(50) | - |
| | 40-60 | - | 14(33.3) | 4(44.4) | 7(87.5) | 10(50) | 1(100) |
| Demand for Labour | Adequate | 1(25.0) | 8(19) | 3(33.3) | 1(12.5) | 6(30) | 1(100) |
| | Normal Demand | 3(75.0) | 24(57.1) | 4(44.4) | 6(75) | 11(55) | - |
| | High demand | - | 10(23.8) | 2(22.2) | 1(12.5) | 3(15) | - |
| Mode of recruitment | Interview | - | 6(14.3) | 2(22.2) | - | 1(5) | - |
| | Contractor | - | 5(11.9) | 2(22.2) | 2(25) | 4(20) | - |
| | Factory gate | 2(50.0) | 13(31) | 1(11.1) | 1(12.5) | 8(40) | - |
| | Recommendation by existing labour | 2(50.0) | 18(42.9) | 4(44.4) | 5(62.5) | 7(35) | 1(100) |
| Basis of selection of workers | Apprenticeship | 3(75.0) | 21(50) | 3(33.3) | 5(62.5) | 13(65) | 1(100) |
| | Technical qualification | - | 5(11.9) | 2(22.2) | - | 2(10) | - |
| | Previous experience | 1(25.0) | 16(38.1) | 4(44.4) | 3(37.5) | 5(25) | - |
| Types of Labour | Skilled labour | 3(75.0) | 27(64.3) | 5(55.6) | 5(62.5) | 9(45) | 1(100) |
| | Semi-skilled labour | - | 9(21.4) | 2(22.2) | 1(12.5) | 6(30) | - |
| | Unskilled labour | 1(25.0) | 6(14.3) | 2(22.2) | 2(25) | 5(25) | - |
| Number of shifts in a day | Two | - | 6(14.3) | 2(22.2) | - | 2(10) | - |
| | One | 4(100.0) | 36(85.7) | 7(77.8) | 8(100) | 18(90) | 1(100) |

*Contd...*

| Factors | | Types of Clay Tiles | | | | | |
|---|---|---|---|---|---|---|---|
| | | *Roofing (n=4)* | *Flooring (n=42)* | *Other tiles (n=9)* | *Roofing & Flooring (n=8)* | *Flooring & Decorative & (n=20)* | *Decorative & other tiles (n=1)* |
| Method of payment of remuneration | Time rate | - | 15(35.7) | 1(11.1) | 2(25) | 5(25) | 1(100) |
| | Time and Piece rate | 4(100.0) | 27(64.3) | 8(88.9) | 6(75) | 15(75) | - |
| Overtime remuneration to workers | 1.5 times of normal rate | 3(75.0) | 26(61.9) | 5(55.6) | 4(50) | 10(50) | - |
| | None | 1(25.0) | 16(38.1) | 4(44.4) | 4(50) | 10(50) | 1(100) |
| Weekend leave with wages | Yes | - | 1(2.4) | - | - | - | - |
| | No | 4(100.0) | 41(97.6) | 9(100) | 8(100) | 20(100) | 1(100) |
| Medical expenditure incurred for accident | Partly beard by unit | 1(25.0) | 16(38.1) | 3(33.3) | 3(37.5) | 5(25) | - |
| | Fully beard by the worker | 3(75.0) | 26(61.9) | 6(66.7) | 5(62.5) | 15(75) | 1(100) |
| Reasons for leave allowed to workers | Shortage of Raw materials | - | 3(7.1) | - | 1(12.5) | 1(5) | - |
| | Inadequate demand for product | - | 1(2.4) | - | - | 1(5) | - |
| | Stoppage of production | - | 2(4.8) | - | 2(25) | - | - |
| | Shortage of working capital | - | 2(4.8) | 2(22.2) | 1(12.5) | 1(5) | - |
| | Not applicable | 4(100.0) | 34(81) | 7(77.8) | 4(50) | 17(85) | 1(100) |
| Workers membership in union | CITU | 1(25.0) | 8(19) | 2(22.2) | 1(12.5) | 2(10) | - |
| | INTUC | 1(25.0) | 10(23.8) | 4(44.4) | 4(50) | 5(25) | - |
| | None | 2(50.0) | 24(57.1) | 3(33.3) | 3(37.5) | 13(65) | 1(100) |
| Performance of labour function [a] | Bad | 2(50.0) | 1(2.4) | 1(11.1) | 2(25) | 2(10) | - |
| | Moderate | 1(25.0) | 7(16.7) | 1(11.1) | 1(12.5) | 6(30) | - |
| | Good | 1(25.0) | 34(81) | 6(66.7) | 3(37.5) | 12(60) | 1(100) |
| | Excellent | - | - | 1(11.1) | 2(25) | - | - |

( )in Percentage Contingency Coefficient ≤ 0.5 P-Value <0.01[a] Contingency Coefficient ≤ 0.5 P-Value <0.05[b]
Contingency Coefficient ≥ 0.5 P-Value <0.01[c] Contingency Coefficient ≥ 0.5 P-Value <0.05[d]

- Most of the units preferred apprenticeship for selection of the workers.
- A majority of units of all the categories have appointed a large number of skilled labourers.
- 6 unit in B, 2 units of C and 2 units of E had 2 shifts a day. All the others had only one shift.
- Paying both by time-rate and piece-rate was favoured by a vast majority of units.
- Regarding overtime payment, 1.5 times the normal wages were paid by 75 per cent of A, 61.9 per cent of B, 55.6 per cent of C, each 50 per cent of D and E. All the other units did not encourage overtime.
- Except one unit of B, no other unit accepted the idea of weekend leave with pay.
- Most of the units of all the categories did not accept to meet the medical expenses of the workers at times of accidents.
- 100 per cent of A, 81, per cent of B, 77.8 per cent of C, 50 per cent of D, 85 per cent of E and one unit of F had no reason to allow leave to workers.
- Sizable majority of the units have no union membership.
- The performances of most of the units have been uniformly good.

Moreover, the results of the contingency co-efficient suggest that the factor of labour namely the performance of labour function was associated with the type of clay tiles manufactured by the units and this was statistically significant at one per cent level.

Table 56 shows particulars of labour on the basis of ownership of the units. The following code is used.

A = Sole proprietorship

B = Partnership

C = Co-operative society

D = Private company

**Table 56**
**Factors of Labour Based on Ownership of the Units**

| Factors | | *Ownership* | | | |
|---|---|---|---|---|---|
| | | *Sole Proprietor (n=48)* | *Partnership (n=29)* | *Co-op. Society (n=4)* | *Private company (n=3)* |
| Number of workers | Below 20 | - | 1 (3.4) | - | - |
| | 20-40 | 25 (52.1) | 18 (62.1) | 1 (25.0) | 3 (100.0) |
| | 40-60 | 23 (47.9) | 10 (34.5) | 3 (75.0) | - |
| Demand for Labour | Adequate | 12 (25) | 6 (20.7) | 2 (50.0) | - |
| | Normal Demand | 25 (52.1) | 18 (62.1) | 2 (50.0) | 3 (100.0) |
| | High demand | 11 (22.9) | 5 (17.2) | - | - |
| Mode of recruitment | Interview | 4 (8.3) | 4 (13.8) | - | 1 (33.3.0) |
| | Contractor | 8 (16.7) | 4 (13.8) | 1 (25.0) | - |
| | Factory gate | 13 (27.1) | 8 (27.6) | 3 (75.0) | 1 (33.3.0) |
| | Recommendation by existing labour | 23 (47.9) | 13 (44.8) | - | 1 (33.3.0) |
| Basis of selection of workers [d] | Apprenticeship | 31 (64.6) | 14 (48.3) | 1 (25.0) | - |
| | Technical qualification | 4 (8.3) | 3 (10.3) | - | 2 (66.7.0) |
| | Previous experience | 13 (27.1) | 12 (41.4) | 3 (75.0) | 1 (33.3.0) |
| Types of Labour | Skilled labour | 32 (66.7) | 14 (48.3) | 2 (50.0) | 2 (66.7.0) |
| | Semi-skilled labour | 7 (14.6) | 8 (27.6) | 2 (50.0) | 1 (33.3.0) |
| | Unskilled labour | 9 (18.8) | 7 (24.1) | - | - |
| Number of shifts in a day | Two | 6 (12.5) | 3 (10.3) | - | 1 (33.3.0) |
| | One | 42 (87.5) | 26 (89.7) | 4 (100.0) | 2 (66.7.0) |

*Contd...*

| Factors | | Ownership | | | |
|---|---|---|---|---|---|
| | | Sole Proprietor (n=48) | Partnership (n=29) | Co-op. Society (n=4) | Private company (n=3) |
| Method of payment of remuneration | Time rate | 13 (27.1) | 8 (27.6) | 2 (50.0) | 1 (33.3.0) |
| | Time and Piece rate | 35 (72.9) | 21 (72.4) | 2 (50.0) | 2 (66.7.0) |
| Overtime remuneration to workers | 1.5 times of normal rate | 28 (58.3) | 16 (55.2) | 2 (50.0) | 2 (66.7.0) |
| | None | 20 (41.7) | 13 (44.8) | 2 (50.0) | 1 (33.3.0) |
| Weekend leave with wages | Yes | - | 1 (3.4) | - | - |
| | No | 48 (100) | 28 (96.6) | 4 (100.0) | 3 (100.0) |
| Medical expenditure incurred for accident | Partly beard by unit | 15 (31.3) | 11 (37.9) | - | 2 (66.7.0) |
| | Fully beard by the worker | 33 (68.8) | 18 (62.1) | 4 (100.0) | 1 (33.3.0) |
| Reasons for leave allowed to workers | Shortage of Raw materials | 3 (6.3) | 2 (6.9) | - | - |
| | Inadequate demand for product | - | 2 (6.9) | - | - |
| | Stoppage of production | 1 (2.1) | 2 (6.9) | 1 (25.0) | - |
| | Shortage of working capital | 4 (8.3) | 2 (6.9) | - | - |
| | Not applicable | 40 (83.3) | 21 (72.4) | 3 (75.0) | 3 (100.0) |
| Workers membership in union | CITU | 10 (20.8) | 2 (6.9) | 1 (25.0) | 1 (33.3.0) |
| | INTUC | 10 (20.8) | 10 (34.5) | 3 (75.0) | 1 (33.3.0) |
| | None | 28 (58.3) | 17 (58.6) | - | 1 (33.3.0) |
| Performance of labour function | Bad | 3 (6.3) | 4 (13.8) | 1 (25.0) | - |
| | Moderate | 10 (20.8) | 5 (17.2) | - | 1 (33.3.0) |
| | Good | 33 (68.8) | 19 (65.5) | 3 (75.0) | 2 (66.7.0) |
| | Excellent | 2 (4.2) | 1 (3.4) | - | - |

( ) in Percentage    Contingency Coefficient ≤ 0.5 P-Value <0.01[a]    Contingency Coefficient ≤ 0.5 P-Value <0.05[b]
Contingency Coefficient ≥ 0.5 P-Value <0.01[c]    Contingency Coefficient ≥ 0.5 P-Value <0.05[d]

- Only one unit of B employed less than 20 workers. 52.1 per cent of A, 62.1 per cent of B, 25 per cent of C and all units of D employed 20 to 40 labourers.
- There was normal demand for labour in majority of units.
- Recommendations by present labourers were mainly considered for recruitment (47.9 per cent of A, 44.8 per cent of B and 33.3 per cent of D). The only deviation is 75 per cent of C which recruited at factory gate (open recruitment).
- Apprenticeship was the favoured basis for selection with 64.6 per cent of A, 48.3 per cent of B and 25 per cent of C. But 27.1 per cent of A, 41.4 per cent of B 75 per cent of C and 33.3 per cent of D all depended upon previous experience.
- Skilled labour formed the largest proportion.
- 6 units of A, 3 units of B and one unit of D had two shifts a day. Whereas all the other units ran one shift.
- Even though 50 per cent of C preferred to pay by time rate, both time rate and piece rate were adopted by a majority of units.
- Overtime payment was 1.5 times the normal wages by a majority of the units (48 out of 84).
- Except one unit of B, no other unit permits weekend leave with wages.
- 31.3 per cent of A, 37.9 per cent of B and 66.7 per cent of D bear the medical expenses of workers party. All the other units did not meet the medical expenses. The employer provides only group insurance claim. This amount contributed by employer and employee.
- 67 units out of 84 had no reason for leave to workers with pay, because there was no shortage of raw materials or labour.
- Regarding union membership, 58.3 per cent of A, 58.6 per cent of B had no membership. C is the most

remarkable with 25 per cent of CITU membership and 75 per cent of INTUC membership. D has equal share of CITU, INTUC and no membership – that is one unit in each.

- Performance has been good, irrespective of the nature of ownership.

Moreover, the results of the contingency co-efficient suggest that the factor of labour namely basis of selection of workers was associated with the ownership of the units and this was statistically significant at five per cent level.

Table 57 examines labour on the basis of the educational qualifications of the owners. The following code is used.

A = Below SSLC

B = Pre-degree

C = Technical

D = Graduate

E = Post-graduate

- 66.7 per cent of A employed more than 40 workers, otherwise a good majority employed 20 to 40 workers.
- There was a normal demand for labour in a majority of the units.
- Factory gate recruitment was the favoured mode with 55.6 per cent each of A and C. But recommendations of present workers weighed with B, D and E.
- Regarding the basis for selection, both apprenticeship and previous experience were equally important.
- Skilled labourers out-number semi-skilled and unskilled labourers.
- Except 10 units, all the other 74 units had only one shift a day.
- Regarding the method of payment, both time rate and piece-rate were followed by a majority of units.
- A majority of units allowed 1.5 normal wages as overtime payment.

**Table 57**
**Factors of Labour Based on the Educational Qualifications of the Unit Owner**

| Factors | | Qualification | | | | |
|---|---|---|---|---|---|---|
| | | *Below S.S.L.C (n=9)* | *Pre-Degree (n=34)* | *Technical (n=9)* | *Graduate (n=29)* | *Post-graduate (n=3)* |
| Number of workers | Below 20 | - | 1(2.9) | - | - | - |
| | 20-40 | 3(33.3) | 17(50) | 6(66.7) | 19(65.5) | 2(66.7) |
| | 40-60 | 6(66.7) | 16(47.1) | 3(33.3) | 10(34.5) | 1(33.3) |
| Demand for Labour | Adequate | 2(22.2) | 11(32.4) | 1(11.1) | 5(17.2) | 1(33.3) |
| | Normal Demand | 6(66.7) | 17(50) | 7(77.8) | 16(55.2) | 2(66.7) |
| | High demand | 1(11.1) | 6(17.6) | 1(11.1) | 8(27.6) | - |
| Mode of recruitment | Interview | - | 1(2.9) | 1(11.1) | 7(24.1) | - |
| | Contractor | 1(11.1) | 8(23.5) | - | 4(13.8) | - |
| | Factory gate | 5(55.6) | 10(29.4) | 5(55.6) | 4(13.8) | 1(33.3) |
| | Recommendation by existing labour | 3(33.3) | 15(44.1) | 3(33.3) | 14(48.3) | 2(66.7) |
| Basis of selection of workers | Apprenticeship | 5(55.6) | 25(73.5) | 4(44.4) | 12(41.4) | - |
| | Technical qualification | 1(11.1) | 2(5.9) | 1(11.1) | 5(17.2) | - |
| | Previous experience | 3(33.3) | 7(20.6) | 4(44.4) | 12(41.4) | 3(100) |
| Types of Labour [d] | Skilled labour | 5(55.6) | 20(58.8) | 5(55.6) | 18(62.1) | 2(66.7) |
| | Semi-skilled labour | 4(44.4) | 3(8.8) | 4(44.4) | 7(24.1) | - |
| | Unskilled labour | - | 11(32.4) | - | 4(13.8) | 1(33.3) |
| Number of shifts in a day | Two | 1(11.1) | 5(14.7) | 1(11.1) | 3(10.3) | - |
| | One | 8(88.9) | 29(85.3) | 8(88.9) | 26(89.7) | 3(100) |
| Method of payment of remuneration | Time rate | 2(22.2) | 9(26.5) | 3(33.3) | 10(34.5) | - |
| | Time and Piece rate | 7(77.8) | 25(73.5) | 6(66.7) | 19(65.5) | 3(100) |

*Contd...*

| Factors | | Qualification | | | | |
|---|---|---|---|---|---|---|
| | | *Below S.S.L.C (n=9)* | *Pre-Degree (n=34)* | *Technical (n=9)* | *Graduate (n=29)* | *Post-graduate (n=3)* |
| Overtime remuneration to workers | 1.5 times of normal rate | 4(44.4) | 19(55.9) | 4(44.4) | 19(65.5) | 2(66.7) |
| | None | 5(55.6) | 15(44.1) | 5(55.6) | 10(34.5) | 1(33.3) |
| Weekend leave with wages | Yes | - | - | - | 1(3.4) | - |
| | No | 9(100) | 34(100) | 9(100) | 28(96.6) | 3(100) |
| Medical expenditure incurred for accident | Partly beard by unit | 1(11.1) | 15(44.1) | 3(33.3) | 9(31) | - |
| | Fully beard by the worker | 8(88.9) | 19(55.9) | 6(66.7) | 20(69) | 3(100) |
| Reasons for leave allowed to workers | Shortage of Raw materials | - | 2(5.9) | 1(11.1) | 2(6.9) | - |
| | Inadequate demand for product | 1(11.1) | - | 1(11.1) | - | - |
| | Stoppage of production | 1(11.1) | 1(2.9) | 1(11.1) | 1(3.4) | - |
| | Shortage of working capital | - | 4(11.8) | 1(11.1) | 1(3.4) | - |
| | Not applicable | 7(77.8) | 27(79.4) | 5(55.6) | 25(86.2) | 3(100) |
| Workers membership in union | CITU | 1(11.1) | 6(17.6) | 2(22.2) | 5(17.2) | - |
| | INTUC | 3(33.3) | 9(26.5) | 2(22.2) | 9(31) | 1(33.3) |
| | None | 5(55.6) | 19(55.9) | 5(55.6) | 15(51.7) | 2(66.7) |
| Performance of labour function | Bad | - | 4(11.8) | - | 2(6.9) | 2(66.7) |
| | Moderate | - | 8(23.5) | 1(11.1) | 7(24.1) | - |
| | Good | 8(88.9) | 22(64.7) | 8(88.9) | 18(62.1) | 1(33.3) |
| | Excellent | 1(11.1) | - | - | 2(6.9) | - |

( )in Percentage Contingency Coefficient ≤ 0.5 P-Value <0.01[a] Contingency Coefficient ≤ 0.5 P-Value <0.05[b]
Contingency Coefficient ≥ 0.5 P-Value <0.01[c] Contingency Coefficient ≥ 0.5 P-Value <0.05[d]

- Except one unit of D, no other unit allowed weekend leave with pay.
- 28 units paid partly the medical expenses of workers, while all the other units did not pay medical allowance.
- There was no reason for leave allowed to workers with pay in majority of 67 units.
- 46 units out of 84 had no union membership.
- Performance has continued to be good in a good majority of the units.

Moreover, the results of the contingency co-efficient suggest that the factor viz., skill of labour was associated with the qualification of the owners of the units and this was statistically significant at five per cent level.

**Table 58**
**Factors of Labour Based on Installed Production Capacity Per day**

| *Factors* | | *Capacity* | | |
|---|---|---|---|---|
| | | *Below 8000 (n=34)* | *8000-16000 (n=33)* | *16000-24000 (n=17)* |
| Number of Workers [a] | Below 20 | - | - | 1(5.9) |
| | 20-40 | 1(2.9) | 30(90.9) | 16(94.1) |
| | 40-60 | 33(97.1) | 3(9.1) | - |
| Demand for Labour [d] | Adequate | 13(38.2) | 7(21.2) | - |
| | Normal Demand | 16(47.1) | 20(60.6) | 12(70.6) |
| | High demand | 5(14.7) | 6(18.2) | 5(29.4) |
| Mode of recruitment [d] | Interview | 1(2.9) | 3(9.1) | 5(29.4) |
| | Contractor | 5(14.7) | 6(18.2) | 2(11.8) |
| | Factory gate | 14(41.2) | 10(30.3) | 1(5.9) |
| | Recommendation by existing labour | 14(41.2) | 14(42.4) | 9(52.9) |
| Basis of selection of workers [c] | Apprenticeship | 23(67.6) | 17(51.5) | 6(35.3) |
| | Technical qualification | - | 2(6.1) | 7(41.2) |
| | Previous experience | 11(32.4) | 14(42.4) | 4(23.5) |
| Types of Labour | Skilled labour | 17(50) | 19(57.6) | 14(82.4) |
| | Semi-skilled labour | 8(23.5) | 7(21.2) | 3(17.6) |
| | Unskilled labour | 9(26.5) | 7(21.2) | - |
| Number of shifts in a day [a] | Two | - | - | 10(58.8) |
| | One | 34(100) | 33(100) | 7(41.2) |

*Contd...*

| Factors | | Capacity Below 8000 (n=34) | 8000-16000 (n=33) | 16000-24000 (n=17) |
|---|---|---|---|---|
| Method of payment of remuneration | Time rate | 10(29.4) | 8(24.2) | 6(35.3) |
| | Time and Piece rate | 24(70.6) | 25(75.8) | 11(64.7) |
| Overtime remuneration to workers[c] | 1.5 times of normal rate | 13(38.2) | 21(63.6) | 14(82.4) |
| | None | 21(61.8) | 12(36.4) | 3(17.6) |
| Weekend leave with wages | Yes | 1(2.9) | - | - |
| | No | 33(97.1) | 33(100) | 17(100) |
| Medical expenditure incurred for accident | Partly beard by unit | 8(23.5) | 14(42.4) | 6(35.3) |
| | Fully beard by the worker | 26(76.5) | 19(57.6) | 11(64.7) |
| Reasons for leave allowed to workers | Shortage of Raw materials | 2(5.9) | 2(6.1) | 1(5.9) |
| | Inadequate demand for product | 1(2.9) | 1(3) | - |
| | Stoppage of production | 1(2.9) | 3(9.1) | - |
| | Shortage of working capital | 2(5.9) | 2(6.1) | 2(11.8) |
| | Not applicable | 28(82.4) | 25(75.8) | 14(82.4) |
| Workers membership in union | CITU | 3(8.8) | 7(21.2) | 4(23.5) |
| | INTUC | 8(23.5) | 10(30.3) | 6(35.3) |
| | None | 23(67.6) | 16(48.5) | 7(41.2) |
| Performance of labour function | Bad | 3(8.8) | 5(15.2) | - |
| | Moderate | 10(29.4) | 3(9.1) | 3(17.6) |
| | Good | 20(58.8) | 23(69.7) | 14(82.4) |
| | Excellent | 1(2.9) | 2(6.1) | - |

( )in Percentage
Contingency Coefficient ≥ 0.5 P-Value <0.01[a]
Contingency Coefficient ≥ 0.5 P-Value <0.05[b]
Contingency Coefficient ≤ 0.5 P-Value <0.01[c]
Contingency Coefficient ≤ 0.5 P-Value <0.05[d]

Table 58 gives particulars of labour on the basis of the production capacity of the units. The following code is used.

A = Units with the production capacity of 8000 tiles a day

B = 8,000 to 16,000 tiles a day

C = 16,000 to 24,000 tiles a day

- Regarding the number of workers, 97.1 per cent of A employed more than 40 workers. Whereas 90.9 per cent of B and 94.1 per cent of C employed 20 to 40 workers only one units of C employed fewer than 20.
- Demand for labour has remained normal in 47.1 per cent of A, 60.6 per cent of B and 70.6 per cent of C.
- Recommendations by the present employees decided the mode of recruitment with 41.2 per cent of A, 42.4 per cent of B and 52.9 per cent of C. Factory gate recruitment figured prominently with 41.2 per cent of A.
- Apprenticeship was the favoured basis of selection of workers (67.7 per cent of A, 51.5 per cent of B, 35.3 per cent of C).
- Skilled labour dominated in 50 units, a majority of 50 per cent of A, 57.6 per cent of B and 82.4 per cent of C.
- Except 10 units of C, all the others run one shift a day (100 per cent of A, 100 per cent of B and 41.2 per cent of C).
- 70.6 per cent of A, 75.8 per cent of B and 64.7 per cent of C favoured payment both by time rate and piece rate according to the circumstances.
- 38.2 per cent of A, 63.6 per cent of B and 64.7 per cent of C allowed overtime payment of 1.5 times the normal wages.
- Except one unit of A, no other units allowed weekend holiday with pay.
- A majority of the units did not bear any responsibility regarding medical expenses of the workers.
- 67 units did not have any problem like shortage of raw materials or working capital or inadequate demand for the product. So, there was no need for allowing leave to the workers with pay.
- Non-membership in trade unions dominated, a majority 67.6 per cent of A, 48.5 per cent of B and 41.2 per cent of C.

- Regarding performance, only 8 units fared badly and 3 units did excellently. The performance had been good in the case of 67 units.

Moreover, the results of the contingency co-efficient suggest that the factors of labour such as number of workers, demand for labour, mode of recruitment, basis of selection of workers, number of shifts in a day and overtime remuneration to workers were associated with the installed production capacity of the units and these were statistically significant at one per cent and five per cent level.

**Table 59**

**Neural Classification Analysis–The Contribution of Various Labour Factors to the Performance of Labour Function in Alagappanagar**

*Dependent variable: Performance of Labour function*

| *Independent Variables* | *Importance Co-efficient* | *Normalised Weights* |
|---|---|---|
| Number of workers in the units | 0.05263 | 5.263 |
| Demand for labour | 0.08772 | 8.772 |
| Mode of recruitment | 0.14035 | 14.035 |
| Basis of selection of workers | 0.05263 | 5.263 |
| Types of Labour | 0.03509 | 3.509 |
| Number of shifts in a day | 0.01754 | 1.754 |
| Methods followed for payment of remuneration | 0.01754 | 1.754 |
| Basis of overtime remuneration | 0.15789 | 15.789 |
| Medical expenditure incurred for accident | 0.10526 | 10.526 |
| Reasons for leave allowed to workers | 0.21053 | 21.053 |
| Workers membership in union | 0.12281 | 12.281 |

No. of hidden layers = 15

Estimation = Sequential Algorithm
Correct classification rate = 91.30%

Table 59 portrays the contribution of various factors to the performance of labour based on the results of neural classification analysis. The factors of labour such as reasons for leave allowed to workers, basis of overtime remuneration, mode of recruitment and worker membership with union attained a greater normalised weights of 21.053 per cent, 15.789 per cent, 14.035 per cent and 12.281 per cent respectively. This shows, among the 12 different factors of labour only the above factors contributed to the performance at a correct classification rate of 91.30 per cent. Moreover the number of hidden layers between the performance of labour function and various factors was 15 and this confirms that there is a non-linear relationship between these two.

Hence, it can be concluded that the level of performance of labour of the units in Alagappanagar was classified by the best discriminating factors such as reasons for leave allowed to workers, basis of overtime remuneration, mode of recruitment and worker membership with union.

**Table 60**
**Neural Classification Analysis–The Contribution of Various Labour Factors to The Performance of Labour Function in Chittissery**

*Dependent variable: Performance of Labour function*

| *Independent Variables* | *Importance Co-efficient* | *Normalised Weights* |
|---|---|---|
| Number of workers in the units | 0.02439 | 2.439 |
| Demand for labour | 0.31707 | 31.707 |
| Mode of recruitment | 0.14634 | 14.634 |
| Basis of selection of workers | 0.17073 | 17.073 |
| Types of Labour | 0.04878 | 4.878 |
| Number of shifts in a day | 0.02439 | 2.439 |
| Method followed for payment of remuneration | 0.02439 | 2.439 |
| Basis of overtime remuneration | 0.02439 | 2.439 |
| Medical expenditure incurred for accident | 0.14634 | 14.634 |
| Workers membership in union | 0.07317 | 7.317 |

No. of hidden layers = 4 Estimation = Sequential Algorithm
Correct classification rate = 84.62%

Table 60 provides the contribution of various factors to the performance of labour based on the results of neural classification analysis. The factors of labour such as demand for labour, basis of selection of workers and mode of recruitment attained a greater normalised weights of 31.707 per cent, 17.073 per cent and 14.634 per cent respectively. This shows that only the above factors emerged and contributed to the performance of labour at a correct classification rate of 84.62 per cent. Moreover the number of hidden layers between the performance of labour function and various factors was 4 and this confirms that there is a non-linear relationship between these two.

Hence, the level of performance of labour function of the units in Chittissery was classified by the best discriminating factors such as Demand for labour, basis of selection of workers and mode of recruitment.

**Table 61**
**Neural Classification Analysis–The Contribution of Various Labour Factors to the Performance of Labour Function in Pudukad**

*Dependent variable: Performance of Labour function*

| *Independent Variables* | *Importance Co-efficient* | *Normalised Weights* |
|---|---|---|
| Demand for labour | 0.05405 | 5.405 |
| Mode of recruitment | 0.18919 | 18.919 |
| Basis of selection of workers | 0.16216 | 16.216 |
| Types of Labour | 0.18919 | 18.919 |
| Methods followed for payment of remuneration | 0.10811 | 10.811 |
| Basis of overtime remuneration | 0.02703 | 2.703 |
| Medical expenditure incurred for accident | 0.13514 | 13.514 |
| Reasons for leave allowed to workers | 0.05405 | 5.405 |
| Workers membership in union | 0.08108 | 8.108 |

No. of hidden layers = 17 Estimation = Sequential Algorithm
Correct classification rate = 95.45%

Table 61 shows the contribution of various factors to the performance of labour function based on the results of neural classification analysis. The factors of labour such as mode of recruitment, types of labour, basis of selection of workers and bearing of medical expenditure attained a greater normalised weights of 18.919 per cent, 16.216 per cent and 13.514 per cent respectively. This shows that only the above factors contributed to the performance of labour at a correct classification rate of 95.45 per cent. Moreover the number of hidden layers between the performance of labour and various factors was 17 and this confirms that there is a non-linear relationship between these two.

Hence, it can be concluded that the level of performance of labour of the units in Pudukad was classified by the best discriminating factors such as mode of recruitment, types of labour, basis of selection of workers and bearing of medical expenditure.

**Table 62**

**Neural Classification Analysis–The Contribution of Various Labour Factors to the Performance of Labour Function in Thrissur District**

*Dependent variable: Performance of Labour function*

| *Independent Variables* | *Importance Co-efficient* | *Normalised Weights* |
|---|---|---|
| Number of workers in the units | 0.11446 | 11.446 |
| Demand for labour | 0.13253 | 13.253 |
| Mode of recruitment | 0.08434 | 8.434 |
| Basis of selection of workers | 0.04217 | 4.217 |
| Types of Labour | 0.09036 | 9.036 |
| Number of shifts in a day | 0.00602 | 0.602 |
| Methods followed for payment of remuneration | 0.06627 | 6.627 |
| Basis of overtime remuneration | 0.08434 | 8.434 |
| Medical expenditure incurred for accident | 0.05422 | 5.422 |
| Reasons for leave allowed to workers | 0.16867 | 16.867 |
| Workers membership in union | 0.15663 | 15.663 |

No. of hidden layers = 23 Estimation = Sequential Algorithm
Correct classification rate = 92.86%

Table 62 explains the contribution of various factors to the performance of labour based on the results of neural classification analysis. It is inferred from the table that the factors such as reasons for leave allowed to workers, workers membership in union, demand for labour and number of workers in the units attained a greater normalised weights of 16.867 per cent, 15.663 per cent, 13.253 per cent and 11.446 per cent respectively. This shows that among the 12 different factors only the above contributed to performance of labour at a correct classification rate of 92.86 per cent. Moreover the number of hidden layers between the performance of labour and various factors was 23 and this confirms that there is a non-linear relationship between these two.

Hence, it can be concluded that the level of performance of labour of the units in Thrissur District was classified by the best discriminating factors such as reasons for leave allowed to workers, workers membership in union, demand for labour and number of workers in the units.

**Table 63**
**Problems in Labour Function Based on the Location of the Units**

| *Problems* | | *Location* | | |
|---|---|---|---|---|
| | | *Alagappanagar (n=23)* | *Chittissery (n=39)* | *Pudukad (n=22)* |
| Inadequate skilled labour | Strongly Disagree | - | - | - |
| | Disagree | 1(4.3) | 2(5.1) | - |
| | Neutral | - | 1(2.6) | - |
| | Agree | 8(34.8) | 15(38.5) | 9(40.9) |
| | Strongly Agree | 14(60.9) | 21(53.8) | 13(59.1) |
| Labour Absenteeism | Strongly Disagree | - | - | - |
| | Disagree | 3(13.0) | 5(12.8) | 2(9.1) |
| | Neutral | 4(17.4) | 3(7.7) | 5(22.7) |
| | Agree | 8(34.8) | 20(51.3) | 9(40.9) |
| | Strongly Agree | 8(34.8) | 11(28.2) | 6(27.3) |
| Expenses involved in training the workers | Strongly Disagree | - | 1(2.6) | 1(4.5) |
| | Disagree | 7(30.4) | 17(43.6) | 6(27.3) |
| | Neutral | 3(13.0) | 9(23.1) | 6(27.3) |
| | Agree | 8(34.8) | 9(23.1) | 6(27.3) |
| | Strongly Agree | 5(21.7) | 3(7.7) | 3(13.6) |
| Interference of trade unions | Strongly Disagree | 8(34.8) | 12(30.8) | 7(31.8) |
| | Disagree | 11(47.8) | 21(53.8) | 13(59.1) |
| | Neutral | 4(17.4) | 6(15.4) | 2(9.1) |
| | Agree | - | - | - |
| | Strongly Agree | - | - | - |
| High compensation | Strongly Disagree | 7(30.4) | 9(23.1) | 8(36.4) |
| | Disagree | 15(65.2) | 27(69.2) | 14(63.6) |
| | Neutral | 1(4.3) | 1(2.6) | - |
| | Agree | - | 2(5.1) | - |
| | Strongly Agree | - | - | - |
| Over expenses due to Excessive Manpower | Strongly Disagree | 8(34.8) | 6(15.4) | 2(9.1) |
| | Disagree | 6(26.1) | 14(35.9) | 8(36.4) |
| | Neutral | - | 2(5.1) | 1(4.5) |
| | Agree | 9(39.1) | 16(41.0) | 11(50.0) |
| | Strongly Agree | - | 1(2.6) | - |
| Labour strikes | Strongly Disagree | 8(34.8) | 11(28.2) | 6(27.3) |
| | Disagree | 15(65.2) | 27(69.2) | 16(72.7) |
| | Neutral | - | 1(2.6) | - |
| | Agree | - | - | - |
| | Strongly Agree | - | - | - |

( ) in Percentage

Table 63 visualises the various problems in labour function based on the location of the units. The locations of the units were classified into three major areas such as Alagappanagar, Chittissery and Pudukad.

Out of 23 units located in Alagappanagar, 60.9 per cent of the units and 34.8 per cent of the units strongly agreed that the problem of inadequate skilled labour and labour absenteeism were existed in their units respectively. The problems of high training cost and high cost due to excessive manpower were faced by 34.8 per cent and 39.1 per cent of the units respectively. 47.8 per cent of the units disagreed to the problem of interference of trade unions. 65.2 per cent of the units disagreed to the problem of high compensation to workers as well labour strike.

Among the 39 units located in Chittissery, more than half of the units strongly agreed that they were facing the problem of inadequate skilled labour. 51.3 per cent and 41 per cent of the units also stated that they were facing the problem of labour absenteeism and high cost due to excessive manpower respectively. The problems such as high training cost and interference of trade unions were not experienced by 43.6 per cent and 53.8 per cent of the units respectively. 69.2 per cent of the units did not experience the problem of high compensation to workers as well as labour strikes.

Finally, out of 22 units located in Pudukad area, 59.1 per cent of the units strongly agreed that inadequate skilled labour problem existed in their units. 40.9 per cent and half of the units stated that they also faced the problems such as labour absenteeism and high cost due to excessive manpower respectively. The problem such as interference of trade unions, high compensation to workers and labour strikes were not experienced by 59.1 per cent, 63.6 per cent and 72.7 per cent of the units respectively. Of the three groups each comprising 27.3 per cent of the units, one group agreed to the problem of high training cost, second one disagreed to this and the third group did not respond to this.

**Table 64**
**Stepwise Multiple Regression Analysis the Impact of Various Labour Problems on the Performance of Labour Function in Alagappanagar**

*Dependent variable. Performance of Labour function (Y)*

| *Independent variable* | *Unstandardised Co-efficient* | *Standard Error* | *Standardised Co-efficient* | *t-value* | *p-value* |
|---|---|---|---|---|---|
| Constant | 0.835 | 0.843 | - | 0.990 | 0.334 |
| Labour strikes ($X_1$) | 0.983 | 0.276 | 0.723 | 3.565 | 0.002 |
| Labour Absenteeism ($X_2$) | 0.283 | 0.129 | 0.444 | 2.189 | 0.041 |

Multiple R = 0.626 F- value = 6.445 d.f. (2,20) P-value < 0.01
R square = 0.392

$$\hat{Y} = 0.0835 + 0.983X_1 + 0.283X_2$$

Where $\hat{Y}$ is the estimated performance of labour.

Table 64 explains the impact of various problems in labour on its performance. The equation describes that, on an average if "Labour strikes" changes by one unit, there will be an increase of 0.983 units in the performance of labour function, when the other problem "Labour absenteeism" is kept constant and vice versa.

The results of the t-test confirm that, the estimated regression coefficients (0.983) and (0.283) are highly significant at one per cent and five per cent level. The multiple R of 0.626 shows that there exists a relationship of 62.6 per cent between the above problem and performance of labour. Moreover, the $R^2$ of 0.392 confirms that these problems only explained 39.2 per cent of variation in the performance of labour. Finally, the result of the f-test signifies that the variations were statistically significant at one per cent level.

Hence, it can be concluded that, among the seven problems identified by the researcher, the "Problem of labour strikes" and the "Labour absenteeism" have significant impact on the performance of labour. This shows that these two problems existed in the units located in Alagappanagar, but they did not affect the performance of labour.

**Table 65**
**Stepwise Multiple Regression Analysis–The Impact of Various Labour Problems on the Performance of Labour Function inPudukad**

*Dependent variable. Performance of Labour function (Y)*

| *Independent variable* | *Unstandardised Co-efficient* | *Standard Error* | *Standardised Co-efficient* | *t-value* | *p-value* |
|---|---|---|---|---|---|
| Constant | 4.720 | 0.396 | | - 11.908 | 0.000 |
| Over expenses due to excessive manpower ($X_1$) | -0.428 | 0.126 | -0.606 | -3.409 | 0.003 |

Multiple R = 0.606 F- value = 11.623 d.f. (1,20) P-value < 0.01
R square = 0.368

$$\hat{Y} = 4.720 - 0.428X_1$$

Where $\hat{Y}$ is the estimated performance of labour.

Table 65 explains the impact of various problems in labour on its performance. The equation describes that, on an average if "Over expenses due to excessive manpower" changes by one unit, there will be a reduction of 0.428 units in the performance of labour function.

The results of the t-test confirm that, the estimated regression coefficient (-0.428) is highly significant at one per cent level. The multiple R of 0.606 shows that there exists a relationship of 60.6 per cent between the above problem and performance of labour. Moreover, the $R^2$ of 0.368 confirms that, the problem only explained 36.8 per cent of variation in the performance of labour. Finally, the result of f-test shows that the variation was statistically significant at one per cent level.

Hence, it can be concluded that, among the seven problems identified by the researcher, the problem of "Over expenses due to excessive manpower" has a significant impact on the performance of labour of the units located in Pudukad.

CHAPTER 5

# Analysis of the Overall Performance of Clay Tiles Manufacturing Units

The chapter deals with the analysis of the overall performance of the units in the major and prominent areas such as Alagappanagar, Chittissery, and Pudukad. The analysis was done at three different stages.

In stage one, simple frequency table was included to show the over all performance of the units. Multiple regression analysis was used to identify the contribution of the performance of various functional areas such as Production, Marketing, Finance and Labour to the overall performance of the units.

In stage two, control chart was used to classify the overall performance of the units into high and low by establishing a cut-off performance. Moreover, one-way Anova was also used to find the difference in the mean performance based on the level of performance of the units.

In third and final stage, discriminant analysis was utilised to forecast the best predictors (performance of various function) that will be discriminated by the performance of the clay tiles manufacturing units into high or low in the future.

Table 1 presents a picture on the overall performance of the clay tiles manufacturing units in Thrissur District. Out of 84 units, nearly three-fourth of the units agreed that the overall

**Table 1**
**Overall Performance of Clay Tiles Manufacturing Units in Thrissur District**

| *Level* | *No. of Units* | *Per cent* |
|---|---|---|
| Bad | 5 | 6.0 |
| Moderate | 13 | 15.5 |
| Good | 61 | 72.5 |
| Excellent | 5 | 6.0 |
| Total | 84 | 100.0 |

*Source:* Primary Data.

performance of units was good followed by 15.5 per cent (13) of the units stated that overall performance level was moderate. Two groups each comprising 6 per cent (5) of the units stated that it was bad and excellent respectively.

Hence, maximum 72.6 per cent of the clay tiles manufacturing units stated that their overall performance was good.

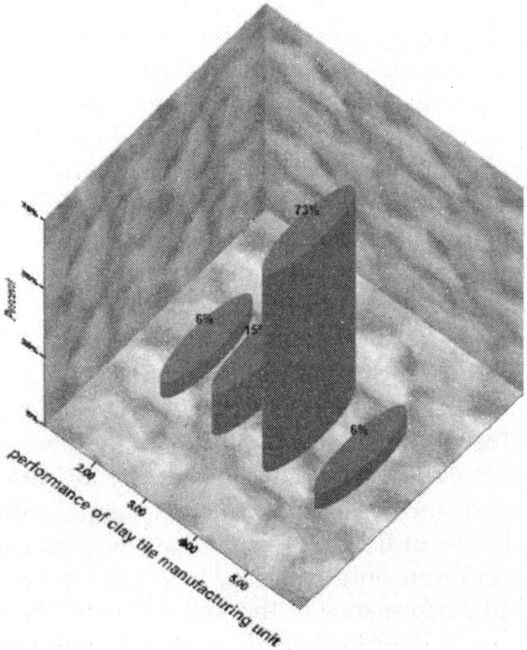

**Table 2**
**Multiple Regression Analysis-The Contribution of Various Functional Areas to the Overall Performance of the Units in Alagappanagar**

*Dependent variable. Overall performance (Y)*

| *Independent variable* | *Unstandardised Co-efficient* | *Standard Error* | *Standardised Co-efficient* | *t-value* | *p-value* |
|---|---|---|---|---|---|
| Constant | 1.382 | 0.791 | - | 1.748 | 0.097 |
| Performance of Production Function ($X_1$) | -0.106 | 0.172 | -0.132 | -0.615 | 0.546 |
| Performance of Marketing Functions ($X_2$) | 0.344 | 0.188 | 0.395 | 1.832 | 0.083 |
| Performance of Finance function ($X_3$) | -0.159 | 0.264 | -0.176 | -0.602 | 0.555 |
| Performance of Labour Function ($X_4$) | 0.556 | 0.281 | 0.581 | 1.979 | 0.053 |

Multiple R = 0.640 F- value = 3.123 d.f. (4,18) P - value < 0.05
R square = 0.410

$$\hat{Y} = 1.382 - 0.106X_1 + 0.344X_2 - 0.159X_3 + 0.556X_4$$

Where $\hat{Y}$ is the estimated overall performance.

Table 2 depicts the impact of the functional areas to the overall performance of the units in Alagappanagar. The equation describes that, on an average "Performance of production function" changes by one unit, there will be 0.106 units reduction in the overall performance of the units when the performance of other functional areas are kept constant; if the performance of marketing function changes by one unit there will be 0.344 units increase in the overall performance of the units when the other functional areas performance are kept constant and so on is presented in the above table.

The result of the t-test confirms that, the estimated regression coefficient (0.556) is nearly significant at five per cent level. The multiple R of 0.640 shows that there exists a relationship of 64 per cent between the over all performance and the performance of various functional areas of the units. Moreover, the $R^2$ of 0.410 confirms that the performance of functional areas were only explained by 41 per cent of variation in the overall performance of the units. Finally, the result of the f-test shows that the explained variation by these functional areas was statistically significant at five per cent level.

Hence, it can be concluded that, among the four functional areas of the units, only the performance of labour significantly and positively contributed to the overall performance of the units located in Alagappanagar.

**Table 3**
**Overall Performance Score and Standard Deviation Based on the Level of Performance of the Units in Alagappanagar**

| *Level* | *No. of Units* | *Performance Score** | *Standard Deviation* |
|---|---|---|---|
| High | 9 | 3.9722 | 0.23199 |
| Low | 14 | 3.1786 | 0.39745 |
| Total | 23 | 3.4891 | 0.51939 |

*F - value = 29.171 d.f. (1,21) P-value < 0.01

Table 3 visualises the mean performance score and standard deviation based on the level of performance of the units. The level of performance of the units in Alagappanagar area was categorized as high and low. Out of 23 units in Alagappanagar, the majority comprising of 14 units achieved a mean performance score of 3.1786 and this reflects that these units attained low performance. Similarly, the remaining 9 units attained high performance and its mean performance score of 3.9722 is higher than the low performing units.

Finally, the result of the One-way Anova shows that the mean performance score differs significantly between the high and low performance units in Alagappanagar area at one per cent level.

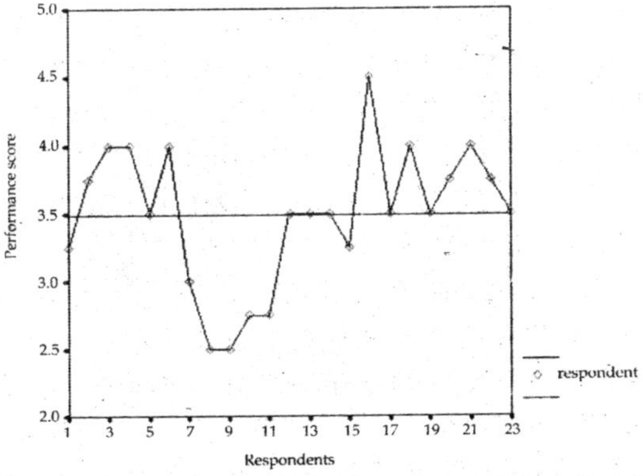


**Control Chart-The Level of Performance of the Clay Tiles Manufacturing Units in Alagappanagar**

## DISCRIMINANT ANALYSIS

Table 4 depicts the mean performance score and standard deviation of various functions based on the level of performance of the units in Alagappanagar. It is noted that, the performance of marketing function achieved a greater score of 4.1111 followed by the performance of production and labour of the units, which attained high performance. Similarly, for the units, which attained low performance, the mean performance score of all functional areas were low when compared to the high performance units. Moreover, Wilks Lambda (0.375) is closer to 0 confirms that the discrimination in the mean performance score of various functions between the high and low performance units were good.

**Table 4**
**Mean Performance Score and Standard Deviation Based on the Level of Performance of the Units in Alagappanagar**

| | *Level of Performance* | | | |
|---|---|---|---|---|
| | *High (n=9)* | | *Low (n=14)* | |
| *Independent Variable* | *Mean Performance Score* | *Standard Deviation* | *Mean Performance Score* | *Standard Deviation* |
| Performance of Production Function ($X_1$) | 4.0000 | 0.50000 | 3.2143 | 0.80178 |
| Performance of Marketing Functions ($X_2$) | 4.1111 | 0.33333 | 3.2143 | 0.69929 |
| Performance of Finance Function ($X_3$) | 3.7778 | 0.44096 | 3.0000 | 0.67937 |
| Performance of Labour Function ($X_4$) | 4.0000 | 0.00000 | 3.2857 | 0.72627 |

Wilks' Lambda = 0.375 Chi-Square value =18.655 d.f. (4) P-value < 0.01

Finally, the results of the Chi-Square test suggest that the mean performance score of various functions differs significantly between the high and low performance units at one per cent level.

Table 5 explains the Canonical and Fisher's Linear discriminant function coefficients in the equation (1), (2) and

**Table 5**
**Canonical and Fisher's Linear Discriminant Function Co-efficients**

| Independent Variables | *Level of Performance* High (n=9) | Low (n=14) | High/Low (n= 23) |
|---|---|---|---|
| Constant | -76.427 | -48.248 | -10.690 |
| Performance of Production Function ($X_1$) | 12.473 | 9.786 | 1.062 |
| Performance of Marketing Function ($X_2$) | 13.990 | 10.997 | 1.183 |
| Performance of Finance Function ($X_3$) | 7.841 | 5.943 | 0.750 |
| Performance of Labour Function ($X_4$) | 3.487 | 3.309 | 0.071 |

Canonical correlation = 0.791 Correct classification rate = 95.7%

$$\check{Z} = -76.427+12.473X_1+13.990X_2+7.841X_3+3.487X_4 \quad (1)$$

$$\check{Z} = -48.248+9.786X_1+10.997X_2+5.943X_3+3.309X_4 \quad (2)$$

$$\check{Z} = -10.690+1.062X_1+1.183X_2+0.750X_3+0.071X_4 \quad (3)$$

(3) respectively. Equation (1) explains that among the four functional areas in clay tiles manufacturing units, the performance of marketing function achieved a greater weight of 13.990 followed by the performance of production. This confirms that in future, performance of Marketing and Production will be the best predictors, which will discriminate the level of performance of the units as high or low. Similarly, equation (2) and (3) explains that among the four functional areas in the units, the performance of marketing function achieved a greater weight followed by the performance of Production. This shows that in future, performance of Marketing and Production will discriminate the performance of the units as high or low.

Finally, the Canonical Correlation of 0.791 explains that there exists a relationship of 79.1 per cent between the discriminatory scores and the performance of various functional areas of clay tiles manufacturing units in Alagappanagar.

**Table 6**
**Multiple Regression Analysis-The Contribution of Various Functional Areas to the Overall Performance of the Units in Chittissery**

*Dependent variable. Overall performance (Y)*

| *Independent variable* | *Unstandardised Co-efficient* | *Standard Error* | *Standardised Co-efficient* | *t-value* | *p-value* |
|---|---|---|---|---|---|
| Constant | 2.496 | 0.615 | - | 4.059 | 0.000 |
| Performance of Production Function ($X_1$) | 0.285 | 0.127 | 0.408 | 2.245 | 0.031 |
| Performance of Marketing Functions ($X_2$) | -0.233 | 0.163 | -0.268 | -1.427 | 0.163 |
| Performance of Finance function ($X_3$) | 0.057 | 0.127 | 0.083 | 0.450 | 0.656 |
| Performance of Labour Function ($X_4$) | 0.284 | 0.141 | 0.376 | 2.015 | 0.052 |

Multiple R = 0.524 F- value = 3.211 d.f. (4,34) P-value $< 0.05$
R square = 0.274

$$\hat{Y} = 2.496 + 0.285X_1 - 0.2334X_2 + 0.057X_3 + 0.284X_4$$

Where $\hat{Y}$ is the estimated overall performance.

Table 6 exhibits the impact of the functional areas to the overall performance of the units in Chittissery. The equation describes that, on an average "Performance of production function" changes by one unit, there will be 0.285 units increase in the overall performance of the units when the performance of other functional areas are kept constant; if the performance of marketing function changes by one unit there will be 0.233 units decrease in the overall performance when the other functional areas are kept constant and it is presented in the above table.

The results of the t-test confirm (0.285 and 0.284) that, the estimated regression coefficients are significant at five per cent level. The multiple R of 0.524 shows that there exists a relationship of 52.4 per cent between the over all performance and the performance of various functional areas of the units. Moreover, the $R^2$ of 0.274 confirms that the performance of functional areas explained only 27.4 per cent of variation in the overall performance of the units. Finally, the result of the f-test shows that the explained variation by these functional areas was statistically significant at five per cent level.

Hence, it can be concluded that, among the four functional areas of the units, only the performance of Production and the Labour significantly emerged and made almost equal contribution to the overall performance of the units located in Chittissery.

**Table 7**

**Overall Performance Score and Standard Deviation Based on the Level of Performance of the Units in Chittissery**

| *Level* | *No. of Units* | *Performance Score** | *Standard Deviation* |
|---|---|---|---|
| High | 28 | 4.0446 | 0.28910 |
| Low | 11 | 3.2500 | 0.22361 |
| Total | 39 | 3.8205 | 0.45142 |

*F - value = 66.933 d.f. (1,37) P-value < 0.01

Table 7 visualises the mean performance score and standard deviation based on the level of performance of the units. The level of performance of the units in Chittissery area was categorized as high and low. Out of 39 units in Chittissery,

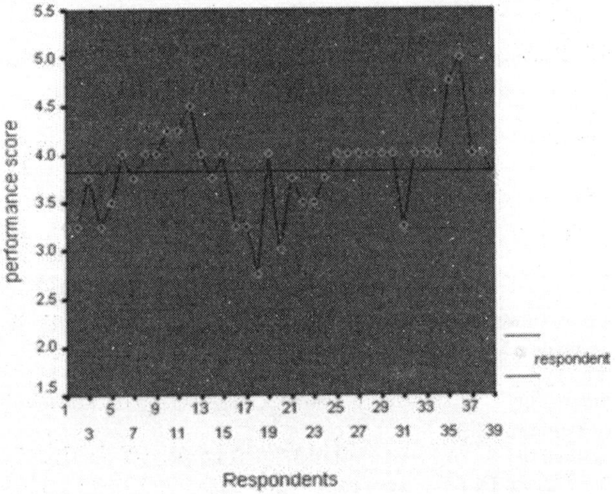


**Control Chart - The Level of Performance of the Clay Tiles Manufacturing Units in Chittissery**

the majority comprising of 11 units achieved a mean performance score of 3.2500 and this reflects that these units attained low performance. Similarly, the remaining 28 units attained high performance and its mean performance score of 4.0446 is high when compared to the low performing units.

Finally, the result of the One-way Anova shows that the mean performance score differs significantly between the high and low performance units in Chittissery at one per cent level.

## DISCRIMINANT ANALYSIS

Table 8 shows the mean performance score and standard deviation of various functions based on the level of performance of the units in Chittissery. It is worth noted that, the performance of marketing function achieved a greater score of 4.1429 followed by the performance of production function attained high performance. Similarly, for the units, which attained low performance, the mean performance score of all functional areas were low when compared to the high performance units. Moreover, Wilks Lambda (0.349) is closer to 0 confirms that the discrimination in the mean performance score of various functions between the high and low performance units were good.

**Table 8**

**Mean Performance Score and Standard Deviation Based on the Level of Performance of the Units in Chittissery**

| | *Level of Performance* | | | |
|---|---|---|---|---|
| | *High (n=28)* | | *Low (n=11)* | |
| *Independent Variable* | *Mean Performance Score* | *Standard Deviation* | *Mean Performance Score* | *Standard Deviation* |
| Performance of Production Function ($X_1$) | 4.1071 | 0.41627 | 3.2727 | 0.90453 |
| Performance of Marketing Functions ($X_2$) | 4.1429 | 0.44840 | 3.4545 | 0.52223 |
| Performance of Finance Function ($X_3$) | 3.8929 | 0.49735 | 3.0000 | 0.77460 |
| Performance of Labour Function ($X_4$) | 4.0357 | 0.42879 | 3.2727 | 0.78625 |

Wilks' Lambda = 0.349 Chi-Square value =36.833 d.f. (4) P-value < 0.01

Finally, the results of the Chi-Square test suggest that the mean performance score of various functions differs significantly between the high and low performance units at one per cent level.

**Table 9**

**Canonical and Fisher's Linear Discriminate Function Co-efficients**

| | *Level of Performance* | | |
|---|---|---|---|
| *Independent Variables* | *High (n=9)* | *Low (n=14)* | *High/Low (n= 23)* |
| Constant | -111.293 | -72.988 | -13.907 |
| Performance of Production Function ($X_1$) | 14.745 | 11.392 | 1.133 |
| Performance of Marketing Functions ($X_2$) | 14.594 | 12.440 | 0.728 |
| Performance of Finance Function ($X_3$) | 13.966 | 10.660 | 1.117 |
| Performance of Labour Function ($X_4$) | 11.531 | 9.535 | 0.675 |

Canonical correlation = 0.807Correct classification rate = 100%

$$\check{Z} = -111.293+14.745X_1+14.594X_2+13.966X_3+11.531X_4 \quad (1)$$

$$\check{Z} = -72.988+11.392X_1+12.440X2+10.660X_3+9.535X_4 \quad (2)$$

$$\check{Z} = -13.907+1.133X_1+0.728X2+1.117X_3+0.675X_4 \quad (3)$$

Table 5.9 explains the Canonical and Fisher's Linear discriminant function coefficients in the equation (1), (2) and (3) respectively. Equation (1) explains that among the four functional areas in clay tiles manufacturing units, the performance of production function achieved a greater weight of 14.745 followed by the performance of Marketing. This confirms that in future, performance of Production and Marketing will be the best predictors, which will discriminate the level of performance of the units into high or low. Similarly, equation (2) explains the performance of marketing function achieved a greater weight followed by the performance of Production respectively. This shows that in future, performance of Marketing and Production will discriminate the level of performance of the units as high or low. Moreover the researcher identified, the performance of Production function will be the dominant factors which will discriminate the level of performance of the units as high or low in the future.

Finally, the Canonical Correlation of 0.807 explains that there exists a relationship of 80.7 per cent between the discriminatory scores and the performance of various functional areas of clay tiles manufacturing units in Chittissery.

**Table 10**
**Multiple Regression Analysis-The Contribution of Various Functional Areas to the Overall Performance of the Units in Pudukad**

*Dependent variable. Overall performance (Y)*

| *Independent variable* | *Unstandardised Co-efficient* | *Standard Error* | *Standardised Co-efficient* | *t-value* | *p-value* |
|---|---|---|---|---|---|
| Constant | 1.504 | 0.838 | - | 1.793 | 0.091 |
| Performance of Production Function ($X_1$) | 0.095 | 0.207 | 0.088 | 0.459 | 0.652 |
| Performance of Marketing Function ($X_2$) | -0.377 | 0.268 | -0.337 | -1.405 | 0.178 |
| Performance of Finance function ($X_3$) | 0.277 | 0.182 | 0.329 | 1.520 | 0.147 |
| Performance of Labour Function ($X_4$) | 0.658 | 0.240 | 0.658 | 2.746 | 0.014 |

Multiple R = 0.720 . F- value = 4.576 d.f. (4,17) P - value < 0.05
R square = 0.518

$$\hat{Y} = 1.504 + 0.095X_1 - 0.377X_2 + 0.277X_3 + 0.658X_4$$

Where $\hat{Y}$ is the estimated overall performance.

Table 10 visualises the impact of overall performance of the units in Pudukad. The equation describes that, on an average if "Performance of labour function" changes by one unit, there will be 0.658 units increase in the overall performance of the units when the performance of other functional areas are kept constant; if the finance performance function changes by one unit there will be 0.277 units increase in the overall performance of the units when the other functional performance areas are kept constant and it is presented in the above table.

The results of the t-test confirm that, the estimated regression coefficients (0.658) are significant at five per cent level. The multiple R of 0.720 shows that there exists a relationship of 72 per cent between the over all performance and the performance of various functional areas of the units. Moreover, the $R^2$ of 0.518 confirms that the performance of functional areas explained only 51.8 per cent of variation in the overall performance of the units. Finally, the result of the f-test shows that the explained variation by these functional areas was statistically significant at five per cent level.

Hence, it can be concluded that, among the four functional areas of the units, only the performance of Labour function significantly emerged as the best contributor to the overall performance of the units located in Pudukad.

**Table 11**
**Overall Performance Score and Standard Deviation Based on the Level of Performance of the Units in Pudukad**

| *Level* | *No. of Units* | *Performance Score** | *Standard Deviation* |
|---|---|---|---|
| High | 9 | 4.0000 | 0.21651 |
| Low | 13 | 3.0000 | 0.46771 |
| Total | 22 | 3.4091 | 0.62937 |

*F - value = 35.455 d.f. (1,20) P-value < 0.01

Table 11 describes the mean performance score and standard deviation based on the level of performance of the units. The level of performance of the units in Pudukad

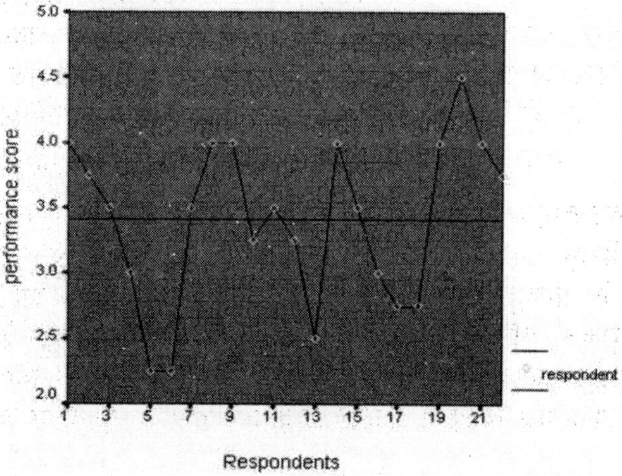


**Control Chart - The Level of Performance of the Clay Tiles Manufacturing Units in Pudukad**

area was categorized as high and low. Out of 22 units in Pudukad, the majority comprising of 13 units achieved a mean performance score of 3.0000 and this reflects that these units attained low performance. Similarly, the remaining 9 units attained high performance and its mean performance score of 4.0000 is high when compared to the low performing units.

Finally, the result of the One-way Anova shows that the mean performance score differs significantly between the high and low performance units in Pudukad at one per cent level.

## DISCRIMINANT ANALYSIS

Table 12 shows the mean performance score and standard deviation of various functions based on the level of performance of the units in Pudukad. It is noted that, the performance of marketing function achieved a greater score of 4.1111 followed by the performance of Production and Finance attained high performance. Similarly, for the units, which attained low performance, the mean performance score of all functional areas were low when compared to the high performance units. Moreover, Wilks Lambda (0.103) is closer

**Table 12**

**Mean Performance Score and Standard Deviation Based on the Level of Performance of the Units in Pudukad**

| | *Level of Performance* | | | |
|---|---|---|---|---|
| | *High (n=9)* | | *Low (n=14)* | |
| *Independent Variable* | *Mean Performance Score* | *Standard Deviation* | *Mean Performance Score* | *Standard Deviation* |
| Performance of Production Function ($X_1$) | 4.0000 | 0.50000 | 3.2308 | 0.72501 |
| Performance of Marketing Functions ($X_2$) | 4.1111 | 0.33333 | 3.3846 | 0.76795 |
| Performance of Finance Function ($X_3$) | 4.0000 | 0.00000 | 2.2308 | 0.43853 |
| Performance of Labour Function ($X_4$) | 3.8889 | 0.33333 | 3.1538 | 0.89872 |

Wilks' Lambda = 0.103 Chi-Square value =40.986 d.f. (4) P-value < 0.01

to 0 confirms that the discrimination in the mean performance score of various functions between the high and low performance units were good.

Finally, the results of the Chi-Square test suggest that the mean performance score of various functions differs significantly between the high and low performance units at one per cent level.

**Table 13**

**Canonical and Fisher's Linear Discriminant Function Co-efficients**

| | *Level of Performance* | | |
|---|---|---|---|
| *Independent Variables* | *High (n=9)* | *Low (n=13)* | *High/Low (n= 22)* |
| Constant | -110.977 | -46.820 | -10.600 |
| Performance of Production Function ($X_1$) | 12.776 | 9.163 | 0.630 |
| Performance of Marketing Functions ($X_2$) | 7.479 | 6.408 | 0.187 |
| Performance of Finance Function ($X_3$) | 38.327 | 20.821 | 3.052 |
| Performance of Labour Function ($X_4$) | -3.855 | -1.634 | -0.387 |

Canonical correlation = 0.947 Correct classification rate = 100%

$$\check{Z} = -110.977+12.776X_1+7.479X_2+38.327X_3 - 3.855X_4 \quad (1)$$

$$\check{Z} = -46.820+9.163X_1+6.408X_2+20.821X_3 - 1.634X_4 \quad (2)$$

$$\check{Z} = -10.600+0.630X_1+0.187X_2+3.052X_3 - 0.387X_4 \quad (3)$$

Table 13 explains the Canonical and Fisher's Linear discriminant function coefficients in the equation (1), (2) and (3). Equation (1), (2) and (3) explain that among the four functional areas in the units, the performance of Finance function achieved a greater weight and this shows the performance of finance function mushroomed as the best predictor which will discriminate the level of performance of clay tiles manufacturing units as high or low in the future.

Finally, the Canonical Correlation of 0.947 explains that there exists a relationship of 94.7 per cent between the discriminatory scores and the performance of various function areas of clay tiles manufacturing units in Pudukad.

**Table 14**
**Multiple Regression Analysis -The Contribution of Various Functional Areas to the Overall Performance of the Units in Thrissur District**

*Dependent variable. Overall performance (Y)*

| *Independent variable* | *Unstandardised Co-efficient* | *Standard Error* | *Standardised Co-efficient* | *t-value* | *p-value* |
|---|---|---|---|---|---|
| Constant | 1.485 | 0.403 | - | 3.686 | 0.000 |
| Performance of Production Function ($X_1$) | 0.113 | 0.086 | 0.132 | 1.315 | 0.192 |
| Performance of Marketing Functions ($X_2$) | 0.028 | 0.105 | 0.029 | 0.270 | 0.788 |
| Performance of Finance function ($X_3$) | 0.150 | 0.093 | 0.191 | 1.607 | 0.112 |
| Performance of Labour Function ($X_4$) | 0.348 | 0.110 | 0.381 | 3.156 | 0.002 |

Multiple R = 0.594 F- value = 10.795 d.f. (4,79) P-value < 0.01
R square = 0.353

$$\hat{Y} = 1.485 + 0.113X_1 + 0.028X_2 + 0.150X_3 + 0.348X_4$$

Where $\hat{Y}$ is the estimated overall performance.

Table 14 shows the impact of the functional areas to the overall performance of the units in Thrissur District. The equation describes that, on an average if "Performance of labour function" changes by one unit, there will be 0.348 units increase in the overall performance of the units when the performance of other functional areas are kept constant; if there is a change in finance function by one unit there will be 0.150 increase in the overall performance of the units when the other functional areas performance are kept constant and it is presented in the above table.

The results of the t-test confirm that, the estimated regression coefficients (0.348) are significant at one per cent level. The multiple R of 0.594 shows that there exists a relationship of 59.4 per cent between the over all performance and the performance of various functional areas of the units. Moreover, the $R^2$ of 0.353 confirms that the performance of functional areas explained only 35.3 per cent of variation in the overall performance of the units. Finally, the result of the f-test shows that the explained variation by these functional areas was statistically significant at one per cent level.

Hence, it can be concluded that, among the four functional areas of clay tiles manufacturing units, only the performance of Labour function significantly emerged as the best contributor to influence overall performance of the units located in Thrissur District.

**Table 15**
**Overall Performance Score and Standard Deviation Based on the Level of Performance of the Units in Thrissur District**

| *Level* | *No. of Units* | *Performance Score** | *Standard Deviation* |
|---|---|---|---|
| High | 46 | 4.0217 | 0.26260 |
| Low | 38 | 3.1382 | 0.38859 |
| Total | 84 | 3.6220 | 0.54813 |

*F - value = 153.295 d.f. (1,82) P-value < 0.01

Table 15 describes the mean performance score and standard deviation based on the level of performance of the units. The level of performance of the units in Thrissur District was categorized as high and low. Out of 84 units in Thrissur District, the majority comprising of 46 units achieved a mean performance score of 4.0217 and this reflects that these units

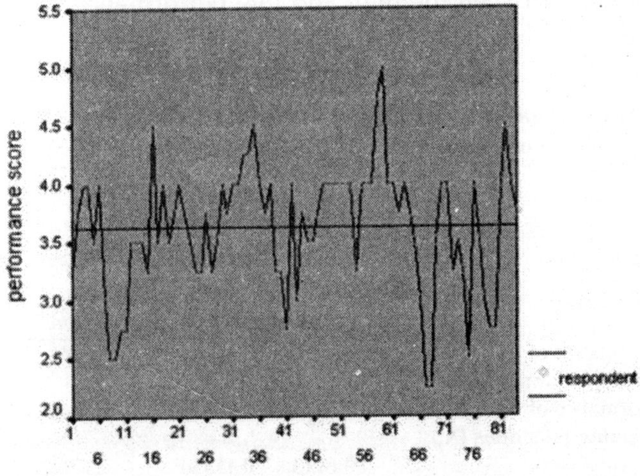


**Control Chart - The Level of Performance of the Clay Tiles Manufacturing Units in Thrissur District**

attained high performance. Similarly, the remaining 38 units attained low performance and its mean performance score of 3.1382 is low when compared to the high performing units.

Finally, the result of the One-way Anova shows that the mean performance score differs significantly between the high and low performance units in Thrissur District at one per cent level.

## DISCRIMINANT ANALYSIS

Table 16 exhibits the mean performance score and standard deviation of various functions based on the level of performance of the units in Thrissur District. It is mentioning to note that, the performance of marketing function achieved a greater score of 4.1304 followed by the performance of production and labour function of the units, which attained high performance. Similarly, for the units, which attained low performance, the mean performance score of all functional areas were low when compared to the high performance units. Moreover, Wilks Lambda (0.307) is closer to 0 confirms that the discrimination in the mean performance score of various functions between the high and low performance units were good.

**Table 16**
**Mean Performance Score and Standard Deviation Based on the Level of Performance of the Units in Thrissur District**

| | *Level of Performance* | | | |
|---|---|---|---|---|
| | *High (n=46)* | | *Low (n=38)* | |
| *Independent Variable* | *Mean Performance Score* | *Standard Deviation* | *Mean Performance Score* | *Standard Deviation* |
| Performance of Production Function ($X_1$) | 4.0652 | 0.44233 | 3.2368 | 0.78617 |
| Performance of Marketing Functions ($X_2$) | 4.1304 | 0.40048 | 3.3421 | 0.66886 |
| Performance of Finance Function ($X_3$) | 3.8913 | 0.43350 | 2.7368 | 0.72351 |
| Performance of Labour Function ($X_4$) | 4.0000 | 0.36515 | 3.2368 | 0.78617 |

Wilks' Lambda = 0.307 Chi-Square value = 94.363 d.f. (4) P-value < 0.01

Finally, the results of the Chi-Square test suggest that the mean performance score of various functions differ significantly between the high and low performance units at one per cent level.

**Table 17**

**Canonical and Fisher's Linear Discriminant Function Co-efficients**

| *Independent Variables* | *Level of Performance* High (n=46) | Low (n=38) | High/Low (n= 84) |
|---|---|---|---|
| Constant | -82.277 | -49.882 | -11.079 |
| Performance of Production Function ($X_1$) | 12.405 | 9.511 | 0.971 |
| Performance of Marketing Functions ($X_2$) | 11.519 | 9.314 | 0.740 |
| Performance of Finance Function ($X_3$) | 12.624 | 8.595 | 1.352 |
| Performance of Labour Function ($X_4$) | 4.054 | 3.935 | 0.040 |

Canonical correlation = 0.832 Correct classification rate = 97.6%

$$\check{Z} = -82.277+12.405X_1+11.519X_2+12.624X_3+4.054X_4 \quad (1)$$

$$\check{Z} = -49.882+9.511X_1+9.314X_2+8.595X_3+3.935X_4 \quad (2)$$

$$\check{Z} = -11.079+0.971X_1+0.740X_2+1.352X_3+0.040X_4 \quad (3)$$

Table 17 explains the Canonical and Fisher's Linear discriminant function coefficients in the equation (1), (2) and (3). Equation (1) clearly explains that the prediction of high-performed units in the future will purely depend on the two major functional areas such as finance and production. Similarly the performance of production and marketing function emerged as significant predictors, which will classify the level of performance of the units as low in the future. Moreover the performance of Finance function and production function were the two major functional areas which will discriminate the level of performance of the units as high or low in the future.

Finally, the Canonical Correlation of 0.832 explains that there exists a relationship of 83.2 per cent between the discriminatory scores and the performance of various functional areas of clay tiles manufacturing units in Thrissur District.

# CHAPTER 6

# Summary of Findings, Suggestions and Conclusion

Based on the analyses, the researcher has summarized the findings of the study according to organizational aspects and the functional areas.

## FINDINGS

### Organisational Aspects

1. A majority of 46.4 per cent of the units were located in Chittisery area.
2. The maximum of 50 per cent of the units were established after 1990.
3. The maximum of 88.1 per cent (74) of the units were located within the jurisdiction of the panchayat.
4. The maximum of 50 per cent of the units manufactured flooring tiles only.
5. The maximum of 57.1 per cent of the units were owned by sole proprietors.
6. 40.5 per cent of the unit owners had education upto pre-degree.
7. 40.5 per cent of the units had the production capacity of 8000 tiles per day.

**Production Function**

1. A majority of 71.4 per cent of the units manufactured 6000 tiles or fewer per day.
2. The maximum of 61.9 per cent of the units were procuring the clay from outside the Panchayat but within the district.
3. 39.3 per cent of the units procure the clay within 10 to 15 kilometres from the factory.
4. The maximum of 71.4 per cent of the units are collecting the clay through contractors.
5. The maximum of 79.8 per cent of the units are using terracotta clay for production of tiles.
6. The maximum 79.8 per cent of the units adopt the heap method to store the clay.
7. 40.5 per cent of the units were using both manual and automatic methods for cutting the clay blocks.
8. 48.8 per cent of the units were procuring the water from their own bore-wells.
9. 48.8 per cent of the units used both manual and machine pressing.
10. A majority of 51.2 per cent of the units used the de-aired vacuum pumps in their production process.
11. 48.8 per cent of the units had both manual and machine trimming.
12. 50 per cent of the units were using light diesel oil in their production process.
13. The maximum of 73.8 per cent of the units used 10 to 20 litres of oil to manufacture a load of 6000 clay tiles.
14. 34.5 per cent of the units were using coir belt for transporting the clay.
15. A maximum of 78.6 per cent of the units were exposing the tiles to natural sunlight to dry them.
16. A majority of 60.7 per cent of the units were purchasing the firewood from outside the panchayat but within the district.

17. The maximum of 61.9 per cent of the units were purchasing the firewood in all seasons.
18. 42.8 per cent of the units were procuring the firewood travelling a distance of 15 kilometres or above from the factory.
19. The maximum of 59.5 per cent of the units used 3 to 6 tonnes of firewood to manufacture a load of 6000 clay tiles.
20. A majority of 60.7 per cent of the units were using sawdust as fuel in their production process.
21. The maximum of 40.5 per cent of the units were using downdraught kiln for burning the tiles.
22. The maximum of 94 per cent of the units were using the practical experience to measure the burning temperature of finished tiles.
23. A majority of 56 per cent of the units used their experienced supervisors to check the quality of finished tiles.
24. 32.1 per cent of the units had an average breakage of 100 to 150 tiles per load.
25. The performance production of 64.4 per cent of the units was good.
26. The results of the contingency co-efficient suggest that:
    (a) The factors of production such as methods adopted for transporting the clay to machines and firewood used per load were associated with the location of the units. This shows that the location of the units played a vital role in determining the methods adopted for transporting the clay and firewood.
    (b) The factors of production namely firewood & oil used per load and test adopted to check the finished tiles were associated with the year of establishment of the units and these were statistically significant at five per cent and one per cent level.
    (c) The factor of production namely distance from the factory to the source of clay was associated with the year of establishment of the units and this was statistically significant at five per cent level.

(d) The factors of production such as methods adopted for procuring the clay, oil used per load, season of purchasing firewood, firewood used per load and performance of production function were associated with the types of clay tiles manufactured by the units and these were statistically significant at five per cent and one per cent level.

(e) The factors of production such as methods adopted for procuring the clay, methods used for pressing the tiles and methods adopted for transporting the clay to machines were associated with the ownership of the units and these were statistically significant at five per cent level.

(f) The factors of production namely methods adopted for procuring the clay, methods adopted for transporting the clay to machines, firewood used per load, breakage of tiles per load and performance of production function were associated with the qualification of the unit's owner and these were statistically significant at five per cent and one per cent level.

(g) The factors of production namely actual production per day, clay used for production, methods adopted for storing the clay, methods of cutting the clay blocks, methods used for pressing the tiles, de-airing machine used in production, methods of trimming the tiles, methods adopted for transporting the clay to machines, methods used for drying the tiles, season of purchasing firewood, distance from the factory to procure the firewood, methods followed for burning the tiles, methods adopted for measuring the burning temperature, test adopted to check finished tiles and breakage of tiles per load - - all were associated with installed production capacity of the units and these were statistically significant at five per cent and one per cent level.

34. The season of purchasing firewood emerged as a best predictor which contributed to the level of performance of

production followed by the factors such as sources of water, methods adopted for measuring the burning temperature and average breakage of tiles per load also contributed to the level of performance of production function in Alagappanagar.

35. The methods of cutting clay blocks emerged as the best predictor which contributed to the level of performance of production followed by the factors such as methods adopted for transporting clay to machines and methods of trimming the tiles also contributed to the level of production performance in Chittissery.
36. The average breakage of tiles per load emerged as the best predictor which contributed to the level of production in Pudukad followed by an equal contribution made by the factors such as the source of clay, de-airing machine used in production and the type of oil used for pressing the tiles.
37. The methods of cutting blocks of clay, average breakage of tiles per load and firewood used per 6000 tiles emerged as best predictor, which contributed to the level of performance of production. Similarly the factors such as methods of drying the tiles, methods of trimming the tiles and principal method of procuring clay contributed to the level of production of the units in Thrissur District.

**Production Problems**

1. The problem of procurement of clay without objection existed in Alagappanagar; it does not significantly weaken the production performance of the units.
2. Among the eight production problems identified by the researcher, only two problems namely "Possibility of pollution created by Kiln" and "Fulfillment of legal formalities in procuring the firewood" have a significant impact on the production performance. Among these, "Possibility of pollution created by Kiln" emerged as the significant problem reducing the production performance of the units located in Chittissery.

3. Among the eight production problems identified by the researcher, only two problems namely "Delay in delivery of clay" and "High price of clay in the market" have significant impact on the production performance. Among these, "Delay in delivery of clay" emerged as significant problem decreasing the production performance of the units located in Pudukad.
4. The problems such as "Procurement of clay without objection" and "High price for clay in the market" positively contributed to the production performance. This shows these two problems existed in the production function of the units located in Thrissur District and these do not significantly reduce the performance of production.

**Marketing Function**

1. The maximum of 69 per cent of the units were getting the orders through the Government contractors.
2. A majority of 73.8 per cent of the units supplied clay tiles to Tamilnadu.
3. The majority of 56 per cent of the units adopted the cost- and demand-based method of pricing.
4. The maximum 69 per cent of the units sold their clay tiles both for cash and on credit.
5. The maximum 53.6 per cent of the units were selling their tiles directly and through the agents.
6. The maximum 35.7 per cent of the units allowed a credit period of one week to their customers.
7. A majority 51.1 per cent of the units faced competition from the nearby units in the Thrissur District.
8. The maximum 77.4 per cent of the units were selling 200 to 400 loads of tiles a year.
9. A majority of 72.6 per cent of the units did not follow any promotional techniques for increasing their sales.
10. The maximum of 57.1 per cent of the units adopted a strategy of timely supply to their customers in order to maintain sales.

11. A majority of 65.5 per cent of the units had stated that their marketing performance was good.
12. The results of the contingency co-efficient suggest that:
    (a) The factor of marketing namely nature of sales was associated with the year of establishment of the units and this was statistically significant at five per cent level.
    (b) The factors of marketing such as methods of price fixation and the nature of sales were associated with the jurisdiction of the units and these were statistically significant at one per cent and five per cent level respectively.
    (c) The factors of marketing such as mode of getting orders and average sales in a year were associated with the type of clay tiles manufactured by the units and these were statistically significant at one per cent level.
    (d) The factor of marketing namely methods of price fixation was associated with the ownership of the units and this was statistically significant at one per cent level.
    (e) The factors of marketing such as location of major competitors, average sales in a year and promotional techniques adopted for selling the products were associated with the installed production capacity of the units and these were statistically significant at one per cent level.
13. The level of performance of marketing of the units in Alagappanagar was influenced by the best discriminating factors such as mode of tile sale, methods adopted for price fixation, average number of tiles sold and location of the competitors.
14. The marketing of the units located in Chittissery was influenced by the best discriminating factors such as credit period allowed to customers, nature of sales, methods adopted for price fixation, location of the competitors, mode of getting work orders and mode of sales.
15. The marketing was influenced by the best discriminating factor "nature of sale" made by the units located at Pudukad.

16. The level of marketing of the units was influenced by the best discriminating factors such as credit allowed to customers, mode of sale of tiles and nature of sale of tiles in Thrissur District.

**Marketing Problems**

1. The problem of "More breakage of tiles" significantly weakened the performance of marketing of the units located in Alagappanagar.
2. Among the various problems in marketing, the problem of "Low profit margin" significantly eroded the performance of marketing of the units located in Chittissery.
3. Among the various problems in marketing, the problem of "Delay in credit collection process" significantly weakened the performance of marketing of the units located in Pudukad.
4. Among the various problems in marketing, the problem of "Incidence of bad debts" significantly decreased the performance of marketing of the units located in Thrissur District.

**Finance Function**

1. 34.5 per cent of the units invested Rs.30 lakhs and above in their business.
2. 36.9 per cent of the units had invested Rs.5 to 10 lakhs.
3. The majority of 82.1 per cent of the units were raising their funds through the Kerala Finance Corporation.
4. 36.8 per cent of the units were raising long-term loans of Rs. 10 to 15 lakhs for their business.
5. 50 per cent of the units paid an interest of 10 to 15 per cent per annum.
6. A majority of 85.7 per cent of the units were receiving subsidies from the State Government.
7. 41.6 per cent of the units were raising their working capital through collection from debtors, cash sales and advances from their customers.

8. A collection period of ten days is allowed by 42.9 per cent of units.
9. A majority of 76.2 per cent of the units were fixing the price for their clay tiles between Rs.2 and 4.
10. A maximum of 59.5 per cent of the units were spending Rs.2000 to 4000 on clay to make a load of 6000 tiles.
11. A majority of 70.2 per cent of the units were purchasing firewood for Rs.2500 to 5000 to manufacture a load of 6000 clay tiles.
12. A maximum of 56 per cent of the units were purchasing oil for Rs.500 to 1000 to manufacture the same number of clay tiles.
13. The maximum of 53.6 per cent of the units were paying Rs. 2500 to 5000 on labour for manufacturing a load of clay tiles.
14. A majority of 52.4 per cent of the units paid Rs.600 to 1200 for electricity to manufacture one load of clay tiles.
15. A maximum 50 per cent of the units had invested Rs.5 to 10 lakhs in land and building.
16. A maximum of 41.7 per cent of the units had invested Rs.9 lakhs and above in plant and machinery.
17. 45.2 per cent of the units had invested Rs.30000 to 60000 in electrical fittings.
18. A maximum of 56 per cent of the units had invested Rs.30000 to 60000 in pallets and frames.
19. 39.3 per cent of the units had invested Rs.3 to 6 lakhs in chimney/kiln.
20. 41.6 per cent of the units had invested Rs.14000 to 21000 in furniture and fittings.
21. The maximum of 91.6 per cent of the units expected a return of 25 to 50 per cent per annum.
22. A maximum of 57.1 per cent of the units achieved only a rate of return of less than 15 per cent.
23. A majority of 51.2 per cent of the units stated that their overall performance of finance was good.
24. The results of the contingency co-efficient suggest that:

(a) The factors of finance such as total capital invested, investment in land and buildings and performance of finance were associated with the location of the units and these were statistically significant at one per cent and five per cent level.

(b) The factors of finance such as major source of borrowed funds, selling price of the tiles, cost of clay, cost of firewood, cost of oil, labour charges and electricity charges per load were associated with the year of establishment of the units and these were statistically significant at one per cent level.

(c) The factors of finance such as major source of working capital, electricity charges per load and furniture and fittings were associated with the jurisdiction of the units and these were statistically significant at one per cent and five per cent level.

(d) The factors of finance namely total capital invested, long-term loan received, selling price of the clay tiles, cost of clay, cost of firewood, cost of oil, labour charges, electricity charges per load, electrical fittings, pallets and frames, furniture and fittings and average actual rate of return were associated with the type of clay tiles manufactured by the units and these were statistically significant at one per cent and five per cent level.

(e) The factors of finance such as major source of borrowed funds, subsidies received from the Government and investment in furniture and fittings were associated with the ownership of the units and these were statistically significant at one per cent and five per cent level.

(f) The factors of finance namely source of working capital and period of credit collection were associated with the qualification of the units owner of the clay tiles manufacturing units and these were statistically significant at one per cent and five per cent level.

(g) The factors of finance such as total capital invested, invested own fund, long-term loan received, cost of oil, electricity charges, investment in land and building, investment in plant, machinery, electrical fittings, pallets, frames, chimney, furniture and fittings, expected rate of return, average rate of return and performance of finance function were associated with the installed production capacity of the units and these were statistically significant at one per cent and five per cent level.

25. The level of performance of finance of the units in Alagappanagar was classified by the best discriminating factors such as costs of oil, clay and labour per load, sources of working capital, investment in land, building and kiln.
26. The finance of the units in Chittissery was predicted by the best discriminating factors such as Sources of working capital, labour charges, cost of clay and cost of firewood per load.
27. The finance of the units in Pudukad was predicted by the best discriminating factors namely investment in electrical fittings, investment of capital, sources of working capital, credit collection period, cost of firewood, cost of oil and electricity per load, investment in plant, machinery, kiln, furniture and fittings.
28. The finance of the units in Thrissur District was classified by the best discriminating factors such as investment in electrical fittings, long-term loans received, costs of oil and labour per load and investment in plant & machinery.

**Finance Problems**

1. The results of contingency co-efficient suggest that there is some relationship between the problems of finance function namely high rate of bank interest & delay in debt collection and the location of the units and these were statistically significant at 5 per cent level.
2. "Shortage of working capital" significantly weakened the performance of finance function of the units located in Chittissery.

3. "Shortage of working capital" significantly weakened the performance of finance function of the units located in Pudukad.
4. Delay in debt collection, shortage of working capital and insufficient subsidy in Thrissur district significantly affected the performance of finance.

**Labour Function**

1. The maximum 56 per cent of the units were employing 20 to 40 workers in their units.
2. A majority of 57.2 per cent of the units had a normal demand for labour in their units.
3. 44 per cent of units were recruiting their workers based on the recommendations by existing labourers.
4. The majority 54.8 per cent of the units selected the workers on the basis of apprenticeship training.
5. The maximum 59.5 per cent of the units employed skilled workers.
6. The majority 88.1 per cent of the units were operating only one shift.
7. The maximum 71.4 per cent of the units were following both time rate and piece rate for paying their workers.
8. The majority 57.1 per cent of the units were paying overtime wages at the rate of 1.5 times normal rate.
9. The maximum 98.8 per cent of the units did not allow their workers weekend off with pay.
10. The majority 66.7 per cent of the units did not meet the medical expenses of the employees incase of any accident.
11. The majority of 79.8 per cent of the units did not give any voluntary holidays to the workers.
12. The maximum 54.8 per cent of the workers of the units in Thrissur District were not members of any of the unions.
13. The overall performance of labour of a majority of 67.9 per cent of the units was good.
14. The results of the contingency co-efficient suggest that:

(a) The factors of labour such as number of workers, membership of workers and performance of labour function were associated with the year of establishment of the units and these were statistically significant at one per cent level.

(b) The factor of labour namely the performance of labour function was associated with the type of clay tiles manufactured by the units and this was statistically significant at one per cent level.

(c) The factor of labour namely basis of selection of workers was associated with the ownership of the units and this was statistically significant at five per cent level.

(d) The factor viz., skill of labour was associated with the qualification of the owners of the units and this was statistically significant at five per cent level.

(e) The factors of labour such as number of workers, demand for labour, mode of recruitment, basis of selection of workers, number of shifts in a day and overtime remuneration to workers were associated with the installed production capacity of the units and these were statistically significant at one per cent and five per cent level.

15. The level of performance of labour of the units in Alagappanagar was classified by the best discriminating factors such as reasons for leave allowed to workers, basis of overtime remuneration, mode of recruitment and worker membership with union.

16. The level of performance of labour function of the units in Chittissery was classified by the best discriminating factors such as demand for labour, basis for selection of workers and mode of recruitment.

17. The level of performance of labour of the units in Pudukad was classified by the best discriminating factors such as mode of recruitment, types of labour, basis of selection of workers and bearing of medical expenditure.

18. The level of performance of labour of the units in Thrissur District was classified by the best discriminating factors

such as reasons for leave allowed to workers, workers membership in union, demand for labour and number of workers in the units.

**Labour Problems**

1. Among the seven problems identified by the researcher, the "Problem of labour strikes" and the "Labour absenteeism" have a significant impact on the performance of labour. This shows that these two problems existed in the units located in Alagappanagar, but they did not affect the performance of labour.
2. Among the seven problems identified by the researcher, the problem of "Over expenses due to excessive manpower" has a significant impact on the performance of labour of the units in Pudukad.

**Overall Analysis**

1. A maximum of 72.6 per cent of the units stated that their overall performance was good.
2. Among the four functional areas of the units, only the performance of labour significantly and positively contributed to the overall performance of the units located in Alagappanagar.
3. The result of the One-way Anova shows that the mean performance score differs significantly between the high and low performance units in Alagappanagar area at one per cent level.
4. The results of the Chi-Square test suggest that the mean performance score of various functions differs significantly between the high and low performance units at one per cent level.
5. The Canonical Correlation of 0.791 explains that there exists a relationship of 79.1 per cent between the discriminatory scores and the performance of various functional areas of the units in Alagappanagar.
6. Among the four functional areas, only the performance of Production and the Labour made almost equal contributions

to the overall performance of the units located in Chittissery.

7. The result of the One-way Anova shows that the mean performance score differs significantly between the high and low performance units in Chittissery at one per cent level.
8. The results of the Chi-Square test suggest that the mean performance score of various functions differs significantly between the high and low performance units at one per cent level.
9. The Canonical Correlation of 0.807 explains that there exists a relationship of 80.7 per cent between the discriminatory scores and the performance of various functional areas of the units in Chittissery.
10. Among the four functional areas, only the performance of Labour function emerged as the best contributor to the overall performance of the units located in Pudukad.
11. The result of the One-way Anova shows that the mean performance score differs significantly between the high and low performance units in Pudukad at one per cent level.
12. The results of the Chi-Square test suggest that the mean performance score of various functions differs significantly between the high and low performance units at one per cent level.
13. The Canonical Correlation of 0.947 explains that there exists a relationship of 94.7 per cent between the discriminatory scores and the performance of various function areas of the units in Pudukad.
14. Among the four functional areas, only the performance of Labour function significantly emerged as the best contributor to influence overall performance of the units located in Thrissur District.
15. The result of the One-way Anova shows that the mean performance score differs significantly between the high and low performance units in Thrissur District at one per cent level.

16. The results of the Chi-Square test suggest that the mean performance score of various functions differs significantly between the high and low performance units at one per cent level.
17. The Canonical Correlation of 0.832 explains that there exists a relationship of 83.2 per cent between the discriminatory scores and the performance of various functional areas of the units in Thrissur District.

## SUGGESTIONS AND RECOMMENDATIONS

Based on the analyses and findings extracted from the study, the researcher gives proper and suitable suggestions regarding the organisational aspects and the various functional areas of the clay tiles manufacturing units in Thrissur district.

### Organisational Aspects

1. Most of the units are located in Chittissery area and this is due to the availability of clay, firewood and other raw materials. The researcher suggests that the new entrepreneurs can come forward to start the clay tiles business in Chittissery due to the feasibility and compatibility of this area.
2. After the year 1985, majority of the units started the clay tiles units. The reason behind this is the increase in demand for the clay tiles products within the State as well as outside the State and the subsidies provided by the State Government at that time. But in later years, the Government stopped providing subsidies. It is suggested that the Government can restore the subsidy provision for this industry. This will trigger the new entrepreneurs to enter into the clay tiles units.
3. Most of the units are located within Panchayat areas because of availability of clay, firewood, water and other raw materials. Therefore the researcher suggests that the new entrepreneurs may start the units within the Panchayat area.
4. The units concentrated on the production of flooring and decorative tiles. The demand for these two products is very

high particularly in South India. So, the units can concentrate more on the manufacturing of flooring and decorative tiles.

5. The new entrepreneurs are advised to set up partnership firm or private companies since the proposed units are small in nature.

**Production Function**

1. In Alagappanagar, the researcher suggests that the units may concentrate more on the production function such as procurement of clay in a lump sum manner, use of machanised methods of cutting & trimming of clay tiles, use of de-airing machine and conduct quality test. This will help to ensure the quality of the final products.
2. Units in Chittissery can concentrate on clay storage, switchover from the traditional method of burning the tiles to adoption of Hoffman type of kiln to burn the tiles. They may follow smoking & stream heating for drying the tiles and finally make arrangement for quality checking of the finished tiles.
3. In Pudukad, the researcher suggests that the units may give equal importance to the production besides the method of burning the tiles. This will lead to the reduction in the cost of oil, firewood and labour expenditure.
4. Finally, the units located in Thrissur district, the researcher suggests that they can take efforts for reducing the cost of procurement of clay and also use the thermocouple instrument to measure the burning temperature.

***Problems in Production***

1. Units in Chittissery faced the problem of "pollution created by kiln". For proper maintenance of kiln can help to reduce pollution.
2. Units in Pudukad can get advance from the customers at the time of taking work order as they supply quality tiles. This will help to procure the clay at the right time and avoid delay in delivery of tiles.

**Marketing Function**

1. In Alagappanagar, the units can concentrate timely supply of tiles to their customers and ensure quality of their product.
2. In Chittissery, the units may adopt the proper promotional techniques such as allowing discount to the customers, compensation for breakage and arrange for transport facilities for their regular customers. In order to sustain the sales the units should extend the credit period for their regular customers.
3. In Pudukad, the researcher suggests that the units have to enhance the mode of getting work orders through agents. In order to meet the competition, the units should extend the credit period to their regular customers. It can boost the sales by following direct sales as well as sale through agents in an effective manner.

*Problems in Marketing*

1. In Alagappanagar, the units may take efforts for avoiding breakage of tiles by adopting mechanisation of the production process and also through adoption of the quality checking of finished tiles.
2. In Chittissery, the problem is "low profit margin", the units may go in for more first quality tiles instead of second quality tiles.
3. For the units located in Pudukad, the problem is "slow credit collection". It is advised that the units may take efforts to speed up credit collection process taking follow up measures.
4. In Thrissur district, it is suggested that the units may evaluate the credit worthiness of the new customers and maintain proper relationship with the existing customers, in order to avoid bad debts.

**FINANCE FUNCTION**

1. The units in Alagappanagar area may give more concentration to the factors namely sources of working capital, cost of

clay, oil & labour expenses, investment make in land & building and furniture & fittings for the effective financial management of the units.

2. As far as units in Chittissery are concerned, the researcher recommends a raised long-term loan regarding increasing the total capital. Moreover, the units can sell their tiles on the basis of credit and extend the credit period allowed to the existing customers for boosting up the sales.
3. In Pudukad, the units may strengthen the owned capital component of the capital structure. They may also allocate adequate amount for meeting the working capital requirements.
4. On the whole units in Thrissur district, pay more concentration on the long-term loans, cost of oil & labour charges, investment in plant & machinery and electrical fittings. Besides these factors, the units may give more importance to the remaining factors in order to improve the financial performance of the units.

### *Problems in Finance*

Shortage of working capital is the major problem for the units located in Chittissery and Pudukad. The units are advised to take remedial measure to increase the working capital. It is suggested that the units can get advance from the customers, try to maintain cash sales and raise short-term loan from the commercial banks.

In Thrissur district, shortage of working capital, delay in dept collection and insufficient subsidies are the major problems in finance function. In order to increase the financial performance of the units, they can increase the working capital by speeding up the debt collection process. The Government may come forward to make arrangement for the provision of subsidies, incentives and loans to the units located in the study area.

## Labour Function

1. Units in Alagappanagar may meet medical expenditure for their workers other than the Group Insurance Scheme at the time of accident.

2. As far as units in Chittissery and Pudukad, they can give weekend leave with wages to the workers. It will boost up the production.
3. Finally, the overall performance of labour in Thrissur district is normally good. All the factors significantly contributed to the level of performance of the units. Besides the units will give equal importance to the all factors, it should enable the performance of labour function.

### Overall Performance

Most of the units located in Alagappanagar declined in the overall performance. In order to improve the performance, the units may concentrate on the production and finance. In the future, the performance of marketing alone will change the overall performance of the units. Therefore, the units should strive hard to increase the efficiency of the marketing performance.

Majority of the units in Chittissery achieved a high level overall performance. In order to sustain the same level of performance, they should give more importance to the marketing performance and also performance of production.

The units in Pudukad should concentrate on marketing and finance functions. It will turn the low performance units into high performance.

On the whole in Thrissur District, the units excelled in the overall performance. In order to enhance and maintain the performance, the units should give more emphasis to the performance of production, marketing and finance.

## CONCLUSION

Based on the analysis and findings the researcher concludes the study on the following grounds of the functional areas.

### Organisational Background

From the study the researcher found out that a majority of the clay tiles manufacturing units are located in Chittissery and they started business after the year 1985. As far as jurisdiction of the units is concerned, it comes under panchayat area.

Moreover most of the units were manufacturing flooring and decorative tiles. Partnership is the predominant of ownership. Similarly, the owners of the units were Graduates. The installed production capacity of most of the units is below 8000 tiles or 8000 to 16000 tiles per day. Finally, the factors such as availability of raw materials, good demand for clay tiles and availability of capital or loan have influenced the owners to establish the units in Thrissur District.

## Production Function

As far as the units located in Alagappanagar are concerned, they mainly concentrate on sources of water and season of purchasing firewood. These two factors significantly determine the production.

The units located in Chittissery are concerned with the source of firewood, methods adopted for transporting clay to machines and methods of cutting the clay blocks. These factors significantly predict their performance of production.

In Pudukad area, the factors such as place of procuring clay, type of oil, oil used per load, methods adopted for transporting the clay to machines, the use of de-airing machine, firewood used, breakage of tiles per load and test adopted to check the finished tiles affected production.

Finally, the production of clay tiles units located in Thrissur district was affected by the methods of cutting the clay blocks, methods of trimming the tiles, methods of drying the tiles and firewood used in their production process. Breakage of tiles significantly determines the production of Thrissur district.

### *Problems in Production*

As far as production function is concerned the researcher explored 8 different problems. In Alagappanagar the problem of procurement of clay existed due to public objection but it did not reduce the performance of production.

In Chittissery, the problem of pollution created by kiln erodes the performance. On the other hand, the problem of fulfilling the legal formalities at the time of procuring the firewood existed but it did not affect the performance.

In Pudukad area, the units strongly agreed that the high price prevailed on the market and delay in delivery significantly reduced the performance of production.

Among the various problems identified by the researcher, the problems of procurement of clay and high price of clay existed in all the units located in Thrissur district. But fortunately these two problems did not affect or reduce the production.

## Marketing Function

The researcher identified 10 different factors which affect the performance of marketing. In Alagappanagar, the performance of marketing was affected by the four major factors such as location of the competitors, nature of sales, methods adopted for price fixation and average sales.

In Chittissery, the methods adopted for price fixation, nature of sales and location of the competitors equally contributed to the performance.

As far as Pudukad is concerned, the factors such as nature of sales, supply of tiles to other States, methods adopted for price fixation, average sales, promotional techniques and strategies adopted for maintaining the sales equally determined the performance of marketing.

Finally, in Thrissur district, marketing performance was purely determined by the three major factors such as mode of sales, nature of sales and period of credit allowed to customers.

### *Problems in Marketing*

The researcher identified 8 different problems of marketing. The problems such as breakage of tiles, low profit margin and delay in credit collection process significantly reduced the performance of marketing function of the units located in Alagappanagar, Chittissery and Pudukad respectively. As far as Thrissur district is concerned the incidence of bad debts prevailed and this affected the performance of marketing adversely.

## Finance Function

The researcher identified 22 different factors of finance. Based on the analysis, it is concluded that in Alagappanagar, the dominant factor was sources of working capital followed by recurring expenditure such as cost of clay, oil and labour per load. Similarly, the units invested their funds in land and buildings as well as in chimney/kiln which significantly contributed to the performance of finance.

As far as Chittissery is concerned, the sources of working capital, labour charges and cost of clay & firewood affected the performance of the units. Moreover, investment in kiln and furniture and fittings emerged as contributors to the financial performance of the units.

In Pudukad, except the investment made in electrical fittings by the units, the other two factors such as funds invested as capital and sources of working capital equally affected the performance. Similarly, the period of credit collection and expenses such as cost of firewood, oil and electricity charges were also equally related to the performance. The investment in plant and machinery, chimney/kiln and furniture & fittings was associated with the financial performance of the units.

Finally, the researcher concluded that the factors such as long-term loans, cost of oil & labour charges and investment made in plant and machinery & electrical fittings have influenced the financial performance of the units located in Thrissur district.

### *Problems in Finance*

Any barrier in the financial function of the units' results in the decline of functional performance as well as overall performance of the units. The researcher explored 7 different types of problems in the units. As far as the Alagappanagar is concerned, there is no problem in the finance function of the units but in Chittissery and Pudukad the problem of shortage of working capital, reduced the financial performance of the units. The researcher also identified 3 different types of problems, which reduced the performance of finance of the units. The problems are shortage of working capital, delay in the debt collection and insufficient subsidies given by the Government.

**Labour Function**

Labour also determines the performance of the units. In order to evaluate the performance of labour, the researcher identified 12 different factors of labour. Among these, the mode of recruitment followed by the units, overtime remuneration given to workers and leave allowed to the workers were the dominant factors of the units located in Alagappanagar.

As for the units of Chittissery, demand for labour, mode of recruitment and the basis of selection of workers determine the performance of labour. Similarly, in Pudukad, the types of labour and medical expenditure incurred by the units influenced the performance of the labour.

Finally, in Thrissur district, the factors such as number of workers and workers' membership in union determined the performance of labour.

*Problems in Labour*

In Alagappanagar, among the various problems, the labour strikes and absenteeism existed but these did not have a significant impact on the performance of labour. As far as Chittissery is concerned, the units were free from problems. The units located in Pudukad faced a problem of over expenses incurred on the excessive manpower employed and the same resulted in the decline of the performance of labour.

Finally, the researcher found out that there were no problems existed in the labour function of the units located in Thrissur district.

## OVERALL PERFORMANCE OF CLAY TILES MANUFACTURING UNITS

The strength and weakness of any manufacturing unit depend on its overall performance of the functional areas. As far as the units located in Alagappanagar, the overall performance was purely determined by the performance of labour. Moreover in this area, most of the units recorded low performance. The researcher predicted that the performance of marketing function will be the best discriminating functional area which will classify the level of overall performance into high or low in the future.

For the units located in Chittissery, the overall performance was determined by production. A majority of the units in Chittissery excelled and achieved a high overall performance. Moreover, the performance of production function emerged as a dominant area, which will classify the level of overall performance of the units into high or low in the future.

In Pudukad the performance of finance played a vital role and it will determine and classify the level of overall performance of the units into high or low in the future.

Finally, the researcher concluded that in Thrissur district, labour significantly contributed to the overall performance of the units. On the whole, a majority of the units achieved a high overall performance. Marketing would be the best and dominating functional area, which will classify the level of overall performance of the units into high or low in the future.

# Bibliography

*Books*

Edward Dobson, "*A Rudimentary Treatise on the Manufacturing of Bricks and Tiles*", London, 1889.

Hoffman, H., "*The Basel Mission Industries*", New Publications, Mangalore, 1913.

Alfred B. Searle, "*Modern Brickmaking*", Ernest Benn Limited, London, 1956.

Alan Muhlemann, John Oakland and Keith lockyes, "*Production and Operation Management*", Macmillan India Ltd, 1998.

Everett. E. Adam, Ponald J. Ebert, "*Production and Operation Management - Concepts, Models and Behaviours*", Prentice-Hall of India Pvt. Ltd., New Delhi, 1998.

Martand Telsang, "*Production Management and Industrial Engineering*", S. Chand & Company Ltd., 1998.

Chary S.N., "*Production and Operation Management*", Tata Mcgraw-Hill Publishing Company Ltd, New Delhi, 2000.

Dr. Aswathappa K., "*Essentials of Production Management*", Himalaya Publishing House, 2000.

Les Galloway, "*Principles of Production Management*", International Thomson Business Press, 2000.

Manoj Kumar Sarkar, "*Production Management*", Crest Publishing House, 2000.

Chary, S.N., "*Theory and Problems in Production and Operation Management*", Tata Mcgraw-Hill Publishing Company Ltd., New Delhi, 2002.

Chanawalla and Patel, *"Production and Operation Management"*, Himalaya Publishing House, 2003.

Shridhara Bhat, *"Text Book of Production Management"*, Himalaya Publishing House, 2004.

James M. Carman and Kenneth P.Uhl, *"Marketing Principles and Methods"*, D.B. Taraporewalla Sons Publishing Bombay, 1983.

Richard J. Semenik and Gray J. Bamossy, *"Principles of Marketing-A Global Perspective"*, South Western Publishing Co., 1990.

William G. Zikmund and Michael d' Amico, *"Marketing"*, West Publishing Company, 1998.

Sak Onkvisit & John J. Shaw, *"International Marketing–Analysis and Strategy"*, Prentice-Hill of India Pvt. Ltd, New Delhi, 1999.

Gary Armstrong and Philip Kotler, *"Marketing An Introduction"*, Addison Wesley Longman (Singapore) Ltd., 2000.

M. J. Xavier, *"Marketing in the New Millenimum-36 Trends that will Change Business and Marketing"*, Vikas Publishing house Pvt. Ltd., 2000.

Rathor and Jani, *"International Marketing"*, Himalaya Publishing House, 2001.

Varshney Bhattacharyya, *"International Marketing Management"*, S. Chand & Company Ltd, 2001.

John C. Hull, *"International to Future and Options Markets"*, Prentice-Hall of India Pvt. Ltd, New Delhi, 2002.

Robert R. Reeder and Edward G. Brierty, *"Industrial Marketing–Analysis, Planning and Control"*, Prentice-Hall of India Pvt. Ltd., New Delhi, 2002.

Krishna K. Havaldar, *"Industrial Marketing"*, Tata Mcgraw-Hill Publishing Company Ltd., New Delhi, 2002.

Monga and Shalini Anand, *"Marketing Management"*, Deep and Deep Publications Pvt. Ltd., 2003.

Prasanna Chandra, *"Financial Management Theory & Practice"*, Tata Mcgraw-Hill Publishing Company Ltd, New Delhi, 1984.

Subir Kumar Benerjee, *"Financial Management"*, S. Chand & Company Ltd., 1999.

James C. Van Horne, *"Financial Management and Policy"*, Prentice-Hall of India Pvt. Ltd, New Delhi, 2000.

Khan M.Y and Jain P.K., *"Financial Management"*, Tata McGraw Hill, New Delhi, 2002.

Kulkarni P.V. and Satyaprasad B.G., *"Financial Management"*, Himalaya Publishing House, 2002.

Pandy I. M., *"Financial Management"*, Vikas Publishing House Pvt. Ltd., 2005.

Ahuja, K.K., *"Advanced Personnel Management"*, Kalyani Publishers, New Delhi, 2000.

Dale Yoder, *"Personnel Management and Industrial Relations"*, Prentice-Hall (P) Ltd., New Delhi, 2002.

Flippo, Edwin B., *"Personnel Management"*, McGraw-Hill Book Company, Singapore, 2001.

Mamoria, C. B., "Personnel Management", *Himalaya Publishing* House, Bombay, 2003.

*Articles and Reports*

Department of Economics and Commerce, Govt. of Madras, *"Manufacturing of Building Materials"*, Unpublished Research Project, Madras, 1957.

The National Council of Economic Research, *"Techno Economic Survey of Kerala"*, A Survey Report, New Delhi, 1962.

Maheswary, U.P., *"Development Research Vs Small Scale Roofing Tile Industry"*, Report of All India Seminar on Ceramic Industries, Small Industries Service Institute (SISI) Thrissur, 1962.

Sorabji, D., *"Brick and Tile Industry"*, Report of All India Seminar on Ceramic Industries, Small Industries Service Institute (SISI) Thrissur, 1962.

Devaraja Iyer, *"Origin, Growth and Present Position of Tile Industry"*, Report of All India Seminar on Ceramic Industries, Small Industries Service Institute (SISI) Thrissur, 1966.

Ghatge, V.K., *"A note on Building Bricks and Roofing Tile Industries"*, Report of All India Seminar on Ceramic Industries, Small Industries Service Institute (SISI) Thrissur, 1966.

*Jain, L.C. and Jain, V.K., "Bricks and Tile Research in India"*, Report of All India Seminar on Ceramic Industries, Small Industries Service Institute (SISI) Thrissur, 1966.

Ananthan, B. R., "Tile Industry in South Kerala District–A Case Study", *Indian Journal of Commerce*, 1975.

Sreedharan Nair, M.R. & Bala Krishnan Nair, M.K., *"Tiles Industry in Kerala - Mangalore Type Roofing Tiles"*, Status report of Small Industries Service Institute (SISI) Thrissur, 1980.

Government of Gujarat, Department of Economics, *"Roofing & Flooring Tile Industry in Morvi"*, Status Report of Government of Gujarat, 1984.

Karnataka State Financial Corporation, *"Modernisation of Roofing & Flooring tile Industry"*, A State Level Seminar Report, Mangalore, 1986.

Thomas, P.F., *"Need for Development of Technology in Tile Industry"*, Status Report of State Product Council, Thrissur, 1986.

National Product Council, *"Productivity of tile Industry in Kerala"*, NPC, Thrissur, 1987.

Nair, M.K., "Modernisation Guide for Clay Products Industry", Study Report of Small Industrial Service Institute, Thrissur, 1991.

Warrier, K.G.K., *"Clay Based Ceramic Products–An Overview"*, Report on Regional Research Laboratory, Trivandrum, 1992.

Dr. Anantha Subramaniam, President, All Kerala Tile Manufacturers' Association, Survey Report on *"Financing for Modernisation of Tile Industry"*, Thrissur, 1993.

Prasad, R. S., *"Cluster Group of Industries on Clay Tiles"*, Study Report of Small Industries Service Institute (SISI), Thrissur, 1994.

Easwaran, V.,*"Improved Bricks and Tiles Through CBRI Research"*, Survey Report of Central Building Research Institute, Trivandrum, 1995.

Narayanan, C.G., Vice President, All Kerala Tile Manufacturers' Association, *"Fuels for Tile Industry"*, Survey Report of Chithra Ceramics, Pudukad, Thrissur, 1995.

KAP India Tiles, *"Present State of the Tile Industry in Thrissur"*, Survey Report, Thrissur, 2001.

*Theses Referred*

Kart, B.G., *"History and Development of the Tile Industry in Mangalore"*, Doctoral Thesis, University of Bombay 1955.

John Thomas Chirayath, "A Study on the Tile Industry in Kerala", *Doctoral Thesis, Calicut University, 1969.*

Mani, K.P., *"Tile Industry in Kerala–Economics, Problems & Prospects"*, Doctoral Thesis, Cochin University of Science & Technology, 1990.

*Office Records*

Geological Survey of India, Department of Mining and Geology, Planning Board.

Regional Research Laboratory (CSIR), Tiruvandrum.

Centre for Earth Science Studies (CESS) Tiruvandrum.

Census of India 2001 and 2002.

Department of Mining and Geology, Government of Kerala, 2001.

District Industries Centre (DIC), Thrissur.

Small Industries Service Institute (SISI), Thrissur.

*Websites*

*http://www.dreadnought-tiles.co.un*

*http://www.handpaintedtiles.org*

*http://www.mrtfla.com/history_clay.htm*

*http://www.mca.tile.com*

*http://www.claymex.com*

*http://www.clayroof.co.in*

*http://www.tileroofing.org*

*http://www.trichur.com*

*http://www.kerala.com*